Enlightenment or Empire

ENLIGHTENMENT OR EMPIRE

Colonial Discourse
in German Culture

RUSSELL A. BERMAN

University of Nebraska Press

Lincoln and London

Library of Congress Cataloging-in-Publication Data
Berman, Russell A., 1950–
Englightenment or empire: colonial discourse in
German culture / Russell A. Berman.
p.   cm.—(Modern German culture and literature)
Includes bibliographical references and index.
ISBN 0-8032-1284-4 (cl.: alk. paper)
ISBN 978-0-8032-2228-1 (pa.: alk. paper)
1. Germany—Colonies.   2. Germany—Cultural policy.
3. Imperialism—History.   4. Nationalism—Germany.
5. Germany—Politics and government—1871–1918.
6. National characteristics, German.   I. Title.   II. Series.
DD220.B48   1998
325′.343—dc21
97-32628 CIP

Ja, wäre nur ein Zaubermantel mein!
Und trüg' er mich in fremde Länder,
[If I only had a magic cloak!
And it carried me to foreign lands,]
Goethe, *Faust I*, 1122–23

The writer speaks without anti-German bias; personally he has deep cause to love the German people. They made him believe in the essential humanity of white folk twenty years ago when he was near denying it.

W. E. B. Du Bois, November 1914

Contents

Acknowledgments

I began this project as a fellow of the Alexander von Humboldt–Stiftung, to which I remain very grateful, and I am indebted to the staff of the Preussische Staatsbibliothek in Berlin, where I completed much of the research. I also received cordial assistance at the state archive in Windhoek. Many colleagues assisted me through discussions and criticism. I want to express special thanks to David Abernethy, Martin Jay, Regenia Gagnier, Peter Hohendahl, Mary Pratt, Klaus Scherpe, James Sheehan, and Wolfgang Winkler. Their aid and encouragement at various stages of this project have been indispensable. My very special thanks and affection go to Aniko, to whom I dedicate this book about travel.

Enlightenment or Empire

INTRODUCTION

"The Kilimanjaro is German; it is a German mountain and, what's more, the tallest one in the German Reich. Eternal snow lies on none of our mountains at home—but it covers the summit of our newly won peak, only three degrees south of the equator!"[1] Such glowing pride in ownership comes from one C. Falkenhorst, an anthologizer and popularizer of the literature of travel and discovery at the end of the nineteenth century. His volumes bear stirring titles such as *Auf Bergeshöhen Deutsch-Afrikas* (On the mountain peaks of German Africa) or *Durch die Wüsten und Steppen des dunklen Weltteils* (Through the deserts and steppes of the dark continent). Published within a series called Bibliothek denkwürdiger Forschungsreisen (The library of remarkable explorations), the books include Falkenhorst's descriptions of various expeditions, which he embellished by cutting and pasting from the reports of the travelers themselves. Robert Flegel, Oskar Lenz, Gustav Nachtigal, Alexandrine von Tinne, Hugo Zoeller, and other *Afrikareisende*, to use the contemporary term, are heroized, excerpted, and presented to a mass reading public, who consume a literature poised ambiguously between popular science and colonial advocacy. Whatever else colonialism may have entailed, it appeared to the reading public as a voyage into an uncharted space, the reports on which could be judged as edifying and instructive, just as they were indisputably thrilling: learn and enjoy.

But let us leave science aside for a moment (although it will concern us often in this book) and return to that hybrid image of the German Kilimanjaro, part European, part African, a mixed-race geography. When Falkenhorst speaks of "our African Alps," we might shrug it off as an innocently descriptive designation of an "alpine region" (as in the alpine meadows of the Sierra) or perhaps an example of the proliferating alpine metaphor, as when one speaks of the "Saxonian Switzerland" in central Germany or even the "Trinity Alps" in northern California. These overly cautious readings would, however, miss the full resonance of the term. For there is more at stake, a more powerful appropriation; these are, after all, "our" Alps in Africa, and Falkenhorst insists on pointing out that Hugo Zoeller had similarly described a peak in the Cameroons as "a west African Montblanc." In the same vein, Falkenhorst discusses the population in the Cameroon highlands using the familiarizing metaphor of Tyroleans—"Die Tiroler von Kamerun"—and he can even predict a future literary history: "The lovely maiden from Bonjongo is a perfect model for a future Cameroon Ganghofer," a reference to Ludwig Ganghofer, the late-nineteenth-century author of popular novels set in Alpine locations.[2] The colonized Cameroon population is thereby rendered as quaint and picturesque as its Austrian doubles: mountain people are mountain people the world over, especially through the unifying power of metaphor.

With this set of Germanizing designations the popular text is, obviously, disseminating an ideology that naturalizes the colonial claim on African territory. German Africa is not merely conquered, occupied, controlled, and owned by Germany; through metaphors like these it becomes like Germany, substantively and affectively. A mirror image of Germany is conjured up, and a new space with which the German public might identify is envisioned. If British colonialism in Africa might at times be driven by the visionary alliteration of Cape and Cairo, German colonialism, as evidenced by this example at least, might rely on an imagination of an Alpine Africa, from Kilimanjaro to Cameroon. This is, of course, quite an odd map with regard to both its topographical creativity and its omission of Namibia, then German Southwest Africa. No matter, though, for ideology is not supposed to be rational or encompassing; it has only to purvey the illusion that it is so, while other matters shape the underlying project. Other matters: the real point is not to collect mountains but to colonize, and in that regard, Falkenhorst points out, highlands are in fact quite important in that they have a climate that might attract a permanent German settlement. Deserts and jungles would, after all, seem less enticing than an African Tyrol.[3]

Yet if settlement, the establishment of permanent colonies, is, so to speak, the ulterior motive of the text, it is not the primary or ostensible topic. The introduction of *Auf Bergeshöhen Deutsch-Afrikas* does not begin with flag waving (or even flag planting on top of a peak). Nor does it spout national or racial superiority, the sort of starting point one might expect in a colonial text. On the contrary, the hierarchy with which Falkenhorst commences is solely spatial: "The high mountain regions have only recently been conquered for science and humanity. In earlier times, a holy fear kept men away from the snowcapped peaks, about the nature of which the strangest opinions held sway. There was nothing to get up there on the glaciers, and the world was blind to the sublime beauty of the mountains. That is why the oceans were crossed and the far North, covered with polar ice, was explored before the highest peaks on the European mountains were climbed."[4] Of course, the perspective is clearly northern and European, since these are the explicit points of reference, but the orientation depends more profoundly on a different narrative: the temporal distinction between the successes of the present and the benightedness of the past, which imply a story of progress. This progress, moreover, entails an ongoing conquest of space. That is, colonial discourse is implicated in some underlying epistemological questions relating to the construction of time and, especially, space, and these issues are prior to any specific or crude program of domination or ideologies of a civilizing mission. For the analysis of colonial discourse, then, the key question is one of space, not race.[5]

Conquest and domination, however, are not far behind the organization of spatiality, and this introduction to the curious construction of the German colonies as an extension of the German Alps proceeds with its history of spatial exploration by dwelling on the history of mountaineering. However, before Falkenhorst's account comes to Horace-Benedict de Saussure's seminal scaling of Mont-blanc in 1787, it identifies an earlier "alpinistic" achievement, the scaling of the volcano Popocatepetl by Cortez's conquistadors prior to their assault on Tenochtitlán. Conquering space is, evidently, more than a matter of sport, and the history of mountain climbing is thereby integrated multiply into a progressive representation of colonialism: travel through space, scientific exploration of the world, European expansion, the progress of humanity.

Falkenhorst's volumes are part of the cultural history of colonialism in the Wilhelmine era, evidence of the popular images that circulated to convince a reticent public of the desiderata of overseas possessions. The manner in which colonialism was represented and addressed, however, points to the larger issues that surround colonialism and that I will explore in this book. Colonial discourse presupposes travel, real or imagined, which in turn necessarily raises questions about the constitution of space: abstract and empty, available for geometric description, or sensuous and populated, more a topic for ethnographers than geographers? Both modes are possible, and both can produce positive knowledge about space, that is, mapping, although it remains an open question as to what sorts of maps might be drawn. A different place might be only another latitude and longitude, or it might be the site of another order of meaning, a cultural alterity, the very difference of which might even be the source, or the incentive, of Enlightenment for the traveler.

So it is not merely a matter of alternative understandings of space; it is rather the experience of space that is at stake and the experience of alterity by the traveler, the subject moving through space. For all the power and violence we may associate with the notion of colonization, colonialism surely also always necessarily entails the encounter—or confrontation or transmission or competition or infusion—between different social systems and cultural paradigms. We may first ask how the metropolitan voyager, for example, the traveler from Germany, understands the space of geography, but once that traveler reaches the foreign land, the colonial territory, or for that matter, any other territory, we have at least to wonder whether that encounter with new material, new people, new ideas, leaves any trace. Does experience matter? Or should we imagine every traveler to be always caught up fully in the codes and models of the metropolis? Are tourists just "programmed" by their presuppositions or can they assimilate something new and different? Some versions of discourse theory and accounts of "orientalism" tend to emphasize the power of overriding paradigms or epistemes, which structure the possibilities of consciousness in advance. In this book the assumption is different, that is, that real travel through space and the encounter with foreign cultures and society certainly has the potential to elicit qualitatively new experiences. By suggesting that humans can learn through experience, that is, encounter the world in ways that change their thinking, I am challenging the contemporary orthodoxy in cultural scholarship that asserts that thought is only a function of paradigms and epistemes, ultimately impervious to experience. When one rejects this sort of academic idealism, the colonial site becomes interesting, not as the location of Fanon's imagined war-unto-death between different races and competing cultures, but rather as a location where, through perpetual acts of cross-cultural contact, transgressive change occurs precisely despite the efforts of colonial regimes to separate and control. There is then a way to hear an unexpected undertone in the oxymoron, "German Kilimanjaro": not a designation of the conquered prize but a formula for a mulatto geography.

The travel through space permits new experiences, even if those experiences and the reactions to them are repressed because of colonial ideology. The written record of that travel is the topic of this book: how German travelers in the non-European world—especially to regions that would come under the sway of European colonization—encountered alterity and came to grips with it (or not). The primary genre of this travel writing came to be narrative, although it stood in a constant competition with systematic description. The difference between the two raises again the question of science, now with regard to the differentiation between a professional and a lay public in scientific matters in the course of the nineteenth century. Narrative is, since the eighteenth century, the more popular option, appealing to a wider public and allowing for identification with the traveler. Nevertheless, the character of the reading public changes, as does the sort of identification or the emotional value attached to a travel text, and it would surely be a mistake to assume that popularization necessarily implies trivialization.

The narratives of travel examined in this book come from different periods, but all are from the past 220 years, surely an age of empire if that is taken to mean the establishment of a thick network of global relations of power and communications. The imperial network, moreover, brings different cultures into unexpected (some heterophobic critics on the right and the left might say unwar-

ranted) proximity, with the possibility of an ensuing dissonance between alternative cultural structures, suddenly juxtaposed. The imperial era includes the "age of discovery," when European voyagers
organized global space into a single cartographic system, then the
age of "high imperialism," marked by the direct political domination of much of the globe by a small number of European states, and
even the "postcolonial" era of some political independence and considerable economic dependence. Viewed from this perspective of
dissonance between alternative cultural structures, this whole era is
then organized around a central problematic—the increased proximity of different cultural orders. In other words, the empire becomes, oddly enough, the prototype of the multicultural setting—
surely not a liberal or happy multiculturalism, for far too much direct power was deployed and too many crude prejudices were current. But it has been multicultural in the sense that wherever different cultures met crossovers have always taken place. Issues of
universalism and particularity—are there norms that prevail
throughout the system or do local determinations always take pre-
cedence?—and the challenge of cultural relativism, indeed, the very
capacity to recognize different cultures, are therefore central to the
discussions in this book.

Enlightenment or Empire: the title of this volume is poised am-
bivalently around the double meaning of the conjunction, suggesting simultaneously an alternative (a choice) and an equivalency.
Shall we think of Enlightenment, the regime of reason, as a potential source of criticism, directed against the arbitrary power of empire? Or are the two terms identical, Enlightenment as the vehicle
through which empire establishes domination and maintains its allegedly insidious control? Much of contemporary criticism would
opt for that latter version, equating the Enlightenment's legacy of
reason and science with the systems of domination for which imperialism might be taken to stand. In a philosophical variant, often associated with deconstruction, the eighteenth-century insistence on
reason is viewed as part of a Western metaphysics, a mode of
thought derived from Socrates (in a genealogy disseminated by
Nietzsche) and organized in terms of logocentrity, that is, the centrality of conceptual thinking. The claim, however, is not merely a

matter of the history of philosophy since the rhetoric of reason is taken to be a vehicle for the suppression of the "other" to reason, alterity, and all that is not rational, according to Western standards. Enlightenment thereby becomes just another name for empire: without Enlightenment, no centralized and rationalized power would have been able to establish networks of control and exterminate everything outside of it that might stand in its path. Historiographical studies inspired by Michel Foucault trace these insinuations of rational power in the detail of modern institutions.

Yet the very drama of the claim that the Enlightenment is implicated in empire derives from the underlying assumption that empire, as domination, is somehow wrong, an affront to expectations about the human condition. It is, however, precisely here that the antilogocentric position begins to surrender some of its credibility, since it obviously relies on claims about a human and therefore universalist condition and, moreover, these claims include a condemnation of domination that in turn implies a norm of freedom. To condemn a collaboration between Enlightenment and empire can only indicate that one has accepted the critical terms of Enlightenment thought. Universalism and emancipation: these are constitutive components of modernity as defined by a legacy of the Enlightenment. In other words, the terms with which empire is criticized derive from precisely that same Enlightenment whose insistence on reason was, a moment ago, attacked as the cause of imperial domination. Deconstructive antilogocentrism is therefore a fraudulent basis for a critique of empire, and imperialism is simply not an essential or necessary feature of Enlightenment.

Contemporary criticism is fraught with tensions deriving from an unresolved evaluation of the legacy of the Enlightenment: as being fully complicitous in structures of power and control, including colonialism, or as the only frame available with which credible criticisms of power and control can be articulated. This book explores that dialectic within Enlightenment as it is played out in encounters between the European and non-European worlds. How can science address qualitatively different cultures? At the same time, however, this book intervenes in the theoretical debates by insisting on the illegitimacy of the antilogocentric denunciation of Enlightenment.

The blanket refusal of reason—and, by extension, of science, progress, and a normative universalism—represents one of the deep-seated failings of contemporary intellectuals and a betrayal of the terms of the scholarly institutions in which they operate. The dismissal of the Enlightenment legacy entails a sophistry that does a disservice to the human capacity to think about the unknown, to pursue curiosity, and to inquire about the world. It is beyond a doubt that knowledge gained is available for abuse: science can be appropriated by political regimes. Yet to endeavor to avoid such appropriation and misuse by avoiding knowledge altogether—or by suggesting the impossibility of knowledge because of the internal complexities of language, as deconstruction would have it—evidences a failure of nerve and a strangely risk-averse fear of life.

The authors whose texts are examined in this book traveled and wrote, and their texts stood in complex relations to the establishment of a global network of European power. Travel, narrative, and empire: how does the construction of space change, and what does it mean to move through it? How is change experienced and how can it be recorded in order to be read in a changed setting again? And, finally, what are the consequences of the encounter with the different culture, the site of the travels, and how do they leave their marks in the text? This book is neither a history of German colonialism nor an intellectual history of the images of non-Europeans in German literature. Instead, it looks at some specific cases in which Germans (sometimes alone, sometimes with others) traveled into that non-European world, gradually coming under the sway of European power. It asks how they wrote about and recorded their encounters with the people they met. At times, the texts are genuine travelogues, whereas others are fictional narratives. In either case, the issue is the encounter with alterity and not simply the literary image of "the other."

A word on method: the topic of this book is colonial discourse, by which is meant the linguistic articulation of the process through which the non-European cultures were integrated into a Europe-based system of administration. It is not a history of colonialism in general, not a discussion of its economic or military or even cultural institutions but an analysis of a set of texts that lend themselves to an examination within the terms of cultural studies. The texts are taken as complex constructions that display political or philosophical issues relevant to the colonial problematic. Therefore, the key topic is not, as it is typically for historians, the biographies of the individual authors (although there is surely much biography in this book) but the precipitation of specific problems within the text.[6] My concern is ultimately not the achievements or failings of individual writers but their capacity to articulate certain fundamental features of the colonial scene in which different cultures collide and intermingle. One can speak of these articulations as colonial discourse, although I do not contend that discourse somehow determines experience. Rather, the modes of expression help objectify key experiences, and the critic's close reading of these texts can ferret out underlying issues.

One might question the choice of texts and authors. I believe that the evidence collected in the book displays a range of crucial phenomena pertaining to colonialism, Enlightenment, and travel. I do not claim to have surveyed the field with these case studies, which, however, have a typological, if not always typical, validity. Thus, Georg Forster, for example (discussed in the next chapter), is surely not typical of the German Enlightenment: he is on its radical end. Nevertheless, the issues from the young Forster that appear in the text are quite characteristic of Enlightenment thinking. In this case, moreover, I have pursued a further strategy to assure objectivity. Here and in some of the book's chapters, I have chosen to bring together texts by different authors in order to better focus on related problems from differing perspectives. By investigating the two accounts of the same incident, one by Forster and the other by Cook, fundamental issues in eighteenth-century thought are exposed with greater objectivity. Ultimately, however, the plausibility of the claims in the book depends on the persuasiveness of the analyses and not on the selection of material.

The topic of the first chapter is an example of the historical Enlightenment, a classic voyage of discovery, begun in 1773, to learn more about the uncharted space of the South Pacific. Of this voyage, Captain Cook's second circumnavigation, we have two narrative records, one by the captain himself and the other by the young

Forster, who accompanied his father, the official scientific officer. The two texts, Cook's and Forster's, are at times uncannily close, betraying the three years they spent together on the *Resolution*. But through a close reading of a particular passage, their first encounter with the inhabitants of the South Island of New Zealand, remarkable differences emerge. Both authors write as Enlightenment thinkers, but the two approach the question of cultural alterity in strikingly different ways, just as they represent diametrically opposed structures of space and understandings of narrative.

The relationship between Cook and Forster is also emblematic of the relationship between England and Germany in colonial matters. The junior partner, Germany, is always lagging behind and increasingly obsessed with a need to imitate. Germany is, so to speak, always the other empire, and the capacity of the German authors to envision a German imperial sweep is often shaped by this secondary status. It is an empire that is staged in opposition to (or in imitation of) England and therefore must sometimes claim to be better; or, it is an empire that is staged differently than the empire of the English and organized around tropes of empathy with the colonized. It is, needless to say, simply self-serving when German authors gloatingly protest that Africans would prefer German to English colonizers. To the extent, however, that German colonial discourse does indeed leave considerable room for direct identification with the colonized—from Forster's cultural hermeneutics to the early-twentieth-century primitivism of the expressionists—this specificity indicates both a different colonial discourse in this, the other empire, as well as a different national self-understanding in Germany, whose *Sonderweg*, its special mode of modernization, rendered it the other in Europe. German colonial discourse is interesting because it is different from the more emphatically universalizing claims of British and French colonial discourses, which in turn is a reflection of Germany's ambivalent situation within Europe. It is emphatically within Europe but also on the margin of the economic and political centers in England and France. This specificity of German colonial discourse, largely ignored by contemporary post-colonial theory, will be examined throughout the book.

After Cook and Forster, the English material recurs in the second chapter, which looks at Gerhard Rohlfs, a German geographer who was attached as the observer of the Royal Prussian Government to the British expedition in Abyssinia in 1868. The chapter describes in some detail the background to that expedition—the diplomatic impasse between Abyssinia and England, the taking of hostages, and the subsequent military action—in order to treat both Rohlfs's report and, a dramatically different approach, the American journalism of Henry Stanley. In addition, Rohlfs's background and his accomplishments as an *Afrikareisender* are discussed, in particular to scrutinize geographic writing—the character of its descriptivism and its objective facticity—as well as the emergent split in the reading public and the consequences of this for scientific writing. The chapter considers the status of science and some of its underpinnings in the nineteenth century as well as Rohlfs's passage from a discreetly unpolitical author to an explicit advocate of the German colonial expansion of the 1880s.

Although the setting is still the same, chapter 3 treats another mode of travel literature, missionary prose, for the missionary under discussion was among the hostages in the Abyssinian fortress of Magdala. Henry Aaron Stern, a German-Jewish convert to Christianity, was preaching to the Falashas when the crisis between Abyssinia and England erupted. An examination of his texts allows for a discussion of an alternative approach to travel: not the descriptivism of the geographer but the imperative of cultural penetration by the missionary. No matter how much the missionary may be a carrier of imperial domination, the nature of the project—the conversion of the local population—requires a measure of cultural empathy foreign, or at least irrelevant, to the natural scientific observer. Indeed, Rohlfs and Stern make up a pair and not only in their crossed Abyssinian paths but in their approaches to writing. The geographer's naturalism and the missionary's historicism represent distinct halves of the same whole that, less than a century earlier, Forster had been able to unite. In addition, Stern's specific function as a converted Jew on a mission to the Jews points to some crucial interrelationships between colonialism and anti-Semitism.

The fourth chapter explores the gendering of colonial discourse, particularly in one of the most widely disseminated German propaganda tracts of the nineteenth century, authored by Ferdinand Fabri. His advocacy of colonialism depends less on rational arguments than on a semiotic system of gendered metaphors and images of bodies flowing between "mother countries" and "daughter colonies," made all the more dramatic by obstetric imagery and anxieties concerning the loss of bodies through emigration to the United States and elsewhere. Fabri, however, is the preface to the more complex gender politics in psychoanalysis. For it was Freud, after all, who linked female sexuality and imperialism by his remarkable use of the metaphor of the "dark continent" (he used the term in English). Is this science, psychoanalysis, as imperialist as Cook's geography might have appeared to be? Or is the entanglement of science and Enlightenment with imperialism more complex? In Freud's case, at least, a close examination of his usage of the term *dark continent* reveals a critical stance, which I then pursue in the rest of the chapter when I examine Freud's own metaphoric identification with Africa: his fascination with Hannibal, recorded in *The Interpretation of Dreams*, and his affinity to Boabdil, the last Moorish king in Spain, in a late essay on "A Disturbance of Memory at the Acropolis"—a location itself overdetermined as an emphatic symbol of Europe.

Chapter 5 continues the gender-theoretical discussion of colonialism through an examination of a counterintuitive relationship between nineteenth-century feminism and empire. The colony appears, at least within colonial discourse, as a site of emancipation for women, allowing for opportunities impossible to achieve in the patriarchal order of Germany. This progressive promise within colonialism is particularly evident in the fictional narratives of Frieda von Bülow, the founder of the German colonial literature, as well as in various vernacular narratives by German settlers in the Africa colonies. For von Bülow the colony is the site of transgender transgression, where women can take on roles previously reserved for men, whereas men are called upon to give up their European role consciousness and develop attributes coded as feminine precisely so the colonial enterprise can be successful. The vernacular evidence, by way of contrast, is considerably more pessimistic, both in an under-lying castration anxiety recurring in several texts as well as in the particular animosity directed toward women in the colonized Afri-can population.

The sixth and final chapter includes a discussion of anticolonial-ism, particularly in the writings of Jean-Paul Sartre and Jacques Derrida, which evince a specific understanding of the colonial set-ting as one of radical and impermeable separation. In addition, their critique of colonialism involves the insistence that Western intellec-tuals and Western culture necessarily lead to the racist hierarchies of the colonies and that an end to colonialism would somehow be tied to an end to intellectuals. Although the first chapter of the book ex-amines texts by two Enlightenment figures, Cook and Forster, in order to explore their relationship to empire, the last chapter re-flects on attacks on the Enlightenment—antilogocentrism—that are tied to political attacks on colonialism. This mixture of anti-colonialism and anti-intellectualism, then, is contrasted with the ev-idence in some various and heterogeneous German texts that con-struct the colonial site as a plausible location for the redefinition of intellectuality. The chapter treats the fictional prose of Leopold von Sacher-Masoch, who provides mid-nineteenth-century accounts of the paracolonial Eastern Europe (territory with a Slavic population under Austrian rule) where the diversity that characterizes the colo-nial setting interacts with particularly peripatetic sexual politics. The putative figure of power displays a fascination with the colo-nized that issues in an inversion. A similar phenomenon can be ob-served in the primitivism of the early-twentieth-century expression-ist painter Emil Nolde, where the empathetic immersion into the cultural sensibility of the colonized people radically transforms the character of "metropolitan" art. It can also be seen in the analysis of colonialism, or, more precisely, the critical analysis of anticolonial-ism, in Kafka's "In the Penal Colony" (1919). As violent and horrify-ing as the administration of colonialism may be on Kafka's island, it is the failure of the anticolonial voyager, a fictional traveler, who cannot genuinely engage with the alterity represented by the back-wardness of the island and therefore must flee back to safety. The text is remarkable because it breaks up the easy opposition between

European and non-European, colonizer and colonized, by recognizing the additional crucial difference between the colonizers and the metropolitan Europeans who regard the immediate colonizers as the real "primitives." Where Sartre and Derrida operated with neat distinctions between colonizer and colonized, or between reason and its other, the German material—Sacher-Masoch, Nolde, and Kafka—displays a more complex and transgressive relation between the poles of the colonial dialectic.

The arguments for the complexity of the colonial scene throughout the book depend on a number of theoretical assertions that are important to underscore at the outset. First, the book participates in the scholarly project that has come to be known as cultural studies, while it simultaneously stakes out a minority position within it—dissident cultural studies, so to speak. In general, cultural studies represents an expansion of the fields of objects of inquiry, challenging disciplines to go beyond the works of canonized literature to examine a wider, perhaps unlimited, set of texts. The goal of such an anthropological redefinition of culture becomes the investigation into the constructions and contestations of group identity, especially through examinations of the deployment of particular discourses, that is, restricted codes of representation. In the wake of structuralist linguistics and the enormous influence of the historiographical work of Foucault, the major tendency within cultural studies scholarship involves the tracing of discourses understood to constitute the experience of subjects. Indeed, subjectivity altogether—not particular versions but the fundamental possibility of subjectivity—is treated as a consequence of discursive structures.

This consistently discourse-theoretical cultural studies is, however, deeply problematic, representing ultimately a return to an idealistic historiography, in that it asserts an overriding zeitgeist or episteme (to use Foucault's term) and then fits the historical data into prescribed frameworks. It thereby loses the sense of an objective historical past as well as the concrete subjectivity of human experience in particular contexts. In contrast, the studies of colonial discourse in this volume impute a quite different status to "discourse," which is understood to designate the social expressions of shared experience. These expressions are necessarily complex, contradictory, and often at odds with experience but nevertheless refer to it. Colonial discourse is therefore the articulation—description, narration, and recollection—of colonial experience; it is not, however, the precondition of colonialism, and it is certainly not identical with colonialism. To the contrary, the complex reality of colonialism leaves its marks in the intricacies of colonial discourse.

The recognition and analysis of complexity and transgression are the major achievements of postcolonial theory, particularly in the notions of hybridity and transculturalism, which have been developed by critics such Homi K. Bhabha and Mary Louise Pratt. This book draws in part on their work. Nevertheless, a second point of theoretical dissension needs to be pursued. Bhabha's work largely, if not exclusively, interprets situations associated with British imperialism; Pratt's work involves Latin America, although it simultaneously derives from structures of British imperialism. Both critics, however, tend to suggest more global claims regarding the relationship between European culture, power, and the colonial world. General statements about Europe are made on the basis of particular national events. The underlying assumption of postcolonial theory appears to be that British imperialism is the normative imperial structure. The point of this book is to argue, on the contrary, that the German experience was quite different, displaying alternative possibilities within the Enlightenment and, more importantly, quite different approaches to alterity. The less stable and more permeable notion of "German," which allows one to include Freud and Kafka in this discussion, results in a greater permeability toward other cultures. The potential for hybridization is consequently not primarily postcolonial but immanent to the colonial situation itself, at least where the colonizing nation has the requisite flexibility of identity. In this German case, however, the understanding of empire requires a deep revision. Although it can entail aspects of violent domination, it also allows for transgression, mixing, and plurality. To represent the colonial scene solely as a Manichaean segregation may be an adequate description of British imperialism, but as a general account it is a sorry misrepresentation and ultimately simply a political effect of a politicized anticolonialism, polemically distorting the scope of differentiation.

Such antinomic misrepresentation is strongly related to the rhetoric of anti-Eurocentrism that marks postcolonialism. The critique of Eurocentrism may have once mediated the literary and political aspirations of intellectuals from the "periphery" of Latin America, especially when they proffered indigenist programs as an alternative to the high culture of the metropolitan centers of London and Paris. However, the appropriation of anti-Eurocentrism as a theoretical (and sometimes curricular) position in the United States is deeply problematic. It surely bolsters a standard American isolationist disregard for the rest of the world, which is never taken quite seriously. Moreover, it is based on a narrow and quite untenable notion of Europe. Given postcolonial theory's extensive dependence on the model of the British Empire—the theory appears to derive from the subjectivity of the Commonwealth—it is particularly strange to translate core problems into a matter of "Eurocentrism" since Britain's relationship to Europe is hardly stable or unambiguous. Postcolonial theory is curiously blind to the distance and difference between Britain and the European continent. If in geographical terms Germany appears to be more definitely in Europe than insular England, the history of Germany's troubled relationship to the European West looms ominously and resists any quick and easy subsumption into a continental identity. During the age of high imperialism, the nation-states of Europe acted less in unison than in antagonism as emphatically individual actors and, even in the 1990s, the project for European unification faces considerable European opposition. Yet if the centeredness of Europe remains so evanescent, it makes little sense to speak of a Eurocentrism.

The third and final point of theoretical clarification involves the understanding of the term *Enlightenment*. It refers most directly to the movement in eighteenth-century European thought that elevated the significance of science and reason in cultural life. Cook and Forster are exponents of the Enlightenment, used in this most restrictive sense. Yet the power of the arguments of the Enlightenment and their consequences have been so important that it would be rather pedantic to limit the usage of the term to a few decades of the Parisian eighteenth century and not see ramifications of Enlightenment—rationalization, the critique of religions and traditionalism, and the spread of scientific norms—as defining features of modernity in general. Rohlfs's geographic objectivism, Stern's universalist faith, Freud's interpretive projects: all these are part of the Enlightenment understood more broadly. The term loses the neatness of the first meaning, the delimited historical period; but it also gains by providing insights into seminal tendencies of the past three centuries.

In the German intellectual tradition, this broader notion of Enlightenment in modernity has been occasionally linked to larger civilizational processes. The work of Norbert Elias comes to mind and, especially, Max Weber's interest in the specificity of an occidental rationality. Enlightenment is given its broadest and most anthropological scope in Max Horkheimer and Theodor W. Adorno's *Dialectic of Enlightenment*, which treats it as the civilizational process itself. For this study, however, it is not the scope of Horkheimer and Adorno's vision that is crucial but rather the particular complexity of the assessment of the Enlightenment, that is, its "dialectic." Although today poststructuralism and deconstruction denounce (in different ways) the Enlightenment as a vehicle of power and domination, Horkheimer and Adorno argued that the project of reason is much more multivocal: potentially a source of domination, it is simultaneously the source of resistance and the vision of a better life. The point is not to find some alternative to Enlightenment but to hold reason to its own standards. It is in this tradition that Enlightenment as colonial discourse is examined here with reference to its multiple valences. This is, however, a potentially quite controversial dialectic since we may find that a colonial discourse derived from the Enlightenment may not only be part of a system of domination, it may also be the vehicle for a genuine knowledge of another culture and the site for fruitful border crossings.

This book, therefore, hardly denies the plausibility of those critiques of Enlightenment that suggest that reason and knowledge may be implicated in structures of power. It is hard to argue with the obvious. The point is rather that such complicity is not at all the whole story, nor perhaps even the most important part of it. Knowledge is not only oppressive power but also the possibility of revising power in order to transform it, perhaps even to overcome it. If one forgets this dialectic, the other side of reason, then one would end up fully in the contemporary cynicism that only describes power with obsessive detailing, but cannot imagine change. Yet that same cynicism also fails to imagine the alterity that is at the core (not the margins) of colonial discourse: the possibility of exploring the world and experiencing something new.

Empire or Enlightenment, colonial discourse or the qualitatively new?: this book explores the labyrinthine dialectics around these terms. It claims that a strand of German culture was quite curious about difference, and this interest produced a particular openness (perhaps less characteristic of the colonialisms of those nations with more rigidly defined identities). The epigraphs with which I have chosen to open the book stage this constellation. Goethe attributes to Faust a nearly unquenchable thirst for experience and for knowledge of the far-flung world. Hence, the urgency of his travel, his pursuit of the large world and—in an anticipation of the malignant side of the Enlightenment—the destruction of the small world of the traditionalism in the story of Gretchen. W. E. B. Du Bois treasured Goethe, indeed urged students at his alma mater to study Goethe in order to support "the rise of the Negro people."[7] Yet even this seminal advocate of Pan-Africanism and ardent proponent of decolonization was not immune to the imperialist allures of Wilhelmine Germany, as Du Bois himself concedes in recalling his student days in Berlin in the 1890s: "Then there was that new, young Emperor, 'von Gottes Gnade, deutscher Kaiser, Koenig von Preussen,' who led and pinpointed the pageantry. Ever and again he came riding ahead of his white and golden troops on prancing chargers through the great Brandenburg gate, up the Linden. . . . I even trimmed my beard and mustache to a fashion like his and still follow it."[8] This is the sort of concrete detail that is erased by the Anglocentrism of postcolonial theory. When the First World War broke out, Du Bois had no particular reason to support an American alliance with the major colonial powers in Africa, Britain and France. Yet he eventually came around to just that position, although he had to address his particular relationship to Germany, which I have chosen as an epigraph to this book, because it expresses a view from a leader in the movement against colonialism that betrays no visceral rejection of Europe, or of Germany. It is worth quoting again here: "the writer speaks without anti-German bias; personally he has deep cause to love the German people. They made him believe in the essential humanity of white folk twenty years ago when he was near denying it."[9]

1

THE ENLIGHTENMENT
TRAVELOGUE AND THE
COLONIAL TEXT

The eighteenth-century Enlightenment, with its emphatic faith in the value of reason, has left a legacy that continues to structure underlying cultural assumptions in many dimensions of social life. To command legitimacy, choices have to appear to be rational; to point to the irrationality of a decision or a judgment is tantamount to denouncing it. Public figures today are surely unlikely to invoke the spread of an idealistic spirit of reason as the core of a Hegelian history. It is certainly the case, however, that much contemporary discourse involves imagery of the rule of law and international regulation, as if particular norms of behavior and codes of action were deemed appropriate to apply around the world. That, however, is little more than a form of the Enlightenment's vision of the universal character of reason's sway, a regime in which the disappearance of prejudice would lead necessarily to emancipation.

Yet from the start, the Enlightenment and its insistence that the institutionalization of reason would further human freedom have been criticized. This critique came not only from traditionalist defenders of the ancien régime of prerational structures but also from others who, very much subscribing to Enlightenment visions of freedom, doubted whether reason could be an effective vehicle for emancipation. Might not the terrorism of reason suppress the imagination, as the German romantics feared? Had not the Napoleonic campaign of reason led to a new imperial tyranny? Might not the world structured around scientific principles become repressive and restrictive, and had not science, knowledge, and reason played central roles in modern structures of domination?

These alternative assessments of reason are crucial to any discussion of colonial discourse since the expansion of European power around the globe has been intimately involved with the expansion of knowledge. Does this complicity, the collaboration of knowledge and power, lead one inexorably to the conclusion, shared by poststructuralists, that the Enlightenment is guilty of colonialism? Or can one separate an emancipatory component of the Enlightenment project from the subsequent history of European rule?[1] This ambivalence in the history of colonialism is, of course, full of implications for the standing, indeed, for the *possibility*, of science in general, and it is with that larger horizon in mind that one can turn with interest to a particular dramatic staging of the tensions within the Enlightenment at a key point in the history of European expansion.

In the course of Captain Cook's second circumnavigation, in March of 1773, an encounter took place on what would become known as the South Island of New Zealand. It involved a group of island inhabitants, on the one hand, and, on the other, the European voyagers, two of whom have left detailed records: Cook himself and Georg Forster, at the time quite young, and who would later become one of the leading authors of classical German literature. The alternative descriptions are extremely close in detail, although their conceptual underpinnings are at considerable odds. In particular, the constructions of space and the related capacity to understand another culture highlight a significant range of possibilities within the Enlightenment itself. In other words, difference or "otherness" is not merely a question of the confrontation of the Europeans with exotic cultures from distant lands; there is an other within the Enlightenment. To the extent that contemporary cultural theory associates alterity solely with non-Western cultures or with marginal groups, it refuses to recognize the diversity within European cultures. It also surrenders the critical capac-

ity that derives from concepts of self-estrangement or alienation, which represent degraded modes of otherness. Precisely
in order to retrieve the complexity of alterity, both within and
outside the Enlightenment, it is important to examine the evidence very closely and to try to draw out the philosophical implications of the two texts.

They did not meet until the stranger's second visit, and, even
then, the misunderstandings seem to have been considerable.
The several records of the encounter are, moreover, not always
in full agreement, which makes it still more difficult to reconstruct the event. What sort of a gathering was it? Two small
groups of people who had never met before struck up a conversation early one evening on a New Zealand beach. Simple
enough and apparently inconsequential, except perhaps for the
fact that it was after all the stranger's second visit; something
had driven him to undertake a rather long voyage in order to
return. Was it noble curiosity? or savage greed? or the swashbuckling adventurism of a buccaneer? And whatever it was that
brought him back to the beach, did it animate or did it distort
the encounter with the newfound friends?

Whatever it was that led him to return, we know for sure that
it was a return, that it was the second visit for the stranger,
Captain James Cook, sailing the South Seas in the service of the
British Crown. Some three years earlier, to be precise on
Wednesday, 14 March 1770, he had sighted this place while he
stood on the deck of the *Endeavour*: "In the PM had a fresh gale
from the Southward attended with squals. At 2 o'clock it
clear'd up over the land which appear'd high and mountainous. At half past 3 double reef'd the Topsails and haul'd in
for a Bay wherein there appear'd to be good anchorage and
into which I had thoughts of going with the Ship, but after
standing in an hour we found the distance too great to run before dark and it blowed too hard to attempt it in the night or
even to keep to windward. For these reasons we gave it up and
bore away along shore. This Bay I have named *duskey* Bay."[2] In
1770, he could only name the bay; in 1773, commanding the *Res-*

olution, he could anchor there and explore the coast, and in the course of these explorations he would be lucky enough to meet some of the local residents. It is this meeting that is of interest here, a genuine and reciprocal discovery the intrusive character of which we should neither deny nor, however, consider as summing up the whole story.

It is, of course, indisputable that the encounter at Dusky Bay entailed something qualitatively new: in the most immediate sense, new acquaintances for all the participants and, more abstractly, an encounter among representatives of two distant and, arguably, different cultures, previously unaware of each other's existence. Yet for all this brilliant novelty, there was history as well on each side. Cook had been there before; he had returned, for reasons yet to be discussed, and for the family he met there—the names of whose members are unfortunately not recorded—this shore was likely part of the home turf and overlaid therefore with memories, practices, and anticipations, the contents of which we can hardly guess. But that there were contents there, indeed, contents on both sides (no matter that we cannot determine them retroactively) is incontestable, which in turn implies that the event itself, the novel encounter, was part of a past for both parties (or rather, for all parties concerned, since there is no reason to assume any sort of monolithic unanimity among the various actors in either the group of travelers or the island family).

So the new event is not unambiguously new: no primal leap, no existential origin here. The event lacks that noble savagery of unquestionable beginnings, onto which an exaggerated sense of originality is sometimes projected by subsequent narrators, anxious to counterfeit some genealogy. For those gathered on a promontory at Dusky Bay on the sixth of April in 1773, what transpired was new but not the commencement of a new age. The groups must have certainly appeared to differ, but there is no evidence that anyone assumed a fundamental incommensurability, let alone an absolute difference. No one records the judgment that it was a meeting of civilization with primitives, or Europe with the East, or a self-conscious self with an exotic other. Ego is not lined up here against id or against alterity; it is a strange encounter but not an estranged one and by no means simply, or brutally, a colonial one.

The complexity of the, let us say, international conclave at Dusky Bay was heightened a bit by the fact that Cook's party was itself no homogeneous self. Among the British captain's companions was the German Johann Reinhold Forster, serving as the scientific expert on the three-year voyage and assisted by his son Georg (nineteen years old at the outset). The young Forster would eventually compose an English-language account of the voyage, which competed with the official version that was authored by Cook and published with the blessings of the Admiralty. Forster simultaneously prepared a German version of his text and, at the risk of succumbing now to the same fascination with origins denigrated a few lines ago, one might treat this voyage and, in particular, the meeting at Dusky Bay, as one of the beginnings of a modern German travel literature. That the German literature of discovery should begin in English as a record of Cook's voyage is itself a trenchant allegory for the origins of modern Germany, German nationhood, and German imperialism—never quite catching up.

Unlike Cook, Forster had never been in the South Seas before (although he was, to be sure, a seasoned traveler). Nevertheless, his description of the natural setting at Dusky Bay has less to do with a romanticism of originality than with a sensuous delight at having returned to land, the first land since leaving Table Bay at the tip of Africa.

> After an interval of one hundred and twenty-two days, and a run of above three thousand five hundred leagues, out of sight of land, we entered Dusky bay on the 26th of March about noon. . . . The weather was delightfully fair, and genially warm, when compared to what we had lately experienced; and one glided along by insensible degrees, wafted by light airs, past numerous rocky islands, each of which was covered with wood and shrubberies, where numerous evergreens were sweetly contrasted and mingled with the various shades of autumnal yellow. Flocks of

aquatic birds enlivened the rocky shores, and the whole country resounded with the wild notes of the feathered tribe. We had long and eagerly wished for the land and its vegetable productions, and therefore could not but eye the prospect before us with peculiar delight, and the emotions of joy and satisfaction which were strongly marked in the countenance of each individual.[3]

Not untouched by the sentimentalism of the 1770s, Forster characteristically integrates an account of emotions, his own and those of his companions, into the narrative of the voyage. How profound is the stirring of his soul, aroused by the prospect of fresh vegetables! (Or was it the stirring of his belly? The history of science enters into this Enlightenment tale here since one positive result of this circumnavigation was the discovery that scurvy could be successfully prevented through a rigorous diet of sauerkraut.)

Few such stirrings are to be found in Cook's record; the cited passage describing the aborted approach in 1770 may be regarded as typical of his prose. For Cook, Dusky Bay is a cartographic fact, a latitudinal item to be entered in the charts and, at best, a way station of solely logistical import for the continuation of an exploratory undertaking that moves along lines drawn from point to point in an empty sea. For Forster, it is an aesthetic experience as well as a natural fact—and more too, since at Dusky Bay an epochal human encounter would transpire. The scientist Cook measures geometric space whereas Forster encounters a life world. The difference between the modes of writing chosen by Cook and Forster—let me label the former geometric and the latter with Forster's own term, a *philosophische Reisebeschreibung*, a philosophical travelogue— the difference between these two versions of rationality in Enlightenment prose sets the stage for a dialectical development of subsequent travel literature, to which I will return presently.[4]

Return: as antithetical as the writers Cook and Forster may be, both were returning—Cook to the place, a lonely spot in the expansive space of the empty southern ocean, and Forster to land and joy and vegetables, a kingdom of sensuous qualities after the emptiness of four months at sea. As new as this topography is for him, it is also familiar. Here too one might be at home, or so the young Forster wishes, and the landscape not surprisingly appears as a montage of quotations: "The view of rude sceneries in the style of Rosa, the antediluvian forests which cloathed the rock, and of numerous rills of water, which every where rolled down the steep declivity, altogether conspired to complete our joy. . . . Such are the general ideas of travellers and voyagers long exhausted by distresses; and with such warmth of imagination they have viewed the rude cliffs of Juan Fernandez, and the impenetrable forests of Tinian!"[5] A postmodern scene, Dusky Bay as the pastiche of a fragmented iconography? Hardly, for this is neither a solely surface landscape nor one marked by a loss of affect (it is not Forster but Cook who excludes sentiment and deflates space into the flatness of a map). On the contrary, the metaphor of art and nature inverts, in a decidedly modern and postclassical manner, the established hierarchy, since it is now nature that is the source of the genuine aesthetic experience and not the conventions of institutionalized art, and this experience is emphatically subjective.

The forests may well be antediluvian; they are not therefore incomprehensibly primitive or dauntingly pristine. Forster is not on a safari for the exotic. Indeed, the stereotypes of wilderness "in the style of Rosa" give way to the actuality of encounter, just as a century and a half later the primitivist iconography of German expressionism, derived from materials in ethnographic museums, gave way to more nuanced representations in the wake of journeys abroad. Evidently, direct experience has the power to transform content and is not fully restricted by codes or discursive paradigms. All that Forster encounters at Dusky Bay, as well as elsewhere on the voyage, is always somehow poignantly familiar in the sense that it is comprehensible to the sentient observer and accessible to some mode of human cognition, be it scientific reason (not unlike Cook's cartography—there is more than a little overlap between the two writing projects), practical understanding, or aesthetic sensibility. The meeting at Dusky Bay is therefore by no means a confrontation with wildly exotic alterity but rather a less than ideal, but much more than failed, communication of worldly enlightened thinkers with other human beings, arguably equally worldly and enlightened. What do they have to tell us?

The *Resolution* entered Dusky Bay around noon on 26 March 1773, and it was not very long before the explorers caught sight of local inhabitants: "We had not been above two days in this bay, before we found that our opinion of its being uninhabited was premature," reports Forster—the expanse of geometric space was not as empty as some had anticipated or perhaps hoped.[6] Nevertheless, both groups are extremely cautious with their curiosity. A small band of officers turns away from "New Zeelanders" who "halloo'd at their approach," for fear of being outnumbered, and later that same afternoon, when Cook landed a party to undertake a visit, "no natives appeared this second time."[7] The mutual observation is evidently tempered by some prudent apprehension since no one wants to be caught at a disadvantage. We know that the officers feared that the rainy weather "might, in case of danger, have prevented their pieces from going off."[8] Still, it is not only danger that fills the air but also the anticipation of a meeting and the initiation of exchange and communication. Finding that the natives avoided the landing party, Cook chose not to search for them, deciding instead to deposit some gifts and "to leave it to time and their own free will to cultivate an intercourse with us."[9] At this initial stage, then, it is clear that, whereas the explorers are prepared to use force if necessary in the case of danger, it is by no means solely in order to force a contact and establish their power that they have come here. The potential interlocutors are presumed to have, as Cook puts it, "free will," which demands respect, and the events at Dusky Bay proceed with tact, not the gunboat diplomacy that would characterize a later era. One would do the Enlightenment explorers and the Enlightenment an injustice, if one were to reduce them to the strategic agents of an imprisoning power, even if a latter-day imperialism would benefit from their research and their science.

The rain held, with barely an interruption, and the travelers could undertake little until the morning of 6 April, when Cook, accompanied by the two Forsters as well as the painter William Hodges—the professional illustrator on the trip—and Anders Sparrman, a young scientist who had joined the expedition at Table Bay, set out in a small boat "to continue the survey of the bay, to copy views from nature, and to search for the natural productions of the country."[10] To the north they entered a "capacious" cove, where "we found a number of wild fowl, and particularly wild ducks, of which we shot fourteen, from whence we gave it the name of Duck Cove."[11] It was, however, on the way back to the *Resolution* that the crucial event, the first substantive encounter between the Europeans and the New Zealanders, took place, and Forster's account of the meeting reveals much about the terms on which it was implicitly based.

In the extensive passage that follows, it is crucial both to follow the narrative and to understand the gravity of the moment: distinct cultures encountering each other and negotiating the terms of their interaction. The invention of language, the deployment of power, the efforts to appeal to a presumed sensibility, and ultimately the very possibility of a cross-cultural, which is to say, universal knowledge—all these are underlying considerations as the Europeans and the Pacific islanders meet, and the plot thickens:

> As we were returning home, we heard a loud hallooing on the rocky point of an island, which on this occasion obtained the name of Indian Island; and standing in to the shore, we perceived one of the natives, from whom this noise proceeded. He stood with a club or battle-axe in his hand, on a projecting point, and behind him on the skirts of the wood we saw two women, each of them having a long spear. When our boat came to the foot of the rock, we called to him, in the language of Taheitee, tayo harre mai, "friend, come hither"; he did not, however, stir from his

post, but held a long speech, at certain intervals pro-
nouncing it with great earnestness and vehemence, and
swinging round his club, on which he leaned at other
times. Captain Cook went to the head of the boat, called
to him in a friendly manner, and threw him his own and
some other handkerchiefs, which he would not pick up.
The captain then taking some sheets of white paper in his
hand, the captain then landed on the rock unarmed, and
held the paper out to the native. The man now trembled
very visibly, and having exhibited strong marks of fear in
his countenance, took the paper: upon which, Captain
Cook coming up to him, took hold of his hand, and embraced him, touching the man's nose with his own, which
is their mode of salutation. His apprehension was by this
means dissipated, and he called to the two women, who
came and joined him, while several of us landed to keep
the Captain company. A short conversation ensued, of
which very little was understood on both sides, for want
of a competent knowledge of the language. Mr. Hodges
immediately took sketches of their countenances, and
their gestures showed that they clearly understood what
he was doing; on which they called him *toa-toa*, that term
being probably applicable to the imitative arts.[12]

This initial encounter establishes mechanisms of reciprocal
comprehension between the two groups. The excerpt from the
narrative of the voyage (representing travel literature as the
prehistory of a subsequent colonial literature, not yet colonial
but occupying the same space) therefore testifies to the construction of the relationship between Europeans and non-Europeans, which is by no means already a colonial one but which
may well contain, as a hidden potential, the possibility of a colonial distortion. The distinction is important. To designate
the encounter as colonial because of subsequent colonial practices is, of course, a case of *post hoc, ergo propter hoc*. Moreover,
such an equation, aside from its logical faults, would effectively represent a severe judgment on the Enlightenment, im-
plying that all science is colonial as are all possible relations be-

tween Europe and the rest of the world. In contrast, a critical
account of colonialism would necessarily have to distinguish
between colonial and noncolonial practices as well as between
valid science and an instrumentalized ideology.

The process at Dusky Bay commences with an invocative use
of spoken language, the man's call to the voyagers. To be sure,
there is no way to determine that his call entailed a salutation;
it may well have been an admonition to ward the presumed in-
vaders off. Since he was swinging a club, his purported greeting was, at best, part of a mixed message. Yet such a counter-
hypothesis is belied, if not conclusively, by the earlier efforts of
the islanders to contact the group of officers on the twenty-
eighth. Not only Cook's party but the indigenous population
as well (or at least part of it) was trying to meet the strangers.
Moreover, there is reason to believe that Cook's party might
have passed by the group without even noticing them had not
the man hailed them. This is at least the implication of a relevant comment in Cook's published account (which, however,
is absent in the journals). So, if the "halloo" was intended as a
warning, it was clearly counterproductive. The obvious conclusion is instead the likely one: that the man was, with both
excitement and trepidation, greeting the strangers and calling
to them. Indeed, it would be fairer to say that he discovered
Cook and company than vice versa.

Cook's reply (and the German text makes it clear that it was
Captain Cook who spoke), the invitation to approach, is similarly a direct invocation, based on the gamble that the language in Dusky Bay might be somehow related to the Tahitian
with which Cook was already familiar. That is, for the Europeans as well as the islanders, the goal appears to have been determining a shared referential language, the initial phase of
which is marked by direct mutual appellation. The first words
are rather close to names (Cook has just named Duck Cove as
he has named many other places, as if the project of discovery
were largely a matter of establishing a serial nomenclature).
This attempt at referentiality is by no means thoroughly unsuc-
cessful. The two men do in fact enter a sort of verbal exchange

that seems to mediate their drawing closer to each other in physical space. It is difficult indeed to imagine Cook's boat approaching the party on shore with everyone, on both sides, guarding a total silence. Moreover, later, once a more solid contact has been established, a conversation takes place in which, to be sure, little is understood—Cook calls it a "chit-chat."[13] Presumably, however, that empirically deficient communication is experienced as such by all concerned precisely because of the shared assumption of a counterfactual ideal of the very possibility of understanding, an assumption established through the initial exchange of invocations. This in turn implies the possibility of shared practices—in this case with regard to language—despite other cultural differences.

Although the invocative referentiality was not a complete failure, it was certainly not adequate to encourage fully cordial relations between the two groups, especially given the degree of fear on both sides. Whereas the man on the shore probably did little to calm the strangers by swinging his club, Cook's behavior too was rather odd. For to the extent that he assumed that his interlocutor understood Tahitian, the suggestion that the latter approach or even enter the boat was sorely inapt: could Cook have truly expected the New Zealander simply to wade out into the water and hop on board? Rather, common sense would dictate that Cook step onto land, which he in fact eventually does. This act, Cook's step forward, begins to break the linguistic stalemate that gives way to a more material exchange: the salutary gesture of rubbing noses and the presentation of gifts. Not any gifts would do, of course. It is hardly incomprehensible that the man refused to stoop for Cook's handkerchief, especially since we soon learn that the local population produces its own textiles. Similarly, they turn down gifts of fish and game, "which the young Woman afterwards took up one by one and threw them into the Boat again giving us to understand that such things they wanted not."[14] Hatchets, spike nails, and a boat cloak, on the other hand, appear to have attracted their interest.[15] The point then is not only that physical touch and material goods considerably augment the fragile linguistic contact but that the character of the trade of the material exchange is one in which the New Zealanders have considerable influence. It is not the case that Cook can arbitrarily dictate its terms. Nor is the opposite true. It is an exchange between shrewd equals engaged in complicated negotiations with much attention to details and nuances. It is here that the still abstract referentiality of the opening invocations begins to be fleshed out with contents as concrete and sensuous as the vegetables whose prospect had so animated Forster's imagination.

Still, it is neither the referentiality of naming nor the materiality of exchange that appears to have been the crux of the matter, but rather Cook's dramatic leap on to the shore and his embrace as a symbolic expression of human solidarity. This is at least the tenor of Forster's account, which leaves no doubt that he considers the "salutation" to have "dissipated" the man's "apprehension." Note, however, that Cook's version leaves room for some ambiguity on this point: "The man could not help discovering great signs of fear when we approached the rock with our boat. . . . At length, I landed, went up and embraced him; and presented him with such articles as I had about me, which at once dissipated his fears."[16] Was it then the symbol of the gesture, as Forster claims, or, as Cook implies, the presence of the articles "which at once dissipated his fears" and produced the ensuing comity? Or did the articles themselves, at least in Cook's eyes, also have a symbolic status? What sort of gift is proper to bring to seaside meetings like the one at Dusky Bay?

Forster alone tells us what those articles were: sheets of white paper, a somewhat strange gift, one might think; indeed, a strange item for Cook to have been carrying with him in the boat. Yet we know that the outing to Duck Cove itself had been undertaken to explore the terrain and "to copy views from nature," a task perhaps not restricted to the artist Hodges. It is not at all implausible to assume that Cook carried paper with him to make notes or sketches since his cartographic task after all involved recording this terra incognita onto reams of blank paper. So it is the writer Cook who jumps ashore with sheets of white paper that he, as writer, recorder, and explorer, naturally has with him, and perhaps even with the covert intention of writing about the encounter. And, so the narrative tells us, before the meeting is concluded, Hodges has indeed captured the new acquaintances, at least on paper—a sort of hieroglyphic writing. What Forster took to be an instance of human solidarity may have entailed a hidden agenda. Where Forster sentimentally sees only an act of fraternization, Cook is driven by a different intention, a grammatology that subordinates all experiences to writing: he quickly reduces his erstwhile "friend" to lines on paper and an object of study. The preceding verbal exclamation of friendship turns out to have been an opportunistic fiction. Power lies instead in the technique of inscription, since everything is about to become a text, a map, or a drawing, all to be turned over to the Admiralty.

For Cook, the inhabitants of Dusky Bay, the New Zealand shore, and the vast space of the South Pacific are, at first, blank and empty, to be filled up and written across by the experience of the traveler. This fundamental asymmetry in the cartographic project depends on a central metaphor of Lockean empiricism. "Let us then suppose the Mind to be," Locke asserted, "as we say, white Paper, void of all Characters, without any *Ideas*; How comes it to be furnished? . . . To this I answer, in one word, from Experience."[17] The question, of course, is whose experience counts, and for the protocolonialist Cook the answer is, presumably, his own, or that of the European voyagers, while the native becomes, metonymically the blankness of the empty sheet of paper.

This difference between the two accounts—Forster's foregrounding of the embrace as an expression of sincerity and brotherhood and Cook introducing the white paper (with the ambiguity of inscription and the potential for hierarchy between the writer as master and his topic as object)—is a permutation of the difference we have already encountered. For the substance of Forster's *philosophische Reisebeschreibung* is the appeal to reason and human experience, whereas Cook's cartographic project of inscription traces an arbitrarily mathematical order in an empty Cartesian space, erasing the materiality of previous experience. Both Forster and Cook report the lability of the initial communication, that is, the weakness of the misunderstood invocations. Their treatments of the New Zealanders' response to Mr. Hodges's drawings, however, which in a sense brings that same lability to a provisional conclusion, vary in interesting ways. Forster translates *toa-toa*, evidently a cognate of the source of the English *tatoo*, as the "imitative arts," but Cook glosses the term as signifying "marking or painting." What Forster, whose susceptibility to aesthetic landscapes we have already encountered, sees as an imitation of nature, Cook treats as inscription and writing. Where Forster locates mimesis, Cook suggests a graphic semiosis. Forster trusts in reflection, authenticity, and communication; Cook's concern is the strategic assertion of a sign system—geography and the power of the Admiralty—by means of writing.

The consequence is a further divergence, a hairline fracture in the composition of the Enlightenment. It should be noted that Cook and Forster enjoyed a by no means antagonistic relation (in contrast to ongoing tensions between Cook and Forster's father, the official scientific expert on board). Indeed, long after the voyage Forster remained a great admirer of the captain. What is at stake, however, is not at all the character of these personal ties between the two but rather significant differences in their accounts—and their manner of accounting—of the voyage and particularly of the events at Dusky Bay. These differences, moreover, have to do with an emerging dialectic of Enlightenment reason, which was after all the motive of the journey, and they frame subsequent transformations of travel literature. The antinomies of that dialectic, evidenced in the alternative translations of the islanders' term as mimesis or semiosis, come to the fore in a further manner at Dusky Bay, shedding light both on alternative assumptions regarding language and the limits of humanist universalism.

The man who hailed down Cook's boat was not alone, as we know; two women stood on the shore with him. In the various

records—Cook's original journals, his published narrative of
1777, an anonymous compilation of 1799, and of course Forster's text—the treatment of the younger woman varies considerably, both with regard to her participation in the conversation and to a dance she apparently performed as the travelers
left. In his journal Cook notes that "the youngest of the
Women bore by far the greatest share" of the conversation,
and, as will be seen in a moment, all the records do present her
as certainly loquacious. In fact, the same sentence appears ver-
batim in the 1777 text. As far as the dance goes, the two texts are
separated by a nuance. In the journal one reads, "Night approaching obliged us to take leave of them, when the young
Woman gave us a Dance but the man view'd us with great attention."[18] If the choice of the contrastive conjunction *but* already suggests a value judgment, counterposing the implicitly
denigrated dance with the "great attention" of the male, the
matter is expressed more forcefully in 1777: "the youngest of
the two women, whose volubility of tongue exceeded every
thing I ever met with, gave us a dance; but the man viewed us
with great attention."[19] The implication of the journal is here
rendered sufficiently explicit: speech and dance are located in a
trivial female realm treated with derision and contrasted with
the presumably silent gravity of age and masculinity. The 1799
text, which draws heavily on the earlier version but attempts
something like a popularization (all three of Cook's voyages
are packaged, posthumously, in the single volume), makes the
matter even clearer: "In this conversation, the youngest of the
women bore the greatest share. A droll sailor remarked, that
the women did not want tongue in any part of the world. We
were obliged to leave them on the approach of night; but before we parted Mrs. Talkative gave us a dance."[20] Women and
speech—or, rather, woman as speech, since they are one in the
figure of "Mrs. Talkative"—are the objects of "droll" humor,
which apparently no longer even has any interest in the erstwhile foil, the attentive man. He has dropped mysteriously out
of sight in this latest version, as if the pejorative presentation
of the native woman derived from an ideological commitment

to denigrate the islanders that would also proscribe any positive representation of a native man.

How does Forster handle the incident? The facts, it turns out, are not in dispute. He too reports that the woman talked a good deal and performed a dance. Yet, as the following passage indicates, the issue is the specific construction of facts, the import projected onto them, since the meaning of a fact is rarely self-evident:

> The man remained silent, and looked after us with composure and great attention, which seemed to speak a profound meditation; but the youngest of the two women, whose vociferous volubility of tongue exceeded every thing we had met, began to dance at our departure, and continued to be as loud as ever. Our seamen passed several coarse jests on this occasion, but nothing was more obvious to us than the general drift of nature, which not only provided man with a partner to alleviate his cares and sweeten his labours, but endowed that partner likewise with a desire of pleasing by a superior degree of vivacity and affability.[21]

One should not be thrown off the track by the adolescent Forster's sentimentalist assumptions regarding the specific content of the role of women. The important point is the discursive context in which he suggests that role is performed. Unlike Cook and his anonymous popularizer, Forster does not deem it appropriate to comment on the young woman's behavior in a derogatory manner. On the contrary, he does his best to make sense out of the scene. Indeed, this is precisely his rationalism, the effort to understand the world, including the dancer, as sensible, no matter how strange from his own standpoint. There is an assumption of a fundamental rationality to the world in general and to human culture in particular. Hence, the possibility of both natural and human sciences. Instead of Cook's account of a silly girl who talks too much and lacks the wisdom of her laconic elder, Forster describes her "superior vivacity and affability" as positive values that complement the seriousness of her "partner," a term, twice mentioned, that after all comes rather close to suggesting equality—a premonition perhaps of Forster's later Jacobinism.

If, then, there is a colonial component in the construction of the relationship between Europeans and New Zealanders at Dusky Bay, it takes the form of the patriarchal judgments on the young woman. The competing versions provided by Cook and Forster indicate divergent possibilities within the logic of the Enlightenment. On the one hand, there is a hierarchical and logocentric contempt for the self-evident irrationality of local culture, that is, the fact the woman would talk on and on despite the less than ideal speech situation, flawed by the lack of a common language. On the other, there is the presumed rationality of human behavior coupled with an undercurrent of egalitarianism. The former option anticipates the paradigmatic tropes of colonial representation that would emerge in the relevant texts of the next century: either vicious vilifications of the colonial population or—as with the disappearance of the wisely silent man from the 1799 text—the invisibility of the natives, a rhetorical extermination. The alternative option, Forster's full and radical Enlightenment, suggests the potential for equality across lines of race and gender.

These contrasts, first, between Forster's multidimensional rationalism and Cook's flattened geometry and, second, between an egalitarian universalism and a cultural blindness are embedded, finally, in alternative assumptions regarding language. Recall that the meeting at Dusky Bay proceeds through various attempts to communicate: invocative referentiality, material exchange, and symbolic expression. The literary attacks on the young woman, which culminate in the caricature of "Mrs. Talkative," are not only a matter of a patriarchal truncation of universalism but are, simultaneously, a judgment on the inadequacy of talk, of speech altogether. One might reconstruct the logic of Cook's position by linking an implicit despair at the failed speech with the man—"half an hour [of] chit-chat, little understood on either side"—to a thorough devaluation of speech in the account of the woman, framed, of course, by the admiration for the profundity of the man's silence: still waters run deep. The good colonial is the silent one (which already anticipates his disappearance in 1799, and later, more elaborate ideologies of silence and domination.

This instrumental aspect, so important as a technique of control, is, however, part of an extensive linguistic trauma, Cook's *Sprachkrise*.[22] Given the manner in which Cook apparently experiences the encounter, he is left, so to speak, speechless, hostile to speech and communication, and it is therefore no surprise that, contrasted with Forster, Cook lends himself as the enfigurement of an instrumental reason. The surprise is rather that this constellation of a suspicion of speech and an instrumentalist reduction of reason—transforming the life world into a map—is so evidently linked to a positive judgment on writing, the translation of toa-toa as "marking," not as mimesis. Cook, the Cartesian cartographer, simultaneously insists on the priority of writing, and it is in this melancholic double function that he circumnavigates the globe, keeping records and drawing charts on white sheets of paper in the service of the Admiralty. The fetishism of writing, the privileging of the written text, and the concomitant denigration of speech—grammatology as a practice of silencing—participates constitutively then in the process of European expansion.

Forster is no enemy of writing; his text is replete with literary allusions and quotations. Nor, however, is he hostile to speech. His construction of language, like his account of the voyage in general, is considerably richer than Cook's one-dimensionality *avant la lettre*. Where Cook shrugs off the woman's speech as pointless and her dance as ludicrous, Forster has the ethnographic wit to consider that neither may be intended for the stranger but, rather, for her "partner." Indeed, Forster's overriding concern throughout the text is the substance of such intentions, the reasonableness or even rationality inherent in the world, including the rationality of social interaction that presumes the possibility of communication by speech. Cook's "chit-chat" and misunderstandings are, for

Forster, "vivacity and affability," the possibility of a public sphere from which, furthermore, women are not excluded. On the contrary, they may even play a centrally constitutive public role by eliciting conversation. In Forster's version the voluble young woman appears as a not-so-distant cousin of the *salonières* of Europe, presumably the butt of the droll quip that Cook records "that women did not want tongue in any part of the world," including London, Paris, Berlin, and Dusky Bay. Clearly, the issues of gender and language are nearly congruent: the misogyny is already a denunciation of speech, and the privileging of writing is a strategy of silencing and an attack on the public sphere of the female salon, the scene par excellence of Enlightenment speech, as well as a technique of colonial domination.

The meeting at Dusky Bay is, however, not primarily an original scene of colonialism, and it is clearly misunderstood if it is reconstructed as a confrontation between the familiar and the exotic, us and them, and so on. What takes place at Dusky Bay on 6 April 1773, is, on the contrary, an early unfolding of the dialectic of Enlightenment, a parting of ways between an emancipatory reason and instrumental rationality. Enlightenment produces both, just as it generates both the colonial project and the anticolonial terms with which it is opposed. If we leave Dusky Bay now and consider Forster's text more broadly, some of these matters can be further clarified with particular regard to the questions of genre, subjectivity, and colonialism.

Although the events at Dusky Bay were not, as I have tried to show, unambiguously new, embedded as they are in multiple historicities, at least Forster understands his own account to depend on a sort of twofold innovation. First, it is framed by an unprecedented curiosity and emphatically eighteenth-century thirst for knowledge, a new era of enlightened discovery. "History does not offer an example of such disinterested efforts towards the enlargement of human knowledge," his preface begins, "as have been made by the British nation, since the accession of his present Majesty to the Throne."[23] For all of its historical erudition, for all of the onerous burden of the past, the Enlightenment entails an invocation of the qualitatively new. To be sure, exploratory expeditions were often undertaken in the past, and their results were hardly trivial, for example, Columbus's voyages to America. But Forster cites the Hispanic age of discovery only as a negative foil—science as it should not be done—since it was fully corrupted by a search for an "evident source of gain." Such by no means "disinterested" exploration apparently stands outside of the history of genuine Enlightenment and, devoid of bona fide rationality, came to a rapid conclusion once the immediate motivation was extinguished. Hence, Forster's superior judgment: "a friendship between Plutus and the Muses was too singular to be sincere; it only lasted whilst they, with no better success than the Danaids, poured heaps of gold into his treasury."[24]

In contrast to the failings of Spanish science, the new, British mode of discovery, devoid of venal intentions, is marked by ideal intentions and material support (rather than avariciousness), both of which Forster praises as "liberal." The novelty of this situation is then quickly doubled—the second innovation associated with Forster's project—by the suggestion that a new mode of writing has become necessary to describe the voyage, "undertaken by order of an enlightened monarch, upon a more enlarged and majestic plan than ever was put in execution before." The new science requires a new expressivity; the corollary to the quantitative scope of the journey is the qualitative enrichment of the autonomy of the Enlightenment subject, the reasoning writer. Free from all merely conventional rules and driven only by a "natural love of science," his sole mission is "to exercise all his talents, and to extend his observations to every remarkable object." Given this new setting, a new sort of authorship emerges that generates a new genre, a "philosophical history of the voyage, free from prejudice and vulgar error, where human nature should be represented without any adherence to fallacious systems, and upon the principles of general philanthropy; in short, an account written upon a plan which the learned world had not hitherto seen executed."[25] It is this innovative text, the narrative of the journey, that Forster presents with due modesty to the public in place of his father, who, because of his official capacity on board, was enjoined from publishing a historical account of his own.

Free from any prohibitions imposed by a higher authority, free of the parochialism that might favor prejudicial accounts, and free to describe the abundance of factual material encountered, the genre is set off from competing texts with alternative constitutions. Indeed, Forster takes pains to set his writing off from all other possible versions of travel prose. Thus, he insists that the indisputable advantage of his own account is that it is both accurate and meaningful, both of which designations are crucial because each points implicitly to alternative generic constitutions. Regarding the norm of accuracy, Forster distinguishes his text from the erroneousness of a surfeit of reports that are, plain and simply, wrong. The polemic is directed against a literary culture, implicitly ascribed to the past, of mutually contradictory geographical claims and flagrant confabulations, that is, a prescientific discourse presumably no longer adequate to the age of reason, "which is too enlightened to credit marvelous histories, which would have disgusted even the romantic disposition of our ancestors." The voyage does not need the embellishments of "fiction" but only a "philosophical recital of facts."[26] Surely, the facticity of Forster's eighteenth-century prose is a far cry from the positivism of the nineteenth, for it still readily encompasses a speculative authorial voice. Nevertheless, it is important to note how a norm of verisimilitude—getting it right—has been established and counterposed prominently to fictionality, which is deemed obsolete.

If this nearly realist insistence on the priority of facts over fiction sets the text off from counterfeit versions—the Enlightenment presumes a self-evident distinction between the genuine and the counterfeit that is lost to postmodern sensibility—it is even more important to note that Forster demands that the recital of facts be the carrier of philosophical meaning. It is here that the demarcation between Forster's project and Cook's cartography, which in terms of factual information is arguably more precise, is played out. For Forster, the object of attention is not the empirical world as a set of isolated facts to be recorded and enumerated, measured and mapped. Rather, it is the life world of the human mind, the subject's growth and journey through by no means merely subjective, private, or ideal experience; as if Forster's *Voyage* were a sort of precursor of Hegel's *Phenomenology of the Spirit*, two variants on a Bildungsroman, travel journals of the soul. Consequently, for all his realism, he rejects the reified accumulation of facts as well as the naturalist reduction (in Husserl's sense) of experience to putatively objectivist data. Indeed, such objectivism is recognized as a scientism, a reified cultivation of accuracy devoid of meaning that has little at all to do with science and that represents a destructive threat inimical to human progress and even more dangerous than either the venal corruption or the marvelous fictions of the past. The greatest challenge to the Enlightenment is its own reductionist consequences, not the ancien régime.

Consider the force of the images that Forster employs: "facts were collected in all parts of the world, and yet knowledge was not increased. They [the learned] received a confused heap of disjointed limbs, which no art could reunite into a whole; and the rage of hunting after facts soon rendered them incapable of forming and resolving a single proposition; like those minute enquirers, whose life is wholly spent in the anatomical dissection of flies, from whence they never draw a single conclusion for the use of mankind, or even of brutes."[27] If fiction is inadequate as a mode of representation because it is inaccurate, fact is inadequate because its version of accuracy prevents comprehension and the rational meaningfulness of Forster's text. Evidently, the prefatory comments on genre are intended to set up the possibility of Forster's writing and his constitution of global space. The new science implies a new philosophy that requires a new genre. Simultaneously, however, one can treat the arguments as rhetorical interventions in a competition with other texts and, especially, their authors, which stand in an agonistic relationship with this text. In other words, the genre-theoretical reflections may be taken on their own terms as an attempt at a reconstituted science or as the philosophical camouflage of a more material and precise gamesmanship with other players. How fair has Forster been to his competitors, and how unimpeachable is his scientific self-assurance?

The structure of Forster's defense of the genre, in particular the location of the privileged term in between two antithetical and degraded alternatives, is deeply indebted to the tradition of German dialectics. On the one side stands excessive imagination; on the other, excessive details, and the synthetic position is occupied by philosophy, combining accuracy with meaning, the concrete and the abstract, body and mind, and so on. Philosophy claims to be more accurate and less invented than the unreliable fictions of the past, just as it is more reflective and less pedantic than scientistic specialization. Yet the terms of Forster's argument for genre are by no means solely philosophical instances. Instead, they represent some very real texts, alternative records of the journey, that threatened to challenge Forster's position on the literary marketplace. The paradigm of fiction can easily be identified as "two anonymous publications" that appeared prior to Forster's and were presumably written by authors who had not taken part in the expedition. Forster characterizes them derogatorily as "marvelous histories."[28] The denigration lies of course in the adjective, for Forster himself presents a narrative with a "historical" character. It is the denigration of the "marvelous," however, that represents both the Enlightenment's victory over superstition and its perhaps excessive confidence in its own ability to separate between the marvelous and the accurate. This rationalistic suppression of marvels is surely the precondition for romanticism as the return of the repressed. In addition, the denunciation of inauthentic representation implies the current polemic against John Hawkesworth, who had composed the account of Cook's first voyage, also without having been on board. Forster may have anticipated a similar substitute authorship for Cook's second account and therefore feels compelled to flaunt his superiority as a firsthand observer. The Enlightenment that would exorcise ghosts appears to have been no more tolerant of ghostwriters, with two distinct motivations. The argument gives expression to a new taste for accurate information that, presumably, is the natural purview of the eyewitness, but it is also strategically a self-interested move on the part of a writer and scholar who has a natural advantage over others who might require assistance in the production of the text. As will become evident later, part of the hidden competition between the two accounts is very much a matter of the tension between the humanist scholar Forster and the technician Cook: *vita contemplativa* and *vita activa*.

The alternative paradigm of a presumably nonphilosophical facticity is, of course, a reference to Cook, but Forster deferentially goes out of his way to avoid criticizing the captain directly. In fact, he superficially separates the genre-theoretical argument regarding the inadequacy of merely factual accuracy from what appears to be a solely descriptive contrast of Cook's perspective and his own. "Many circumstances familiar to the navigator, who has been bred on the rough element, strike the landman with novelty, and furnish entertainment to his readers. The seaman views many objects on shore with a retrospect to maritime affairs, whilst the other attends to their oeconomical uses. In short, the different branches of science which we have studied, our turns of mind, our hands and hearts have made a difference in our sensations, reflections, and expressions." So far, so good, it would seem: the two authors simply provide two different points of view—different tropes for different folks. Yet this disarming simplicity barely conceals the tactful cleverness of the argument, since Forster may have reasonably calculated that there were more landmen than seamen in the literary public, even in Britannia. That is, he is essentially claiming for himself the status of generalist with an interest in "oeconomical uses" while relegating Cook to the margins as an overspecialized nautical expert on "maritime affairs." Hence, he can in fact augment the comparative value of his own text by proferring the tongue-in-cheek alibi that he has omitted considerable material that, should someone care to seek it out, can be pondered in the tedious textual competition:

> I have slightly passed over all regulations relative to the interior economy of the ship and the crew: I have studiously avoided nautical details both at sea and in harbour, nor ventured to determine, how often we reefed, or split a sail in a storm, how many times we tacked to weather a point, and how often our refractory bark disobeyed her Palinurus, and missed stays. The bearings and distances of projecting capes, of peaks, hills, and hummocks, of bays, harbors, ports, and caves, at different hours of the day, have likewise been in general omitted. These instructive particulars thrive in the proper field of the navigator.[29]

They may therefore be properly gleaned from the navigator's text, and readers with burning interests in bearings and hummocks at different hours of the day are directed there, but otherwise the philosophical recital is recommended as superior. What appeared to be a casual matter of different perspectives and alternative interests proceeds directly to a distinction between particular and general interests and thereby to a hierarchy of one perspective, putatively general, over the other.

The point here is neither to denounce nor deny the distinction Forster has been describing. Cook's text is indeed much more a maritime account than is Forster's. Nor is it relevant to express particular approval for the one mode of writing or the other. The issue is that evidently much more is involved than accidental perspectives or literary styles. Forster is correct in his contrast of the two narratives, but he is wrong in his explanation that the differences are due to differing psychologies or temperaments. The difference is a much deeper one, a division of labor within the Enlightenment itself, so that the two authors, for all their shared eighteenth-century presuppositions, in fact set out on widely divergent undertakings. Where Forster, as the autonomous subject, directs "his observations to every remarkable object," the royal subject Cook concentrates from the start on a precise and delimited cartographic undertaking. The sole question that concerns Cook is stated baldly in the introduction to the 1777 text: "Whether the unexplored part of the *Southern Hemisphere* be only an immense mass of water, or contain another continent, as speculative geography seemed to suggest, was a question which had long engaged the attention, not only of learned men, but most of the maritime powers of Europe." The unabashed link between knowledge and the military concerns of "maritime powers" makes it clear that the undertaking was considerably less "disinterested" than Forster had imagined. Its goal was nonetheless an increase in knowledge, as Cook continues: "To put an end to all diversity of opinion about a matter so curious and important, was his Majesty's principal motive, in directing this voyage to be undertaken, the history of which is now submitted to the public."[30] The phrase is quite remarkable: to end "all diversity of opinion" means achieving the accuracy of a definitive determination that will prove useful to the "maritime powers."

Unlike Forster, who posits a radical break between the rapacious and therefore prescientific Spanish expeditions and his enlightened present, Cook proceeds by placing himself comfortably in a lineage of discoverers from Ferdinand Magellan and Alvara Mendaña through Abel Tasman and Louis de Bougainville. One would misread this list if one were to understand it solely as an empty chronicle of events. Cook's point, on the contrary, is to establish the status of cartographic knowledge regarding the South Seas in order to proceed in a methodical and scientific manner. The names have the same function as footnotes in today's scientific journals: citations of authority and collections of state-of-the-art research, as both a rhetorical legitimation of the text and as a genuine measure of cognitive reliability. His masses of nautical details—which Forster marginalized as merely consequences of the specialized standpoint of the "seaman"—are by no means dead facts or "disjointed limbs" but bits of information crucial to the rational, if nonspeculative, execution of the Enlightenment project as cartography. Consequently, it is not quite adequate to follow Forster and concentrate solely on a distinction between philosophical and nonphilosophical accounts since there is obviously at least one other relevant dimension.

In addition to the contrast between the factual and the philosophical modes, which has to do with the relative importance of empirical details and rational argument in the texts, a second, more thematic contrast operates between the specifically cartographical material and other content. This is Forster's "every remarkable object," including natural scientific data as well as social-anthropological observations and records of aesthetic and other subjective experiences. Tending to collapse the critique of empiricism, that is, the proliferation of factual details, with the critique of cartography, as a specific organizational strategy for the presentations of some of those details, Forster misses the scientific and argumentative value of the nautical material, just as he misunderstands the specific character of his own generic innovation.

In other words, the difference between Forster and Cook is not, as Forster suggests, his own philosophical superiority over Cook's realm of mere facts; for it is hardly the case that Cook is somehow less rational than Forster. At stake is rather a differentiation within the Enlightenment between alternative rationalities, the object of one being the control and domination of nature—the fully mapped-out globe—the object of the other maintaining an interest in alternative regions of human experience. There can be no doubt that within the cartographic project, that is, on its own terms, Cook's text is the technically more competent one, in a contemporary scientific sense. It attempts to answer the question of a southern continent soberly, without the sort of aestheticizing interjections and literary allusions that Forster so evidently enjoyed. Yet Cook's scientific success hides a double irony. He was ultimately forced to see his success in negative terms, the presumed nonexistence of *terra australis*, and that success would later be erased, long after Cook's death, by the determination of an antarctic continent beneath the polar ice. Modern science, despite its taste for footnotes, proceeds without respect for its authorities.

Despite such failing, Forster can hardly claim scientific superiority to Cook. Given the sentimentalism of Forster's text in many passages, the opposite would be a more likely conclusion. Forster's text is different from Cook's, not because his voice is more (or less) rational but because the scope of his vision—the scope of the genre—is wider, apperceiving a more differentiated life world than the geometry of navigation might allow. Forster's text presents a multidimensional, non-disenchanted world where there is always meaning in excess of the cartographic items, and this excess nourishes a perpetual optimism and good will. It is this surplus of meaning that points toward an emancipatory character in Enlightenment subjectivity.

Enlightenment subjectivity oscillates between the models suggested by Cook and Forster, between scientific expertise and empathetic sentimentalism, the one measuring the outer world accurately, the other responding to that outer world enthusiastically as well as to inner dimensions of experience. Yet Forster's polemical claim to philosophical, that is, scientific priority is evidently untenable. The situation is much more complicated than a simple binary opposition. As a rationalist, Forster claims a more powerful command of the facts that otherwise tend to overwhelm the mere empiricists of Cook's ilk. That his rationalism is ultimately little more than the pretense of a narrative cohesion—against the "disjointed limbs" of the factualists—is of little concern. More important is that this initial juxtaposition of an abstract rationalism and a concrete empiricism is simultaneously undermined by a countertendency. For it is after all Cook's geometric project that is genuinely a process of abstraction, an evacuation of experience, the metamorphosis of the world first into white paper and then into the sign system of nautical charts. In contrast to this scientific abstraction, Forster's tenacious protection of the diversity of human experience—the materiality of physical experience, sociocultural pragmatics, aesthetic interiority, and religious experience—is extraordinarily rich and concrete, like that kingdom of sensuality to which the sailor returned for vegetables. Obviously, the poles are reversed here. It now appears that Cook, the modern scientist, engaged in a theorizing of experience, the capacity for rationalization in modern science, whereas it is Forster who holds onto the life world as the locus of sensuous experience and human creativity. The tension between Cook and Forster repeats, in the new context of the Enlightenment of the eighteenth century, a conflict constitutive of modern science between a Neoplatonic model of mathematic description (crucial for Galilean physics and, therefore, for Cartesian logic) and a tradition of Aristotelian empiricism. Forster writes as both rationalist and empiricist: as the rationalist eager to construct a cohesive narrative dubbed "philosophical," yet also as the empiricist eager to account for every object while excluding no subject of human experience.

Who is the subject of Forster's *Voyage*? Since its publication, the question of authorship has been repeatedly raised by various critics unwilling to believe that the young traveler, only a teenager at the start of the journey, could have composed such an impressive account. Instead, they attribute the text to his father who, owing to the dispute with the Admiralty discussed later, could not appear in public as the author. Nevertheless, Forster himself promptly countered all the relevant arguments, and no new evidence has appeared that significantly undermines his claim. Of greater interest, however, than the personal determination of the author is the structure of authorship or, rather, the constitutive subjectivity of the text, and on this score the son's relationship to the father is indeed consequential. Writing in place of the father, overcoming the authority of the undoubtedly domineering father, the son as author displaces the father in an oedipal gesture and carries out an act of emancipation, an act, moreover, with ramifications far beyond any personal psychological realm. The subject of the text thereby becomes the emancipatory subject of the Enlightenment, inimical to the restrictions of empirical authorities and endowed with a universalist and transcendental structure. Where does this endowment come from? Is there another father waiting in the wings?

Forster himself does not offer the best explanation. We have already seen him willing to trivialize the distinction between Cook's narrative and his own by writing off his perspective as accidental and personal, the point of view of a "landman." Expressing opinions and describing sentiments beyond an impartial reportage of facts, he feels compelled to relativize his comments with an apology: "I have sometimes obeyed the powerful dictates of my heart, and given voice to my feelings; for, as I do not pretend to be free from the weaknesses common to my fellow creatures, it was necessary for every reader to know the colour of the glass through which I looked. Of this at least I am certain that a gloomy livid tinge hath never clouded my sight."[31] If this brief comment were adequate, then Forster's optimism, the presumably rosy tinge of his glasses, would not be preferable but only different from gloomy pessimism, his universalism only one stance among many: egalitarianism of equal validity with elitism and transcendental subjectivity ultimately always only the expression of particular interests. Yet the strength of Forster's account—which is stronger than his explanation of its status—derives precisely from an implicit utopia of disinterestedness and universalism, clearly much more than from an arbitrary point of view.

Reviewing the *Voyage*, Christoph Martin Wieland put a twist on the distinction between "seaman" and "landman" that sheds important light on this problem. Recall that Forster introduced the distinction to suggest a division of labor that could account for the differences between his own and Cook's—again, just perspectival variants. In contrast, Wieland ascribes to Forster the status of general humanist, since he took part in the expedition "not as a seaman but as natural scientist, and as a human—*wie ein Mensch*—moreover as a young man, whose reading of ancient and modern poets was still fresh in his mind." As a scientist presumably rational, as a reader receptive to aesthetic phenomena, and, above all, as the representative of humanity, Forster is for Wieland the prototype of the participant in the public sphere whose comments are, far from being merely private and personal, of general import.

Hence, the special status of his prose is universally interesting: "Professional seamen are too used to the storms and hardships that a terrestrial animal—man—must endure at sea, and they are usually too unskilled in writing to provide us landlovers the sort of vivid and detailed description of those scenes which we would want. Here [Forster's account] one from our midst describes for us what every one of us would have felt in his place; this feature of course makes every line of his narrative doubly interesting for the reader with heart [*Leser von Gefühl*]."[32]

Forster's counterposing "landman" and "seaman" as equal if different perspectives is now transformed explicitly into the alternative between narrow and distorting specialization, on the one hand, and general universalism, on the other. Wieland's characterization of Forster clearly suggests a notion of subjectivity as the representative of the bourgeois public that is considerably more substantial than, to recur to Forster's image, the color of the author's glasses. Nevertheless, the passage makes equally clear the weak point of the public sphere, where the process of its structural transformation would quickly commence.[33] As important as universalism may have been for Wieland, Forster is "from our midst," and the implied "we" is constructed through a double exclusion according to the criteria of *Besitz und Bildung*, property and education. The seamen are marginalized, if not thoroughly excluded, from the community of bourgeois humanity not only because of their specialization but also because they are too accustomed to work and—therefore?—they cannot write well. The putatively general appeal of Forster's text is obviously restricted to the educated minority of the literary public, the readers with heart who have the leisure to be sentimental.

Wieland's comment indicates how Forster may have undervalued his own text to the extent that he suggested that his judgments were, in the final analysis, solely personal and particular. Still, Wieland's appreciation turns out to be, implicitly, a mixed blessing since it constructs the authorial subjectivity as parochially bourgeois, one whose universalism ultimately only masks a narrow class interest. If this diagnosis were valid, then

Forster's text would indeed stand clearly at the beginning of colonial literature, the bourgeois vision appropriating the globe for its own economy. Such a conclusion, however, is so blatantly counterintuitive, conflicting as it does so emphatically with Forster's egalitarianism and anticolonialism, that it would be prudent to push the matter further. We have seen that the generic imperative of the "philosophical recital" implies a cohesive narration, as opposed to a disjointed collection of facts, in order to achieve a total view rather than a fragmentary perspective. Yet the very tenability of such a narratological distinction between cohesion and collection, totality and fragment, has still to be demonstrated. Forster, it turns out, solves this problem and, with it, the question of the subject, without even knowing it in the passages immediately preceding the relativist metaphor of the colored glass. "The traveler was no longer to trust to chance for a variety of occurrences, but to make use of his first discovery, as the thread of Ariadne, by the help of which he might guide his steps through the labyrinth of human knowledge."[34]

The thread of Ariadne is, obviously enough, the metaphor for narration as rational and continuous inquiry, which might lead one out of the confusion of the labyrinth (in which, according to the myth, the body of youth or the body of knowledge would become "disjointed"). If, however, the labyrinth is itself "human knowledge," then the activity of the rational subject, explicitly counterposed to the labyrinth, implies surpassing or overcoming merely human knowledge (or the knowledge of mere humans) and is consequently somehow dependent on some nonhuman, supramundane instance, no matter how much the activity itself transpires within the natural world. In other words, it appears as if the generic self-understanding of the text as well as the construction of a transcendental subject depend on a dialectic between this-worldly and otherworldly spheres. Indeed, Forster tells us as much directly: "I have always endeavored in this narrative to connect the ideas arising from different occurrences, in order, if possible, to throw more light upon the nature of the human mind, and to lift the soul into that exalted station, from whence the extensive view must 'justify the ways of God to man.'" Thus, there exists an intimate link between a generic imperative of rationality, that is, the narrative of a coherent itinerary of the mind, and a religious faith in a providential deity, the source of the rationality of creation. The subject who rationally explores the world, the rationality of which is of divine origin, is certainly no merely private person (and by no means a mystic, passive vessel of illumination) nor a representative of a localized group, but a universalist of Forster's persuasion: "Accustomed to look on all the various tribes of men, as entitled to an equal share of my good will, and conscious, at the same time, of the rights which I possess in common with every individual among them, I have endeavored to make my remarks with a retrospect to our general improvement and welfare; and neither attachment nor aversion to particular nations have influenced my praise or censure."[35]

The Enlightenment subjectivity of Forster's text therefore depends on a religious dimension for both the rationality of the judgments and for the politics of universalist emancipation, just as the corollary, the generic definition of narration, depends on theological underpinnings. That religious arguments might have very different consequences in the cultural history of colonialism could be explored with regard to the Spanish Conquest in the Western Hemisphere. Here the point is that the supramundane deity renders the undertaking—rational human practice—more than terrestrial, more than the disenchanted geometry of Cook's cartography, and it can thereby surpass the twin temptations of avarice and fragmentation. Lacking Forster's transcendentality, Cook's more radically secularized Enlightenment ends up impoverished, always tending to collapse into the one-dimensionality of instrumental reason, always potentially a fetishization of worldly detail. Forster's ability "to lift the soul into that exalted station," in contrast, lifts the subject off the ground and opens it to a variety of modes of rationality: scientific considerations of flora and fauna, practical discussions of social institutions, and expressions of aesthetic pleasure at natural wonders—for example, the exuberance of his record of his first sight of Tahiti.

A similar variegation characterizes the range of topics in the text, especially in the ethnographic passages, where Forster pays attention to the physical settings, economic organizations, and cultural customs. When he suggests comparisons with Europe—the best example perhaps is the discussion of the Tahitian fleet as being comparable to the navy of ancient Greece—the point is never a denigration of the Pacific islanders in terms of Western norms.[36] The opposite is more often the case, since Forster participates to some extent in a Rousseauist glorification of "primitive" society as a mechanism to criticize European civilization. Yet this is by no means the overriding tendency of the narrative. Forster encounters various societies with little need to lock them into a hierarchy. Instead, he views them all, including Europe, as various paths on which the potential of human life has been realized in divergent natural settings. This is far from an "anything goes" relativism; human life always implies, Forster is certain, the parameters of reason and happiness, even if there is never a global standard for either. But the parameters evidently do imply that a society that organizes itself rationally is better than one that makes less sense, for the former would be nonexclusive, given the fact that reason is taken to be a universal human faculty. And a society in which more participants are happy is better than one in which fewer are, although it goes without saying that happiness too is dependent on local norms and values.

This dialectic of universalism and relativism, a universalist justification of particularity, is grounded in the same deism discussed earlier. Forster concludes an extended ethnography of Tahiti with the following credo: "The ideas of happiness are infinitely various in different nations, according to their manners, principles, and degrees of civilization. As the productions and apparent good qualities of our globe are either profusely or sparingly distributed, on its different parts, the diversity of human opinions is a convincing proof of that paternal love, and unerring wisdom, which, in the plan of this world, has provided for the good of mankind, alike in the torrid and the frigid zone."[37] The supramundane agency, God the Father, who allowed for the internal differentiation of the Enlightenment subject, also guarantees the multiplicity of human cultures, even if, in all their diversity, all display a divine provenance manifested both in the rational activity of the mind and the desideratum of pleasure. Given this universalism, it comes as no surprise that the Enlightenment, at least in Forster's version, generates a decidedly anticolonialist politics.

Or is this result not indeed rather surprising? The Enlightenment expedition, the voyage itself, was undertaken at least in part with regard to power politics. We know this from Cook's introduction. There can be little doubt, furthermore, that the sort of knowledge collected on the voyage and on others like it contributed significantly to military technology and naval competence. Without Captain Cook Britannia would not have ruled the waves in quite the way she did. Mapping the world made policing it possible: the Enlightenment of the panopticon corresponds, presumably, to a global expansion of administrative power and the geometric organization of space. Knowledge, it turns out, is not disinterested (as Forster imagined) when it is interested in particular colonies. Yet unless one is satisfied with the frivolous conclusion that in order to avoid colonialism one must therefore avoid knowledge, one does well to turn to Forster for an alternative version of the Enlightenment. If policing requires maps, maps are hardly only there for the police alone. If the Enlightenment is admittedly never free of particular interests, neither is it fully coincident with them, and its pursuit depends on a categorical disinterestedness, both as a regulative principle and as a source of egalitarianism. The dialectic of Enlightenment means universalism as the simultaneity of authoritarian surveillance in a transparent world and unbroken human solidarity hostile to authoritarian domination. This emancipatory Enlightenment potential explains Forster's anticolonial judgments: the critique of the Portuguese administration on the Cape Verdes, the nasty comments about conditions at the Cape of Good

Hope, and the impassioned denunciation of European explorers as the likely source of venereal disease on the islands.

Since colonialism and anticolonialism are both linked to the categories of the Enlightenment, it may be useful to return one more time to a contrast between Cook and Forster, not the two persons, but the variations within the Enlightenment project, which leave telling tracks in the two authors' texts. The drama of the argument derives in part from the situation of writing. An original plan, according to which Forster senior and Cook would collaborate on a single account, collapsed. The reasons proposed to explain the disagreement range from Forster's faulty English and impersonable character to the Admiralty's reluctance to cooperate with an author of Forster's radical views. The matter has been discussed at length in the critical literature and need not be rehashed here.[38]

As far as the situation of writing goes, however, it is important that father Forster appeared contractually bound to refrain from publishing a "narrative," that is, a cohesive account of the journey. The Admiralty clearly wished that such a publication be reserved for Cook, perhaps solely to reward the national hero with the income from the royalties that were likely to be considerable. However, Forster junior was in no way bound by his father's contracts, and he could therefore undertake to write a narrative as he explains in the context of the discussion of genre. Indeed, his elaborate discussion of the status of his text and its relationship to narrativity is itself a function of the legal dispute. If his father was prevented from composing narrative, Forster was perhaps all the more eager to insist that his own text was, in terms of narrativity, generically superior to Cook's maritime facticity.

So soon after their return from their years together at sea, we have to imagine Cook in Portsmouth and Forster in London, each seated before piles of white paper, probably not unlike the paper that Cook carried with him at Dusky Bay, scribbling hastily and copying out of diaries, each frantically hoping to be the first to publish an account of the sensational voyage. It appears that Forster won the race; his text was probably published on 17 March 1777, and Cook's not until a month or so later.[39] Nevertheless, the Admiralty had granted Cook all of Hodges's illustrations at no cost, which of course rendered this text much more attractive and the profits presumably more handsome. The crucial issue, however, is that this race to write left marks in the two texts and not simply in the sense of a plethora of printing errors in the published volumes. Forster takes pains, as we have seen, to shrug off Cook's prose as excessively concerned with specialized nautical details: literary criticism as market competition before the background of legal limitations. Cook also tries to package his product in order to gain an advantage, and these efforts clarify further differences—less between Cook and Forster than between versions of the Enlightenment.

Cook's introduction is dated 7 July 1776, some nine months before the volume was published. At the time, Cook was preparing for his third expedition (in the course of which he would eventually lose his life) and left "this account of my last voyage in the hands of some friends, who in my absence have kindly accepted the office of correcting the press for me." Proofreading or ghostwriting: did this "office" take all of nine months or was some considerable writing undertaken? Since the Hawkesworth account (of the first voyage) had been subjected to criticism for precisely that reason, Cook immediately goes out of his way to insist that the yet-to-be-published (indeed, yet-to-be-edited) text is authentically his own work: "what I have here to relate is better to be given in my own words, than in the words of another person; especially, as it is a work designed for information, and not merely for amusement; in which . . . candour and fidelity will counterbalance the want of ornament."[40] The passage reads like a strange reversal of Forster's polemic against facts. For Cook, the sober report, marked by candor and fidelity, accuracy and transparency, is counterposed to a denigrated zone of ornament. Is "ornament" Cook's pejorative characterization of Forster's perhaps all too precious notion of a "philosophical recital"? Or is it the appearance of sentimentalism, viewed from the standpoint of information? Yet in July of 1776, it is impossible that Cook could have seen any of Forster's manuscript; on the contrary, it was not until July that Forster commenced work on his version.[41] Could Cook have surmised what Forster's text would turn out to be like on the basis of their years together on the *Resolution*? The answer is certainly yes, for given considerable textual similarities we can only assume that the diaries written on board during the voyage circulated freely and the published accounts drew extensively from the diaries. Authorship is therefore clearly hybrid: Cook's voice ends up in Forster's text and vice versa. Yet precisely this contamination makes the differences all the more stark because the points of divergence are more obvious.

If one ascribes to Cook this sort of speculation, then the critique of ornament in his introductory remark turns out to be a proleptic literary criticism of Forster's text. Just as Forster has been observed trying to stake out a "philosophical" high ground against Cook's merely factual maritime interests, we now find Cook engaging in a similar operation with an antithetical valorization. Facticity is candid, whereas poor philosophy, implicitly, is little more than ornament. In this case, the phenomenological opposition heretofore presented between the one-dimensionality of Cook's cartography and Forster's multidimensional life world is reconfirmed but now with an important revaluation. What appeared to be the mathematical reductionism of a truncated Enlightenment turns out to be the fidelity to the facts of a serious scientist; and Forster's transcendental subjectivity with all its aestheticizing embellishments—the classical allusions and polished phrases—collapses before Cook's Puritan accusation of a nonproductive "amusement." Now Cook emerges as the advocate of a radical scientific modernization and Forster as a representative of a conservative traditionalism: the mathematical Neoplatonism of a maritime Galileo versus a still medieval Aristotelianism. If this inversion rescues Cook, however, it surely abuses Forster, not an opponent of science but the proponent of a different, more humanistic structure of science.

Yet this argument is itself highly speculative given the history of the texts. More to the point is the following passage in Cook's introduction, the importance of which depends in no way on an alleged familiarity with Forster's work-in-progress but solely on the likelihood that Cook presumed that one or the other of the Forsters would be preparing a competing volume. For read against the background of the situation of writing, the passage is clearly intended to muster various loyalties in the recipient for Cook as preferred author:

> I shall therefore conclude this introductory discourse with desiring the reader to excuse the inaccuracies of style, which doubtless he will frequently meet with in the following narrative; and that, when such occur, he will recollect that it is the production of a man, who has not had the advantage of much school education, but who has been constantly at sea from his youth; and though, with the assistance of a few good friends, he has passed through all the stations belonging to a seaman, from an apprentice boy in the coal trade, to a Post Captain in the Royal Navy, he has had no opportunity of cultivating letters. After this account of myself, the public must not expect of me the elegance of a fine writer, or the plausibility of a professed bookmaker; but will, I hope, consider me as a plain man, zealously exerting himself in the service of his Country, and determined to give the best account he is able of his proceedings.[42]

The text may of course be taken as a blanket apology for the inadequacies of a volume, certainly a conventional gesture. Yet given the interlinear competition with Forster, it may be wise to ask whether more is at stake. Has Cook foregrounded the specific character of his prose in order to present himself as the simple Englishman, salt of the earth, who has worked all his life and, moreover, in the service of his country? Such a strategy would hardly have been pointless, especially given the opponents: learned gentlemen who, in addition, were not even British. The suggestion then is that Cook may have been attempting to touch on chords of anti-intellectualism and patriotism in order to promote himself against the intellectual foreigners, who just happened to be his competitors in the business of producing literary travelogues for sale.

To the extent that such undertones are indeed present in the passage, some additional light is shed on the central philosophical problem. I have discussed the divergence between a geometric cartography involving, on the one hand, the production of empty space from which sensuous detail—vegetables—has been evacuated and, on the other, the "philosophical" narration (with its putatively coherent organization of details). This divergence turns out to be complexly embedded in sociohistorical contexts. If Cook can plausibly present himself as the plebeian technician, true to the hard facts and armed with a no-nonsense disregard for ornament and amusement, then Forster is cast as the privileged, which is to say elite, scholar, the work-shy perpetual student who, as a familiar saying goes, ought to get a job (best of all, perhaps, as an apprentice in the coal trade). No matter that the Forsters were in fact far from well off. On board, they belonged to the class of gentlemen, not the sailors, and the consequences of this class structure include the disruption of the universalist Enlightenment project itself. If Forster, at least for Wieland, is "from our midst," he is automatically counterposed to a "them," the others who stand outside. As if the classical counterpoint of Odysseus and his sailors had been played out on the *Resolution*, Cook—despite the fact that he was captain and therefore counted as a gentleman—can suggest that "plain men," like himself, are deaf to the sirens and loyal to the fact and not to the luxuries of a noninstrumental rationality. (Obviously, it is Forster and not Cook who is cast here in the role of the privileged sovereign Odysseus, at least according to the reading by Horkheimer and Adorno.)[43]

In this reading, despite Forster's professed egalitarianism and subsequent Jacobinism, his material entanglement in the existing social structural hierarchy subverts the plausibility of his progressive claims: the elite's critique of elitism is necessarily suspect. Thus, Cook can imply that Forster's projection of an emancipated subjectivity is just a figment of a social privilege and that a genuinely leveled society of "plain men" would necessarily entail a leveling of the Enlightenment as well. Yet this is precisely Cook's tragedy. Without a doubt, he is the better scientist in the normal sense of the term: he gives us the facts and leaves the rhetorical figures to Forster. The reduction of the world to facts, however, is a process of flattening and exclusion. Both Forster and Cook report the discovery of the medicinal value of sauerkraut, but only Forster's text has room for the delight over vegetables, just as it is only Forster's text that records the intimacy of the climactic embrace in the meeting at Dusky Bay, the rubbing noses. Cook in effect represses the human proximity that his enthusiastic admirer celebrates, and he, Cook, thereby maintains a distance to the islander, just as, as captain, he presumably maintained a distance to his crew, despite the retrospective self-staging as a "plain man." The universalist solidarity that Forster imagined and projected on to the captain is rejected by Cook himself as just another communicative fiction: the fiction that humans might communicate or imagine equality. With the wisdom of age, of the scientist, and the writer, he knows that it is all just a matter of markings on paper: *toa-toa*. Hence, his loneliness in an empty space that he compulsively charts; hence also the anxiety in his prose when the itinerary leads to land and to developments potentially beyond his control and beyond his text.

Loyal to facts, "plain men" are also loyal to their country, Cook suggests, and he thereby marginalizes the Forsters as foreigners. The anti-intellectualism goes hand in hand with a xenophobic innuendo, another promising marketing device, but of particular note in a text concerned with the circumnavigation of the globe. Just as the cohesion of the Enlightenment is shattered by the class division of society, its very universalism runs afoul of national particularity. Does the difference between the two narratives, Cook's and Forster's, turn out to be a national difference, a difference between a practical British empiricism and the stereotypical profundity of German "philo-

sophical" thought? An inkling of these images may hide between Cook's lines, and the competition between the texts
might be viewed as a prologue to subsequent conflicts between
English and German imperialism (an issue that will recur in the
following chapters). The British Empire acts in the name of
science, progress, and humanity, and German colonialism,
playing a no-win game of catch-up, tries to imitate England, as
envy turns into enmity. With this subsequent history in mind,
it is particularly interesting to begin this inquiry with an example in which the German author is watching the British traveler
interacting with the non-European world.

If, however, the issue of national difference is to be taken seriously, it is more important to return one final time to Forster,
whose deep-seated and sincere admiration for England was
eventually soured by the dispute between the Admiralty and
his father. Although the history of that transformation can
hardly be traced in the text of the *Voyage*—written, after all, for
a British public—it is all the more prominent in some letters to
his German friend Adolf Vollpracht from the period of his
work on the volume in 1776 and 1777. In the letters one can trace
the progress of his work—a work undertaken, so to speak, expressly against the wishes of the royal government—and, at
the same time, the shift in his political judgment: from an initial Anglophilic hostility to the American revolutionaries to an
explicit solidarity with their "good struggle," which any
"friend of freedom" ought to support.[44] Has the Admiralty
spoiled Forster for England? Is his opposition to the foreign
policy of the British Empire solely the self-serving repercus-
sion of the altercation with Cook? Does he support the American Revolution only because the British Crown opposed his
father's publication plans? That would indeed be an instrumentalist reading of the constellation, reducing politics to immediate self-interest in the most parochial sense. The implication would be that political or even philosophical positions are
always only the expressions of interest, despite universalizing
pretensions, which are themselves merely pretexts. In that case
little would be left of Forster's own aspirations for the Enlight-

enment. Can one, however, imagine a noninstrumental practice, a not solely self-interested motivation? Is there ever more
at stake than personal power? One need not transform Forster
into a disinterested saint in order to suspect that more was indeed at play there and that the critic of colonialism in the South
Seas and advocate of human equality everywhere could have
plausibly held, in the name of a benign creator and a universal
Enlightenment, principled reasons to support the first anticolonial uprising of the modern age. Forster stands for a capacity within the Enlightenment to recognize and appreciate
other cultures, not because he represents some sort of exception to an otherwise domineering rationalism, but because this
emancipatory possibility was and remains a potential for the
Enlightenment and its exploration of the world.

2

GERHARD ROHLFS AND
GEOGRAPHIC WRITING

Cook and Forster were engaged in the practical Enlightenment of discovery: the production of knowledge through the exploration of the world. Both could presume that the advance in science entailed an advance in civilization with results that could only be beneficial to all. The meeting at Dusky Bay is interesting because, despite its successful conclusion—contact is made, goods are exchanged, and the feared violence does not come to pass—the limits of understanding become evident, staged by the incomprehensibility of the woman's dance. It is after all a radically different culture that thrives on the South Island of New Zealand, and it is not immediately transparent to the European travelers. That is, of course, hardly surprising. The material becomes dynamic, however, because of the differences among the Europeans, the alternative castings of Enlightenment universalism. On the one hand, there is Cook's elaboration of a universal space of the physical cosmos in which cultural material plays at best a peripheral role and, on the other, Forster's universality of a human capacity for culture, that is inherently rational even if it is not directly comprehensible. This duality, corresponding to what in contemporary philosophical discourse would be played out as the distinction between Kantian and Herderian descriptions of culture, points directly to the key issue for European colonialism. The spatial expansion of European power—with travelers in the vanguard and followed by missionaries, traders, and gunboats—had as a direct consequence contact, not necessarily always confrontational, with other cultures. Would these cultures, which would always and necessarily appear as local and particular in contrast to the self-appointed universalism of Europe, be granted a local legitimacy or would they be denounced as less than universal and therefore less than rational? Can the Enlightenment tolerate alterity?

In Forster's case, the answer is clearly yes. For Cook the cultural question is effectively sidestepped, although the vicissitudes of the silent, older man at Dusky Bay and his eventual disappearance in the posthumous anthology can be read as an initial obliteration of the native population from textual memory. By the middle of the nineteenth century, however, this capacity to denigrate the other populations had magnified, as the eighteenth-century mercantile Enlightenment, concerned with mapping the world, gives way to the project of founding territorial empires (as if British, French, and then German imperialisms were intent on returning to the Spanish model denounced by Forster) and, more broadly, establishing firm networks of military, commercial, and diplomatic power. This transition is particularly clear in the prose accounts of geographic travelers such as Gerhard Rohlfs, whom I discuss in this chapter. A corollary version is to be found in missionary narratives, an example of which will be discussed in the next chapter, which is devoted to Henry Stern. Rohlfs and Stern are particularly useful examples for the examination of the transformation of colonial space and the reduction of alterity because they are both Germans observing different aspects of the British Abyssinian expedition of 1867. Yet individual biography is no more the key issue than it was in the discussion of Cook and Forster. The individual actors participate in larger discourses (which they may certainly nuance or even undercut), but it is these discourses, not the singular persons, that are the topic of cultural studies.

This chapter therefore describes a British context for a German discourse, including the debate on Ireland and the issues at stake in the Abyssinian expedition. In general, Forster's relation to Cook, the German observing British power, is repeated structurally, although the discourses of Rohlfs and Stern have little in common with his. The structural continuity has to do with the relationship of Germany to England, the former's junior status in the project of European colonial expansion, and the imitative admiration it directed to England, at least until the era of the First World War. If colonialism raised the question of the relationship between a putative universal rationality and the apparent irrationality of local culture, and if this antinomy would be played out as the conflict between England and its overseas subjects, the German voice is particularly interesting because of its liminal location. Was it one of irrational particularity or was it enlightened and European? That choice eventually becomes the frame for twentieth-century debates over German identity: was it driven by its own peculiar character along a separate path, a *Sonderweg*, toward a special destiny or was it simply another nation, one among many, equally obligated to universal norms? Representing "maritime powers," Cook found only irrationality at Dusky Bay, whereas Forster could recognize a cultural rationality with which he could identify. Eventually, the same antinomy would be mapped onto Europe, as the opposition between a normative West and German irrationality. The categories of colonialism are repeated in the fissures of European space, disaggregated by the disruptions of Enlightenment. Yet if Europe too is remapped by the process of imperialism, and if this remapping includes decenterings—between West and East, center and periphery— then anticolonial accounts of a centered and monolithic Europe threatening the rest of the world are sorely inadequate. Such postcolonial fantasies of "Eurocentrism" ignore the dramatic diversities within Europe, just as they refrain from inquiring into the way similar processes of cultural transformation operate in European and non-European contexts.

This chapter focuses on the nineteenth century and its changing understanding of local practices and local freedom, both seemingly incompatible with the desiderata of national unification—it is the moment of Otto von Bismarck and Ca-

millo di Cavour—let alone imperialism. Within Europe the
process of state-building and national unification continued a
history of erosion or suppression of local traditions. Globally,
European civilization, as heir to the Enlightenment, claimed a
similar superiority over the local cultures of colonized peoples.
Yet precisely that assertion of superiority could require a re-
course to violence or, at the very least, an arrogant intolerance
that sensitive observers could recognize as the sign of a dis-
turbing illiberalism. The Enlightenment as the assertion of the
priority of science began to undercut the Enlightenment as an
unprejudiced curiosity, open to the world. Forster, we have
seen, presumed an underlying rationality in the incomprehensibility of the dance. By the middle of the nineteenth century
such a presumption was no longer commonplace, as John
Stuart Mill underscored in his polemic on England's Irish policy. I want to consider Mill's text, with Forster in the background, in order to measure the shifted status of alterity and
local culture within the context of an expanded colonial discourse. From Mill's account of Ireland, I will turn to the contemporary British incursion into Africa and only then to
Rohlfs's remapping of African space.

Fenian activity in both England and Ireland in 1867, which
culminated in the sensational killing of a police officer in Manchester, added fuel to the ongoing debate on the Irish question.[1] Mill's pamphlet, "England and Ireland," which appeared
in February of 1868, concludes with hopes for comity and con-
ciliation, suggesting that a separation of the two countries
would be disadvantageous for both. However, the central
theme of the text and the course of the furor that it provoked
entailed a bitter attack on the character and consequences of
the British administration. Although Mill by no means advo-
cated Irish independence, neither did he apologize for a status
quo that had been detrimental to the population in ways he
enumerates with both polemical ardor and moral passion. Mill
mounts arguments to demonstrate "that there is probably no
other nation of the civilized world, which, if the task of governing Ireland had happened to devolve on it, would not have

shown itself more capable of that work than England." One argument is of particular interest in this context because it has to do with the sort of cultural assumptions governing the relationship between a hegemonic metropolitan power and its paracolonial subjects, that is, the relationship between the universalism of power and the peculiarities that appear to adhere to any local culture.[2]

"There is no other civilized nation," Mill writes, "which is so conceited of its own institutions, and of all its modes of public action, as England is." One does well to pay attention to the complaint Mill is addressing to the ideologues of British power. British laws may or may not be appropriate and effective in Britain, but the sheer fact of their acceptance in Britain is not alone proof of their applicability elsewhere. The argument here is neither objectivist nor materialist, that is, Mill's point does not depend on, say, differences in physical geography that might imaginably correspond to alternative social organizations. Nor is it yet a genuinely utilitarian argument (although, to be sure, it takes a utilitarian turn in the course of the essay). His concern is not the relative efficacy of particular regulations in the production of a universal good in variously structured contexts but, instead, the insistence on different cultural settings, marked by different ideas and values, and hence different visions of a good life and a desirable social organization.

> If suitability to the opinions, feelings, and historical antecedents of those who live under them is the best recommendation of institutions, it ought to have been remembered, that the opinions, feelings, and historical antecedents of the Irish people are totally different from, and in many respects contrary to those of the English; and that things which in England find their chief justification in their being liked, cannot admit of the same justification in a country where they are detested. But the reason which recommends institutions to their own supporters, and that which is used to stop the mouths of opponents, are far from being always one and the same.[3]

Reason, in other words, is necessarily the ultimate value for the public sphere to which Mill addresses himself, but reason is simply not as monologic as a common sense might assume: one man's reason is another man's violence. This is surely far from a postmodern relativism because reason remains the undisputed desideratum, but the imperial situation—or rather a network (administrative, economic, and symbolic) that has become transcultural and is characterized therefore by a plurality of value systems—induces a plurality of rationalities as well. Cultural difference is not irrationalism, but rationality has surely ceased to be solely British. This was Forster's point in his interpretation of the dance. Later, Hannah Arendt would similarly underscore that "the Irish example proves how ill fitted the United Kingdom was to build an imperial structure in which many different peoples could live contentedly together."[4]

The radical answer to the Irish question is evidently based on certain presumptions regarding cultural differences and international relations, presumptions that are symptomatic of the transformation of the character of the relationship between Europe and the non-European world in the middle of the nineteenth century. Mill's essay is, in effect, a liberal critique of imperialist structures and, as such, deserves more extended comparison with Forster's universalism. As we have seen in the previous chapter, Forster makes several universalist assumptions, all in the spirit of the Enlightenment: the importance of reason as a crucial human faculty; the normative status of social equality; and the possible perfectibility of social institutions, that is, progress. At the same time, however, this universalism is by no means linked to the assertion of a particular normative model. Forster is far from regarding Europe as an example for the New Zealanders to follow. On the contrary, it is a universalism that is compatible with—perhaps even constitutive of—a local cultural autonomy. Universalism is not a rigid hierarchy of norms to which global validity is ascribed but rather a recognition of the constant human capacity for culture, that is, the production of meaning, in particular, the elaboration of meaningful solutions to the challenges of the physical cosmos.

Alterity derives from the shared human capacity for meaning, especially for meaning different contents.

For Forster, in other words, Enlightenment universalism is the grounding for any local difference. This heterophilic vision of heterogeneous cultures all engaged in parallel projects of social progress with no universally valid solution appears to be so self-evidently correct that Forster barely mentions alternative and less admirable versions of heterophobic European behavior abroad: the brief, introductory dismissal of Spanish colonialism as a solely venal endeavor or the caustic remarks on the abusive demeanor of European sailors in the Pacific. Mill's stance is not far from Forster's; he too suggests the importance of recognizing cultural differences while simultaneously assuming the universality of progress and equality (his term is *democracy*), no matter how dissimilar the paths to reach them may be. Democracy, in other words, is taken to be a universal good that permits particularity and difference, for it entails the expression of the specific experiences of a people rather than a momentary arithmetic accident. Yet how different are the two argumentative contexts and the assumptions the writers could make about their respective publics. Forster wrote presuming that an age of reason was dawning as rosy as the morning sun in Tahiti, while Mill engages in a bitter polemic against a false universalism that, instead of recognizing a shared social condition within particular cultural settings, remains blind to every local particularity.

The enlightener Forster cannot get enough of foreign cultures, while Mill complains that his contemporary advocates of British rule cannot even note the presence of alternative institutional projects except perhaps as a threat to which the only imaginable answer is military force. This fundamental inequality in the new structure of international relations—inequality was not the key issue at Dusky Bay—obviously precludes any equal communication. "The reason which recommends institutions to their own supporters," Mill writes, "and that which is used to stop the mouths of opponents, are far from always being one and the same"—as if the relationship between supporters and opponents, colonizers and colonized, was always necessarily violent and their interests profoundly incompatible. The moral force of Mill's text derives instead from the tension between an Enlightenment universalism that provides a norm of egalitarianism and the keen understanding of a really existing politics of domination. This tension characterizes the transitional period of the mid-nineteenth century, when enlightened ideals were still near enough to exercise influence while the brutality of extraterritorial domination was increasingly recognized as part of a modern present. Unlike Forster Mill cannot relegate colonial excesses to the distant past of the Spanish age of discovery.

At this penultimate moment, just before the full institutionalization of the system of the modern European colonial empires and the "scramble for Africa," one can investigate this proximity of science and power, universalism and parochialism, in the accounts of the two German witnesses to the British expedition to Abyssinia that transpired in the first months of 1868, just as Mill was intervening in the Irish debate. That I focus again on German observers of British expansionism indicates the belatedness of German colonialism and the importance of an intra-European mimicry in establishing the German imperial aspirations. Before turning to those texts, however, it is worthwhile to take a look at the event itself and its own textual construction, which exemplifies the emergent imbalance of power. The colonialist event had its own communicative and discursive character that requires some detailed description. Against this background I will then proceed to Rohlfs's texts to explore the peculiar features of geographical writing and its participation in colonial discourse.

RHETORIC AND IDEOLOGY IN THE ABYSSINIAN EXPEDITION

The story begins with an unacceptable delay: the failure of Queen Victoria to reply in a timely fashion to a cordial letter from Tewodros (Theodore), the king of Ethiopia. "No release until civil answers to King's letter arrives"—thus, the laconically desperate text that the British consul, Charles Duncan Cameron, smuggled out of the fortress of Magdala where he and a group of other Europeans were being held captive. The recipient of the note, Hormuzd Rassam, the British First Assistant Political Resident in Aden, had been charged by the Foreign Office with a mission to rectify the Abyssinian situation and obtain the release of the hostages through the delivery of a belated answer from London. Although Rassam's efforts would eventually fail (indeed, he too ends up a prisoner), he set off sharing Cameron's understanding that the British abuse of the conventions of epistolary diplomacy could be put right with relative ease through a completion of the exchange, better late than never: "The undertaking at the outset involved no higher function than the delivery of a letter to the Abyssinian Sovereign. It was generally believed, and with good reason, that a courteous reply from Her Majesty to Theodore's letter would effect the immediate liberation of the captives, and put an end to all the difficulties in that quarter."[5] Enlightenment optimism of the purest sort: the inadequacies of the world would melt away if people would only communicate properly and reason together.

Rassam's failure to free the hostages through diplomatic channels, which set the stage for the dramatic military conclusion—the costly invasion, the storming of the fortress, and Tewodros's suicide—indicates how inadequate was the postponed text as a substitute for the missing one. At the very least, the deferral slighted the king who, arguably the diplomatic peer of Victoria, had attempted to institute an equal exchange. Indeed, Tewodros's unanswered letter included a proposal to regularize such an exchange through the establishment of an Abyssinian embassy in London. London's disregard for Tewodros's offer effectively prohibited communication on equal footing (and we can therefore view this disrupted exchange as the negative counterpart to Cook's embracing his interlocutor and rubbing his nose on the promontory at Dusky Bay). One might well conclude that British behavior demonstrated to Tewodros that Europeans were more likely to respond to force than to friendly communication. Much more than a faux pas in the Foreign Office is at stake, then. The "King of Kings" had been mistreated by subaltern diplomats, the disrespect exhibited by the British might well contribute to the subversion of his tenuous domestic legitimacy, and, in any case, he certainly had good reason to suspect that the British inability to reply indicated a potential foreign threat to his disputed Sudanese border. Why would Victoria ignore his cordial message unless a plot was underway, directed against his sovereignty? To quote Sven Rubenson, a biographer of Tewodros, "it was not a negative reply but the failure of Cameron to deliver [Tewodros's] letter [to Victoria] in person, the nonexistence of a reply, and the recall of the British Consul that caused the detainment and imprisonment. In the circumstances, this amounted to the 'breaking off of diplomatic relations,' and Tewodros can hardly be blamed if he suspected that the British and French actually contemplated siding with the Turks against him, as they had done against Russia in the Crimean War."[6]

Early in 1864 Tewodros imprisoned Cameron and his staff along with some missionaries active in the kingdom (one of whom, Henry Aaron Stern, is one of the two German chroniclers of the Abyssinian events and is discussed in the next chapter). They would not be freed until the fall of the fortress of Magdala four years later in April of 1868. All this for the sake of a missing text, the refusal to conclude an equal exchange of letters? Lest this account be judged excessively literary because of the concentration on the status of writing in the context of extraterritorial politics, let me cite a contemporary observer, Clements Markham, who celebrates the expedition: "The cause of quarrel [freeing the hostages] was absolutely just"; and he only regrets that the invasion had not been launched earlier.[7] So although he was hardly an opponent of the undertaking, he too locates the source of the conflict in the distorted communication generated by the Foreign Office and not in the Abyssinian court. In Markham's words,

> It does not appear that the conduct of Consul Cameron, in the course of these transactions, is open to censure. . . . The main cause of the imprisonment of the English Consul was the omission to take any notion of Tewodros' letter; and it is as ungenerous as it is erroneous to attempt to throw any portion of the blame on the unfortunate victim of this omission. The dis-

courteous omission to answer the letter was a perfectly just reason for Theodore's anger; and there can be no doubt that, if he had received a civil reply, which would have had the effect of explaining away Cameron's visit to the Turks, there would never have been any reason for spending several millions on an Abyssinian expedition.[8]

In fact, the bill was worse than Markham imagined. Rubenson puts the price of the expedition at nine million pounds, but more is at stake here than the cost of the invasion in monetary or other terms. Just as Mill would complain that the British, or rather their "ruling classes," could not even recognize the presence of "opinions, feelings, and historical antecedents" other than their own, Lord Russell was not able to recognize the king of kings of Ethiopia as a valid interlocutor for the British head of state. The complicated efforts to establish communication at Dusky Bay are simply no longer representative of international politics ninety years later; in their place come staid silence and, then, disproportionate conflict. A history of colonialisms might proceed from an account of Cook's willingness to embrace the islander at Dusky Bay to the Foreign Office's refusal to answer Tewodros's letter. In both instances, German observers looked on, and an understanding of the specific character of colonial discourse in German culture depends on taking such displacements into account. It might almost seem that it is not the British but Tewodros who, assuming the possibility of equal exchange and rational communication, is the heir of Forster and the Enlightenment in this story: as if the emancipatory ideals of European culture were forced into exile from Europe and found a home in radically different settings.

Tewodros is a much debated figure in the history of Ethiopia. "His name in the past was almost a byword for terror," Rubenson notes, and there can be little doubt that his career was one of military expeditions and nearly constant civil war, often accompanied by mass killings and cruel mutilations of prisoners.[9] Nevertheless, as Rubenson comments, "there is a tendency among the younger generation of Ethiopians today to see him as the symbol of all that is dearest to their hearts: equal opportunity for all, bold and progressive policies, and the unity and greatness of Ethiopia."[10] If the two characterizations of the figure seem incompatible, it is in part due to the extreme nature of the context in which Tewodros emerged. During the last third of the eighteenth century the Gondarine Empire fell into a state of irreparable decline, marked by an almost complete disappearance of central authority and, consequently, perpetual fighting among local governors. This was exacerbated, moreover, by doctrinal disputes within the Abyssinian church and a reassertion of Islam, both inside the country and beyond its borders. The period has come to be called Zamana Mesafent, the age of the judges, a reference to the Old Testament designation of the political constitution of ancient Jewry before the establishment of a royal dynasty with the anointment of Saul. The metaphor is part of a crucial political symbolism since the nominal rulers, no matter how insignificant their powers, always insisted on claiming descent from the Axumite dynasty, presumably founded by Menelik I, the son of Solomon and the queen of Sheba. Tewodros too would eventually insist on this tradition. By the end of his reign he included "the son of David and Solomon" among his royal titles, even though it is perfectly clear that his path to the throne depended much more on military success than on a fiction of genealogical legitimacy.

Born around 1820, Kasa (his name before the coronation) gradually emerged as one of many feudal political leaders, but he was the one leader whom the first British Consul in Massawa, Walter Plowden, identified as the likely agent of Ethiopian progress: "Should Kasai be the victor," he wrote in 1854, "I shall then hope that something may be effected for Abyssinia, even in its internal administration, by the destruction of the feudal system, the introduction of paid Governors and Judges."[11] As Plowden hoped, Kasa was indeed the victor at the battle near Deresge on 9 February 1855, and two days later he was crowned "King of Kings" by the Abun, the head of Ethiopian Orthodoxy, in the Deresge Maryan Church. The throne name that he adopted, Tewodros, was indicative of his proud intentions, taken as it was from the apocalyptic text Fikkare Iyesus. There Tewodros is the promised king who puts an end to long years of corruption and establishes a peaceful, just, and moral order.

It is clear that Tewodros failed to live up to the standards set by his own chosen name. His reign was a violent one, and after the fall of Magdala, Ethiopia was as disunified as before the coronation. Nevertheless—this is the argument of recent historians—Tewodros in effect initiates the reestablishment of an Ethiopian state through his vision of centralized authority as an agency of technical and administrative modernization. Thus, his policies included attempts to abolish slavery and polygamy, to reduce corruption, to separate church and state, to unify the Ethiopian church as a potential symbol of national cohesion, and to develop closer ties to Europe. In Europe his prime concern seems to have been to gain access to technical material assistance, which he received largely from the lay Protestant missions of the Saint Chrischona Institute. Given these components of a domestic modernization policy, it is no surprise that Tewodros imagined the possibility of an equally modern foreign policy, entailing the assertion of national sovereignty (rather than dynastic continuity) within an international diplomatic community that Abyssinia would enter on equal terms while fostering connections to the relatively advanced societies of western and central Europe.

It is in this context that he directed his letter to Victoria (as well as another to Napoleon III) in an appeal for the establishment of ties to Europe and to gain, at the very least, British moral support in the war with the Ottoman Turks to the north. This conflict was by no means solely a matter of a marginal border dispute but impacted directly on the very possibility of Abyssinian national sovereignty and on Tewodros's modernization policies, which were, for symbolic reasons, couched in religious terms. Thus, the conclusion of his letter: "I fear that if I send ambassadors with presents of amity by Consul Cameron, they may be arrested by the Turks. And now I wish that you may arrange for the safe passage of my ambassadors everywhere on the road. I wish to have an answer to this letter by Consul Cameron, and that he may go with my Embassy to England. See how the Islam oppress the Christian."[12] Tewodros has coupled minimalist requests with the maximalist urgency of a fellow Christian beleaguered by heathens, and London's rebuff is consequently all the more painful, suggesting an implicit rejection of the modernist politics and religious solidarity on which Tewodros has counted. In other words, as a modernizing Christian and enlightened head of state, Tewodros expected a response as an equal from a Europe that first chose instead to ignore him and later cast him in the role of terrorist, primitive, and barbarian. Yet if Tewodros was presented as the enfigurement of an exotic irrationality, it is not because of his initial intentions (which, on the contrary, concerned the amelioration of irrational conditions) but because exoticism and irrationality turn out to be the ideological product of a European civilization that projected them abroad.

After clumsy diplomacy failed, the British sent an army to rescue the hostages. In January 1868, the force of thirty-two thousand, mainly Indian troops under the command of Sir Robert Napier, landed at Zulla near Massawa, proceeded through the Senafé Pass and headed toward Magdala. Just below the fortress, on the Plain of Aroge, the single battle of the campaign took place on Good Friday, 10 April 1868. Of the four thousand Abyssinians, all that remained of Tewodros's once much greater army, nearly eight hundred were killed and twice that number were wounded. The British mounted a force of two thousand, of whom twenty were wounded and two died. Defeated at Aroge, Tewodros promptly released the captives the next day. Because of a final misunderstanding regarding the terms of a peace settlement—another textual confusion—the British stormed Magdala on Monday, 13 April, where they discovered that the king had taken his own life. The fortress was razed, and by 2 June most of the British troops had left Abyssinia via Annesley Bay.

Despite the obvious imbalance of firepower; despite, also, the emergence of an imperialist system of international relations and the consequent detriments to the African state, the Abyssinian expedition of 1868 cannot be strictly labeled a colonial undertaking. Neither its intentions nor its result entailed the establishment of a permanent British settlement in the region. Nevertheless, even this abbreviated recapitulation of the events indicates an underlying asymmetry that presumably could provide the political alibis or cultural rationales for a full-fledged colonialism. Tewodros initially proposes a model of equal communication, equal exchange (of letters), and equal or at least common interests of modernization and

Christianity. The world of spatial expanse becomes imaginably open and transparent. The momentary internal cohesion of the state corresponds to the "safe passage" that Victoria is requested to guarantee for Tewodros's ambassadors. Language too is transparent. Claiming the name "Tewodros," he becomes Tewodros, a perfect referentiality, the apocalyptic king at the end of history, charged with founding the final just and stable order. Yet things turn out to be far less clear than that. The African head of state is not accepted as an equal partner by the British Foreign Office, and his communicative model is displaced by misunderstanding and force. British policy pushes Tewodros beyond the margins of a common humanity. The point is not that he is strange but that he is made strange by a structural imbalance that subverts the plausibility of normative equality. Egalitarianism cedes to exoticism.

The Abyssinian material is important in this context because it demonstrates in an exemplary manner the production of the exotic. For Forster, Dusky Bay was new but never strange. For the travelers in Abyssinia, nothing is ever really new. It is a landscape of postromantic antiquity, dotted with timeless ruins, and all encounters confirm long-held prejudices. But it is all always strange, no longer belonging to a sphere of experience for which one might ever develop empathy. The insistence on an absolute otherness is implicated, here, either in a compulsive destructiveness, leading to the king's death and the razing of Magdala, or in an equally compulsive effort to integrate and equalize: the king's eight-year-old son, Alamayahu, was taken to England and sent to school at Rugby, where he died in 1879 and was buried at St. George's Chapel in Windsor.

The Abyssinian material is a complex resource for the study of colonial discourse. It is somewhat unique in that there is a clear record of the voice of the other, in this case, Tewodros himself. Interestingly, his initial position appears hardly disruptive or existentially different; it is he who appeals to norms and values he imagines to be shared. It is only through the imbalance of power that he becomes a textual construction of frightening exoticism, a monstrous Macbeth besieged in his castle—absolute difference. Tewodros's voice is intertwined and ultimately overcome by the colonial discourse of European power, including the specific character of German perspectives.

Two Germans watched the siege of Magdala in 1868. Their narratives might be read, of course, as further sources of information regarding the details of the Abyssinian campaign. Yet they are more important as representative samples of emerging colonial discourse, more precisely, examples of travel literature in two variants: science as geography and religion as missionary activity.

Gerhard Rohlfs was, at the time, a celebrated explorer of Africa. The Prussian government attached him as an official observer to the expedition, which was itself no easy task, and Bismarck's personal intervention was in fact necessary. It is not absolutely clear why Berlin was interested at all: what concern did the king of Prussia have at all with the heir to the queen of Sheba? Of course, Tewodros may have included Prussia in his European diplomatic offensive, and British and French interests had begun to clash in the region (a point probably not lost on Bismarck). In addition, Abyssinia belonged to the sphere of influence of the Anglican bishopric of Jerusalem, which, founded in 1841, stood under the joint patronage of the British and Prussian monarchs. In 1844, the first bishop, Michael Solomon Alexander, had ordained Henry Aaron Stern as deacon (both Alexander and Stern were German-Jewish converts). Some twenty years later, Stern, who had been involved in missionary activity in Abyssinia, ended up among the captives in Magdala. Whatever the Prussians' motives may have been, the Abyssinian texts by Rohlfs and Stern exemplify two mid-century versions of European accounts of non-Europeans within an ideational context in which Forster's universalism had given way to a structural asymmetry producing a growing contempt for the Africans. On that point, Rohlfs and Stern concur, as they do in political questions; neither takes Tewodros's side.

Yet there is a world of difference between the writings of an author of descriptive geography and the missionary narratives of the prisoner. The watchword for the former is the natural fact, for the latter a universal faith as a measure for historical culture. Within the overall process of the establishment of a language of colonialism, it is important to distinguish between science and religion, or more generally between naturalism and historicism, and the alternative sorts of texts each generates. They are both embedded in the same European culture of imperialism, increasingly growing as strange to itself as its science and religion are to each other, and which may therefore be unable to construct an epistemological subject adequate to the task of grasping qualitative difference—Africa—that is instead perpetually denounced as exotic, barbaric, and incommensurable. To be sure, Forster's Enlightenment might be accused of imagining everyone to be rational; nevertheless, we have seen his capacity to respect difference. In contrast, it is precisely colonial discourse that produces the notion of absolute difference, which may be occasionally fascinating but more typically beneath contempt.

Among the many German authors of African travelogues—from Friedrich Hornemann, Gustav Nachtigal, Heinrich Barth, and Georg Schweifurth to the colonial propagandist Carl Peters (to mention only a few representatives of a genre extremely popular in the nineteenth century and effectively ignored by literary history)— Rohlfs is of particular interest. This is so not solely because of the celebrity status he enjoyed in the late 1860s but, above all, because in his texts one can trace the specifically colonial turn. Setting off as an adventurer, his success won him recognition in the scientific community without, at first, any political overtones, but by the end of his career he had come to advocate the establishment of the German colonial empire. In this study, however, neither his scientific contribution nor his political allegiances are of primary concern but rather the process by which allegiance to scientific facts, a presumably objectivist descriptivism, metamorphoses into colonial agitation.

The biographers of Rohlfs are, by the way, far from unanimous about his political profile. In 1940, in the midst of the Nazi era, Ewald Banse counted him among "Our great Africans," part of a tradition of grand German Africanists, in order to criticize British and French colonialism with the argument that the Germans were the first explorers and the better rulers. As such, they could raise a substantively more legitimate claim to a colonial empire than their opponents who had confiscated the German colonies in the Versailles Treaty. In contrast, a 1982 East German biography by Wolfgang Genschorek treats Rohlfs as a progressive figure, allied to the democratic movement and a critic of imperialist adventures (including the Abyssinian expedition). Both tendentious accounts are quite tenuous, and both are ultimately more interested in the person than in the rhetoric of the written texts or the transformation of ideology. They concur, however, with other biographical accounts in the description of a narrative of a labile, undisciplined youth, born in Vegesack near Bremen in 1831, who ran away from school and nearly succeeded in signing on as a hand on a ship about to leave Amsterdam for the East Indies; who enlisted as soon as he could in the German regiments fighting in the Schleswig-Holstein War; and who studied medicine for only three semesters at three different universities before running off again and eventually ended up in the French Foreign Legion in Algeria in 1855.[13]

Banse explains this trajectory by presenting Rohlfs as a daring adventurer, a sort of Nazi hero *avant la lettre*. Somewhat more convincingly, Genschorek attributes it to a deep despair over the German conditions, especially the outcome of the war in the reactionary context of the suppression of the Revolution of 1848. It would go beyond available evidence to state forcefully that Rohlfs traveled to Africa to escape the postrevolutionary conservatism in Germany, although the corollary would certainly be an attractive argument: extraterritorial expansion as a consequence of disappointments with domestic political processes. One can speculate, however, on the basis of the scant biographical data about young Rohlfs's restlessness and the particular manner he chose to resolve conflicts: running away to sea, to war, to the Foreign Legion. Apparently at the last minute, he abandoned the medical profession pursued by his grandfather, his father, and his two brothers and disappeared for years. Much more than momentary political items, this pattern may explain an aspect of his work; escaping conflicts by avoiding authority, he avoids carrying out a conflict with authority and thereby, in a sense, accepts it. This acceptance fundamentally grounds his purportedly scientific descriptivism as a mode of writing devoted to the passive reproduction of observed data.

This descriptivism is often accompanied by a sense of danger, a pervasive threat, that Rohlfs tends to project onto the African population. Underneath that projection, it is presumably the unresolved conflicts with authority, which he had escaped but never overcome, that account for the sometimes ominous atmosphere of his descriptions. The Abyssinian narrative is a good example. On this score, the difference between Forster and Rohlfs is immense. Writing in place of his father, Forster effectively displaces him and emerges in public as the more interesting partner in the father-son team. Leaving authority intact, Rohlfs changes his own place and continues to wander and to write about wandering. If the geographical descriptions sometimes have a nervous undertone, it is because the author is, apparently, always on the run.

When Forster describes an extreme situation, for example, a storm at sea, he is likely to include an account of the crew's emotions, which may even be embellished with classical literary allusions. To touch on a very different case, C. Falkenhorst, who compiled popular accounts of explorations—the Bibliothek denkwürdiger Forschungsreisen (1890)—chooses extreme conditions to flush out the limits of descriptivism where one could only speak, negatively, of the *unbeschreiblich*, the indescribable heights, indescribable lushness, indescribable heat, a formula repeated stereotypically. Descriptivism is thereby pushed beyond itself and falls victim to its own sensationalism in what one might call a colonial sublime.

Consider now Rohlfs's handling of an extreme situation, the *samsun*, a sandstorm in the Sahara, in an 1881 collection of essays. The power of nature is immense, and the prose even falls into an excited cadence. Yet Rohlfs neither addresses any internal agitation (as Forster might have), nor does he retreat at all from the project of scientific observation; nothing is indescribable, not even the *samsun*. Indeed, the essay commences with a suggestion of heightened visibility; the Sahara's sunlight becomes diffuse, and "It no longer strains the eye to look into the otherwise blinding heaven, even without colored glasses."[14] Rohlfs proceeds to detail the natural signs indicating the approaching storm, and when it finally arrives and forces one to close one's eyes, even then Rohlfs only comments on the change of temperature. The observer's temporary loss of sight never calls into question the basic observability of the world as an object of scientific study. "In order to protect the skin from the truly painful effects of the coarse grains of sand and small pebbles that are tossed around vehemently, even man himself covers his head and all exposed parts of the body. He too has nothing to do but wait and accept his fate with patience."[15]

The response to the mortal threat is simple patience, not fear and trembling, not an appeal to God. In contrast to Forster's deistic trust in Providence, a source of emancipatory ideals, Rohlfs displays a positivist equanimity with minimal affect. The scientific descriptivism, an apparently complete objectivity, is external and terrestrial, without either an internal psychological or a transcendental dimension. In a thoroughly illuminated world of facts, Rohlfs collects details and presents reports that are, if anything, *sachlich*, objective and sober. Yet this objectivity is precisely the mystery, a particularly salient example of nineteenth-century positivist compulsion to accumulate and horde disenchanted details. Instead of naively accepting such realistic description as somehow natural, it is crucial to inquire into the conditions and motives underlying the production of this sort of text and its naturalism.

In the same 1881 volume, an important piece of evidence can be found in the essay on "Tripolitania and Its Importance for the History of the Discovery of Africa." At a time when public attention was directed to more distant regions of central and eastern Africa, Rohlfs's manifest concern here is to underscore the significance of this region, less removed from Europe but, according to Rohlfs, not adequately studied. In this context, he invokes some relevant predecessors, including Hornemann, whom he labels "the father of German Africa-travellers."[16] Other fathers follow, including Eduard Vogel who, Rohlfs tells us, was murdered at Uadai in 1856 and Moritz von Beurmann, murdered in 1861 in the Sudan. This necrology might be shrugged off as innocent if lugubrious professional history (like Cook's invocation of the discoverers who went before him), except for the fact that a paratextual aspect places Rohlfs himself in direct connection with the two victims. On the cover of the volume one finds a picture of Mohammed el Gatroni, the North African guide and servant who accompanied Vogel, Beurmann, and others, as well as Rohlfs, on their journeys. Through the presence of the servant, Rohlfs finds himself haunted by some deceased colleagues, a situation whose importance is perhaps always implied by the cliché of following in the footsteps of great predecessors. Do the fathers cast a shadow on the prose of the isolated and itinerant son? If one could answer affirmatively, then one would be able to explain both Rohlfs's anxiety as well as, more broadly, the construction of colonial literature as a series of narratives of martyred colonizers.

Soon after this trace, Rohlfs presents the mandate of the professional explorer: "A discoverer should and must go everywhere. He should provide as exact as possible information about topography, orographic and hydrographic conditions of the terrain, as well as generally report on the geology, the plants, animals, and peoples."[17] Ubiquity, exactitude, generality: Rohlfs sets himself high goals, but he has not actually determined whether they are mutually compatible. By invoking the imperative of collecting data, Rohlfs can articulate an excuse for his never-ending wanderings. Yet even the exigencies of science, as presented here, are indicative of a threat. Rohlfs, the traveler who pursues general, if precise, examinations everywhere, understands that he can never compete with the specialist, the *Fachgelehrter*. On one level, Rohlfs's point is correct in a platitudinous sense, for it is obvious that general travelers may precede specialists into new regions (although one can easily imagine the opposite to be true as well). More significantly, however, we find Rohlfs here beleaguered by an image of the better qualified and better trained scientist: not only the specialist who might follow him but the better educated explorers, including Vogel and Beurmann, who preceded him. His own descriptivist discipline may be a generalist knowledge that is less than disciplinary and therefore by no means an unproblematic mirror of the world. On the contrary, Rohlfs, the university dropout, reduces the world to a set of reportable data—Forster's "disjointed limbs"—as a concession to the challenge posed by imagined competitors, past and future. It turns out that his scientific objectivity is, on a deep level, a response to a threat, his positivism, one might say, just a symptom of his fear of ghosts.

A different enfigurement of threat appears even more clearly in the important earlier text, *Quer durch Afrika* (Straight through Africa), the account of his journey of 1865–67 from Tripoli to Lagos. This trip, much touted as the first north-south traversal of the Sahara by a European, made him famous (and lent him the credibility that explains his selection by the Prussian government to accompany the British expedition in 1868). After relating the preparations for the journey, he expresses his delight at returning to Africa: "With what exuberant feelings does the Africa-traveler land, after having plowed through the floods of the Mediterranean, on the African continent, which he will, in a certain sense, regard as his home for the duration of his journey. Here he hopes to open up new lands, new mountains, rivers, and lakes for geographical knowledge; he hopes to find new peoples with different customs and religions. Africa is indeed the Dorado of the traveler."[18]

Certainly, one hears the energetic traveler, eager to find and describe new landscapes and new cultures, and there is no reason to diminish the value of that sort of curiosity, which had inspired Forster as well. Yet the curiosity has undergone subtle cultural-historical shifts, and it is therefore important to inquire into the specific form—psychological, social, or literary—taken by such curiosity and to determine, furthermore, whether this structure of the cognitive impulse somehow hinders or distorts its own realization. In this vein, one is struck by a particular dissonance in the credo. If Africa is to be his home, his *Heimat*, can it also be a Dorado? For the latter designation implies both an object of discovery of the new as well as an imperial incursion, an allusion borrowed from that age of Spanish exploration that Forster treated so dismissively. It is not at all clear how the explorer can be returning to an African home, an odd sort of proprietary claim and—simultaneously—intending to extract a wealth of new knowledge to bring home, as from an El Dorado. The tension between these two poles, these conflicting constructions of expeditionary space—at home in Africa while exploiting it—generates new forms of anxiety.

Rohlfs immediately glosses the ebullience of the previous passage with a cautionary note. As happy as the traveler may be to set foot in Africa, he always needs to have his wits about him (exploitation may have undesired consequences). The terrain is dangerous, and to avoid succumbing to external threats, one must first of all know how to keep internal threats under lock and key: "The primary quality that an Africa-traveler, indeed everyone intending to explore unknown regions, must possess is that he know himself through and through; for only after an exhaustive and objective self-analysis can one hope to have acquired sufficient understanding, and that is nowhere more important than in travels in Africa, where one must constantly be able to judge correctly strange peoples and individuals."[19] This is quite an admission, one that tends to justify the interest in Rohlfs's psychology and his relation to paternal authority. Only by mastering oneself, Rohlfs seems to be saying, will one be able to master Africa and therefore anticipating, in reverse, Freud's usage of the metaphor of a "dark continent." External travel demands internal analysis.

There is a double terrain to explore, geographic and psychological, but it is always threatening, and the threat is always human. Thus, Rohlfs continues, "Danger has only one source: man. The climate of the region can be effectively resisted with quinine, and the threat posed by wild animals is next to nothing. But as difficult as it is here to separate friend from foe, it becomes even more difficult, the higher the level of so-called civilization occupied by the parties in question." The discipline he demands of himself and that determines the rigor of his descriptivist prose, always close to the facts, is a strategy to avoid danger, which lurks everywhere, within and without. His objectivity betrays a paranoid streak. If one were to treat him and other expeditionary authors as instrumental in the construction of colonialist ideology, it is not because their observations contribute directly to the military surveillance of the terrain but because the very notion of facticity with which they operate and which they disseminate presumes a threatening nature that has to be subdued by Enlightenment as domination.

Rohlfs's prose, as an example of the genre of scientific expeditionary literature, evidences a paranoia of objectivism, Cook's geometry gone mad. A legitimate human curiosity takes on the distorted form of a compulsive wandering driven by anxieties involving an inability to address authority, professional competition, a repression of personal subjectivity, and an omnipresent fear of foreign peoples. A fear of the foreign has emerged as a consequence of one's own alienation. These features, well documented in the case of Rohlfs, are indicative of European and, specifically, German society by the middle of the nineteenth century. The result is a travel literature that anxiously attempts to remain calm in the face of panic by fleeing into an ostentatiously scientific posturing to suppress the threat; hence, the never-ending descriptions (the rhetorical corollary to the poetic realism of fictional authors). Nevertheless, this suppression comes to the fore occasionally, leaving traces in the objectivist text of the social alienation that generated it. I want to explore several aspects of this problematic.

Rohlfs's ethos of objectivity assumes a model not unlike Tewodros's understanding of communication. The world is what it seems to be and language is transparent, an unproblematic vehicle of information. We have already seen how Tewodros was disabused of this illusion. In the case of Rohlfs, the whole project of verisimilitude, describing the newfound terrains truthfully, is based on a fiction, his deceptive assumption of a false identity. Serving in Algeria and taking part in the wars with the Kabyls in the late 1850s, he apparently learned Arabic and became very familiar with North African customs. The editor of a recent reedition of *Quer durch Afrika* claims that "no other European researcher of the period succeeded in understanding so completely the life style and mentality of the North African population and adapting to it so well that he could eventually be taken for an Arab."[20] At stake is not the historical veracity of the claim nor even the unquestioned value of the desirability of geographical penetration of the unknown but the construction of the explorer as a figure of deceit.

When Rohlfs left the Legion in 1860, he traveled into Morocco, a feat at that point nearly unheard of for a European, by undergoing a pseudoconversion to Islam and adopting the name Mustafa Bey or Mustafa Nemsi, that is, "the German." Not all but much of his journeys in the 1860s (the important and most productive decade) depended on this ruse. Some of his mentors, including both Barth and Mahmud-Pasha, the governor of Tripoli (later naval minister of the Ottoman Empire), had concerns and doubts about the deception and its ethical implications. Rohlfs's own account indicates how, in some places, doubts were raised about the genuineness of the conversion. He responded with all the more vigorous displays of piety.[21] (The question of conversion, of a "genuine conversion," and the relationship to the itinerancy of wandering will recur in the discussion of Stern, the other traveler at Magdala.)

There is no reason to relate these incidents in detail or to retrace Rohlfs's path since what is at stake here is a dynamic that threatens to destabilize and invalidate the objectivist text itself. Let us leave aside the ethical question of whether it was proper to carry out this masquerade and, for example, to accept hospitality (which Rohlfs generously acknowledges) on the basis of a lie. Suffice it to note that he apparently had no ethical reservations. A graver issue is the epistemological quandary we confront as soon as we juxtapose the descriptivist claims with the deceptive practice. If Rohlfs could be mistaken for an Arab what may he have mistaken to be a fact? Because in a world of spies anyone may be a double agent, Rohlfs's admitted behavior is good reason not to trust his account. Were one to ignore such epistemologically pessimistic considerations, one could still not help but wonder how a traveler constantly concerned with maintaining a false identity could have the peace of mind to describe his encounters while maintaining a naive faith in the accuracy of language. If we are thereby drawn away from the information value of the text, we find that it is engaged in another, very intriguing sort of production. Pushing into Africa, Rohlfs becomes exotic and dons a primitive mask. As in the discussion of Tewodros, exoticism turns out to have little to do with the real character of life outside of Europe but is rather itself a European product.

The problem of the mask might be formulated as a split between performative and expressive forms of identity, terms chosen to suggest a radicalization of the more familiar polarity of public and private. Rohlfs's prose suggests another split, however, a second indication of a fundamental structure of social alienation. For the issue of deception, as discussed so far, bears largely on the subject of the text, the narrator, and one has good reason to inquire as well into the addressee, the reading public. Consider for a moment the following comment in the introduction to the 1874 German edition of Schweinfurth's *Heart of Africa* (it had appeared in English the year before): "No matter how one-sided it may be, it is specialized natural-historical research that is able to provide genuinely positive information regarding an unexplored territory. On the other hand, a large part of the readers rightly demands *narration* in addition to *description*; out of the authors' own experiences emerges the backdrop of the grand stage on which he played out his role as a researcher."[22] In her rich study of German *Afrikareisenden*, Cornelia Essner identifies this passage as indicative of a crucial juncture between a classical travel literature and a colonial literature in a strict sense. As description was replaced by narration, the literary precondition was met for the generation of heroic narratives rather than of systematic scientific accounts. In fact, public taste in the nineteenth century gradually shifted away from serious geographic or ethnographic reports and toward the records of exhausting and exciting trips, preferably with some novel character capable of catching the public imagination. Professional science appealed less and less to a consumerist public with its taste for adventure: Livingstone's 1852 traversal of southern Africa from Loanda to Quelimane; Stanley's later expeditions; and, in the German setting, Hermann Wissmann's trip described in his *Unter deutscher Flagge quer durch Afrika von West nach Ost* (1881; Under German flag across Africa from west to east). Rohlfs's trans-Saharan journey to Lagos certainly belongs in this group. Although many of the routes he took were in fact not at all new (they were old trading routes), the novelty of the traversal and the appeal of narrative won him mass acclaim.

As a generic problem, the distinction between narration and description played a role, of course, in the construction of Forster's text. Forster senior was prohibited by the Admiralty from publishing a "narrative," a task then taken on by his son, while he restricted himself to taxonomic descriptions. Moreover, in the preface to the narrative the son attempted to marginalize Cook's account as primarily scientific, that is, nautical description best suited for specialists. This by no means implied that Forster's version lacked scientific content or was solely an individual story. Furthermore, the tension between the accounts by Forster and Cook appears to have taken place in the context of a still relatively homogeneous public prepared to engage itself with serious scientific reports. For Rohlfs and Schweinfurth, the case is evidently very different, and the distinction between narration and description is by no means solely a matter of form. The scientific community—the specialized public—demanded a reliably descriptive text, increasingly incompatible with the sort of narrative presumed necessary for the commercial market.

This split in the structure of the reading public, and its consequences for the internal construction of expeditionary literature, can be demonstrated with exemplary clarity by contrasting two versions of Rohlfs's trip. Although *Quer durch Afrika* appeared in book form in 1874, he also published a version entitled "Reise durch Nord-Afrika vom Mittelländischen Meere bis zum Busen von Guinea: 1865–1867" (Journey through North Africa from the Mediterranean Sea to the Bay of Guinea: 1865–1867) in the scholarly *Mitteilungen aus Justus Perthes' Geographischer Anstalt* (Communications of Justus Perthes's geographical institution), commonly referred to as Petermann's *Mitteilungen*, after the editor, August Petermann. This second version appeared in two separate supplementary volumes in 1868 and 1872. Needless to say, the sober and precise title of the periodical version appears rather dry next to the sensational *Quer durch Afrika*, the subtitle of which underscored the drama of the event even more: "Die Erstdurchquerung der Sahara," a phrasing surely worthy of Stanley.

Yet the difference between the two versions goes far beyond the titles. Although on occasion the prose is identical or nearly so, the overall structure and stylistic flavor of the two are at considerable odds. The 1868 publication, the academic version, commences in Fesan, omitting the passage from Tripoli through Ghadames, Misda, and Mursuk, these areas not being particularly new to the geographic public; that is, publication decisions are made on the basis of scientific interest. In contrast, the 1874 volume commences with Rohlfs in Tripoli (indeed, even before, since the preparation for the journey is described as well). In this second case, travel literature is no longer primarily a matter of describing new material to benefit the progress of science but is rather a narrative of the progress of the traveler on adventurous paths through exotic countries. Consequently, the periodical publication tends to report factual data more extensively. For example, although both include accounts of meteorological conditions in Fesan, the 1868 text treats the consequences for agriculture, and especially the complex irrigation system, at great length. Alternatively, in the book publication, one finds considerably more discussion of Rohlfs's personal circumstances—his finances, accommodations, even erotic innuendoes and the like—since the tendency in this text, written for the general public, is the construction of a cohesive narrative organized around the figure of the traveler.[23]

This split between narration and description corresponds, in sociological terms, to a dichotomy between a mass public and an educated elite and, in philosophical terms, to the tension between subject and object. This is no longer Forster's world of universal reason and empathy. The subject encounters a world of objects as a stranger without any promise of reconciliation. One response to this condition is the preference for masks; another is belligerence, a further textual trace of alienation. Reading Rohlfs's prose, one cannot help but be struck by the frequency of derogatory comments, fully absent in Forster's, that stand out from the otherwise neutral and objective tone. Not that Rohlfs engages in the sort of consistent racism expected from high imperialist discourse; far from it. On occasion, he will even express considerable admiration for African culture and society, as in his account of Bornu. Yet it is precisely such admiration that prefigures a desire for the colonial object, and in any case the text is sprinkled with asides such as "the indolence of the population at the oasis Derdji" or "of course, because the Rhadamans are Mohammadan, they do not lack those dirty insects that always accompany unhygienic people." Also in Rhadames, he takes note of "unattractive head shapes, and facial features [that] indicate frequent crossings with Negroes," just as in Gatron he finds "ugly faces" and a music described as "horrible noise."[24]

Although such judgments are by no means typical of Rohlfs's prose in general, neither are they mere accidents that one can skim

over and ignore. On the contrary, their marginality in the text is itself an indication of their importance; he has included them even
though they are not structurally required by the narrative. Just as
the neutral objectivity of descriptivism not only tolerates but depends on the deception of the mask and the dichotomy of the public, it also thrives on these assertions of aggressive disdain. The mask
splits the subject internally, the public is split horizontally, and here
humanity is split into us and them, self and other, Europe and Africa. This potential for antagonism, held in check at the borders of
the descriptivist text, comes to a head when an external political
constellation, like the Abyssinian campaign, provides an opportunity for an unbridled articulation of aggression.

I return now to his account of the 1868 campaign because it demonstrates how at an early date, at the height of his career as *Afrikareisender*, but in a unique setting, he was susceptible to ideological
pressures not unlike those that some fifteen years later pulled him
conclusively and definitively into the colonialist camp. In the preface, Rohlfs comments that English readers may feel that he has
judged Napier too harshly. The East German critic Genschorek
quotes the remark and in his subsequent recapitulation of the campaign implies that Rohlfs's admittedly critical observation referred
to the British force's excessive brutality on its passage through
Abyssinia and in the storming of Magdala—as if Rohlfs could be
cast as an incipient critic of British imperialism. Nothing could be
further from the truth. Rohlfs himself points out in the lines that
immediately follow that his judgments were, if anything, milder
than those of the correspondents of the *Times* and the *Daily Tele-
graph*. Moreover, he proceeds directly to rebut allegations in the
German press that the British forces had behaved improperly. Because of Genschorek's tendentious distortion of this matter, the
passage is worth quoting in full: "Recently, voices in the German
press have even tried to suggest that Sir Robert treated Tewodros
dishonestly; those are malicious denunciations. The English army
itself has been accused of poor conduct with regard to the natives,
but all foreign officers—representatives of nearly all nations were
present in Abyssinia—know that not only was the private property
of every Abyssinian protected but also that every small item was

paid for in cash and not even the smallest bit of arbitrary violence was tolerated." Despite Genschorek's Cold War imagination—searching for German opponents of British imperialism—Rohlfs turns out to be a defender of Napier on precisely those points that were at stake in the claim: the treatment of the population on the way to Magdala and the exchange of notes preceding the storming of the fortress.[25]

Yet if Rohlfs was willing to testify in favor of Napier on these controversial points, why did he fear that his judgment might be regarded as too harsh? The text does indeed entail a bitter critique of the general, but it is by no means an obviously tendentious one and certainly not one compatible with an East German vision of anti-imperialism. Instead, Rohlfs, observer and scientist, expresses complaints regarding inefficiency and incompetence. It is not the Abyssinian war in general or the British military presence as such that he castigates but the embarrassing lapses in Napier's personal leadership abilities. Thus, for example, he sarcastically describes the commencement of the bombardment of Magdala by recounting Napier's scrupulous placement of the artillery, carried out "with all the precision and tact as if it were an exercise." The caustic implication that Napier may not be quite up to performing well in a real battlefield situation (rather than in an exercise) is confirmed by the result: "unfortunately, not a single Armstrong cannon ball hit its target, not a single rocket ignited even one of the many straw roofs of Magdala." Rohlfs does not end the polemic with the meager conclusion that Napier is a poor shot, for the general's incompetence deserved at least another ironic twist: "yet it was lovely, the shots were so regular and exploded in the air and the rockets hissed so nicely that Sir Robert appeared to feel an extraordinary contentment and satisfaction, if he was awake at all. For his eyes were shut fast as I watched him."[26]

The passage is indicative of the sort of criticism Rohlfs directs at Napier. His concern is not brutality but inefficiency (anticipating a subsequent kind of critique of British imperialism: the Germans would make better colonizers). It is, of course, also indicative of Rohlfs's own valorization of observation: watching the general, he complains that the general is not watching Magdala. Given Rohlfs's descriptivist stance, we can imagine that ideally this Argus would never close his eyes, and he would not do so, presumably, because an enemy fortress is always nearby.

In the account of the Abyssinian campaign, the tendency already inherent in *Quer durch Afrika* for descriptivism to turn into belligerence becomes predominant. Indeed, compared with the travelogue, even with its surfeit of pejorative remarks as discussed earlier, the viciousness and antipathy that Rohlfs expresses in the Abyssinian text seem shockingly incomprehensible, until one recognizes that the military setting must have encouraged this sort of aggressive prose. Unlike Napier, Rohlfs keeps his eyes open, but everything he sees is judged to be either disgusting or threatening. Even the Egyptian coast puts him off: "Although noteworthy thanks to a few buildings and antiquities, such as the pillar of Pompey and the needle of Cleopatra, the view of Alexandria is not at all attractive and even less impressive. To be sure, the masses of ships, mostly from Mediterranean countries, is significant, but everything seems dirty, an impression magnified by the many small boats rowing around, handled by tattered, half-naked Egyptians."[27] Matters get worse when "hungry urchins came on board and tried to seize the travelers and their baggage; only with the help of strong language and strong beatings, which they accepted quite patiently, could one remain in control of oneself and one's possessions." And so forth: he refuses to hand over his passport for fear that the policeman would soil it, the railway is so dirty "that it could only be compared with the government," and Cairo proves to him that "in a Mohammedan city, dirt and grime are as unavoidable as ruins."[28] At Zula, Arabian music is a "torture" (and this from a traveler who had spent more than a decade in North Africa, often under an Arab alias), any significant works of art in Ethiopian churches are attributed to Venetians or Portuguese, Abyssinian priests are hopelessly venal, and Abyssinian Christianity strengthens his conviction that "Christianity, left to itself without the classical traditions of the Greeks and Romans, degenerates as quickly into an empty superficial form as do the other two mainly semitic religions, Judaism and Islam."[29]

The narrative of the Abyssinian campaign is important for an understanding of Rohlfs because it magnifies these sorts of judgments. It is here that his ideology becomes clearest. He has his eyes open, while Napier keeps his shut, but both are waging war. This belligerence is, moreover, not a merely peripheral feature; on the contrary, it is part of the descriptivism that is at the very center of Rohlfs's writing and that is always driven by an experience of threat. The threat, however, is not only external, not only Alexandrian beggars, Arabian musicians, and Abyssinian priests. The text simultaneously suggests an internal threat—fractures in the composition of European identity—particularly during the voyage on the Péluse across the Mediterranean, from one continent to another. Perhaps because the catastrophic ending, the razing of Magdala, casts a shadow backward to the beginning, the description of the passengers unintentionally conveys a sense of danger. Rohlfs is uncomfortable with the French passengers and their display of their government medals, and although he is delighted to find some "German-speaking gentlemen," he can report nothing that was spoken. Instead, he recurs three times to "a fine Parisian *Lorette* of the demimonde," who, drinking too much, always kept the conversation going. Rohlfs regrets that he never learned her name, but he does know that she "was going to Egypt to make her fortune, perhaps she was speculating on the harem of some pasha, perhaps even of the highest one."[30]

As short as the passage is, it is curious that Rohlfs has included it since, as he points out, Mediterranean cruises were by then nothing new, and he was eager to begin with an account of the actual African journey, his Dorado. It is nevertheless included, and in a fairly prominent location, and it betrays an anxiety about the passage from Europe to Africa that takes the shape of Rohlfs's fantasy that the *Lorette* was heading for the viceroy's bed. At stake then is the construction of a polar opposition between European and non-European identity (a distinction thoroughly foreign to Forster's universalism), which accounts for the brutality of Rohlfs's treatment of the Egyptians, as if he were punishing them for welcoming his unnamed erotic companion. It also accounts for another critique directed at Napier.

Although Genschorek imaginatively envisions the British fighting their way through Abyssinia, ruthlessly suppressing widespread resistance, in fact the invading force proceeded largely on the basis of negotiations with regional governors, many of whom were, by then, in open rebellion against Tewodros. Rohlfs focuses on such negotiation with the Prince of Tigre in order to express several complaints: the two-week delay caused by the meeting was excessive and logistically unnecessary; Napier accorded the prince, officially still a subordinate of Tewodros, a diplomatic treatment appropriate for the sovereign monarch; and Napier's approach to the prince on an elephant was ridiculous, and the use of elephants in general (brought from India) costly and inefficient. As interesting as it would be to clarify the character of Rohlfs's judgment on all these points (and to contrast it with evidence from competing accounts), one aspect of his interpretation is of particular importance now. Repaying the prince's morning visit, Napier entered his tent in the evening, was offered a meal, and then the prince presented him with an Abyssinian costume, a sword, and a donkey. Rohlfs's comment: "Thus transformed into an Abyssinian chief, Sir Robert left the tent, to which he had come riding on an elephant. The comedy could not have been more complete."[31]

If one recalls the fact that Rohlfs himself had traveled extensively in disguise, his contempt for Napier's donning the local dress must seem strange indeed. If Mustafa Bey can wear African clothes, why not General Napier? The difference is that Mustafa Bey was alone and vulnerable and adopted a mask to escape a perceived threat, whereas General Napier stood at the head of an army, the mission of which was to rescue the representatives of Europe from their imprisonment at the hands of an African king. Fearing the dissolution of identity, threatened from without by Alexandrian beggars, from within by the Parisian demimonde, Rohlfs insists on a rigid assertiveness, imagines that Napier is "going native," as anthropologists put it, and hence has little appreciation for what actually must be regarded as a successful diplomatic encounter on Napier's trek to Magdala.

This insistence on preserving a beleaguered identity has direct consequences for Rohlfs's politico-economic ideology. We have already seen how, Rohlfs insists against critics in the German press that the British army respected the private property of the Abyssinian population. What happened to property at Magdala? Entering the king's chambers, Rohlfs is overwhelmed by the treasures: silver crosses, golden crowns, rifles, sables, rugs, and more, "a real used furniture store, wholesale," and everyone, clearly including Rohlfs himself, took several objects, "crosses and incense holders to bring home as souvenirs."[32] He returns his booty, however, when he learns that when a British army conquers a city, all conquered goods customarily belong to the troops to be sold off and the profit divided. Although Rohlfs reluctantly conforms to this practice, he quickly gets a sort of vengeance when he argues with a British officer that gifts from Tewodros previously given to a German resident of Magdala were not subject to British appropriation.[33] In both passages and in the introduction, Rohlfs appears as an adamant defender of private property momentarily threatened by the masses in the form of the multiracial British troops.

To measure the specific character of Rohlfs's expeditionary prose, it is useful to set as a norm the prose of that member of the press corps accompanying Napier's army who would later become the most famous: Henry Morton Stanley. The differences between the two tell us a good deal about the contrast between German and American literary culture in the middle of the nineteenth century, and they equally help us grasp the specificity of Rohlfs's position and German colonial discourse more generally. Stanley's book, *Coomassie and Magdala: The Story of Two British Campaigns in Africa*, appeared in 1874; the section on the Abyssinian war was later republished as a single volume. In the first chapter, he provides a substantial review of the events leading up to the invasion, whereas Rohlfs, curiously, is nearly silent on the political context. In general, Stanley seems eager to present an exciting or, better perhaps, thrilling story, whereas Rohlfs is a much more reticent observer, restricting himself largely to the reporting of the minutiae of technical details and strategic developments. The point of juxtaposing the two texts then is not to contrast possibly different political judgments, since Rohlfs by and large refrains from explicit statements on this issue, but rather to raise the question of Rohlfs's reticence itself. To the extent that the German *Afrikareisender*, to use the contemporary term, prefers to maintain a descriptivist stance, what is the nature of the facts he describes and what are the generic and ideological consequences of such facticity?

Stanley immediately introduces himself as a brash American journalist, drawn to excitement and sensation: "Before proceeding to Abyssinia as a Special Correspondent of the 'New York Herald,' I had been employed by American journals—though very young—in the same capacity, and witnessed several stirring scenes in our Civil War. I had seen Americans fight; I had seen Indians fight. I was glad to have the opportunity of seeing how Englishmen fought. In Abyssinia I first saw English soldiers prepared for war."[34] He is a witness, therefore, not of just any "scenes" but of "scenes" that are "stirring," and these make up the high points of his text. Yet if he enjoys the view as a sort of aesthetic spectator, the agonistic pleasure is linked directly to a larger evaluative framework: the soldiers who fight well are engaged in the good fight "which England undertook in Africa, in behalf of her honour, her dignity, humanity, and justice; and more brilliant successes . . . are not recorded in history."[35]

Such pompous rhetoric and the superlative claims are absent in Rohlfs's prose. Is it a matter of the difference between American journalism and German science? commerce and culture? Perhaps not solely. For although Rohlfs had previously received support and encouragement from figures as prestigious as the explorer Heinrich Barth and the geographer August Petermann and was therefore arguably a recognized member of a scientific community, he was, at best, a lay member without formal academic training. One comes closer to grasping the key issue by considering the titles of the two volumes, which demonstrate perspectives at considerable variance from each other. Stanley's *Magdala* draws attention to the political center and military climax of the campaign, without a doubt a "stirring scene." The full text on the title page of Rohlfs's volume reads as follows: "In Abyssinia: In the service of His Majesty the King of Prussia with the English Expeditionary Force in Abyssinia. With a Portrait of General Napier and a Map of Abyssinia." The reference to the map and the threefold mention of the name of the country clearly underscores the value of the text as geographical information. (Or does the repetition of the geographical name betray an anxiety on the author's part regarding his own geographical credentials?) Where Stanley's title cut to the chase by focusing on the dramatic climax at Magdala, Rohlfs's title suggests a primarily geographic concern.

In addition, the title indicates the author's status as an observer accompanying the English force as a foreigner (and elsewhere Rohlfs explicitly underscores the hospitality he received).[36] After Forster and Cook, the constellation of Rohlfs and Napier indicates again how the emergence of German colonialism is, at least in part, a matter of an intra-European dynamic of imitation and competition. Most important in the title, however, is the invocation of two authoritative figures, the general and the king, as if the validity of colonial authorship depended on the goodwill of superiors. Yankee Stanley writes for a mass public, and in his later career he certainly produces himself as a hero for—and above—the masses. Rohlfs's prose is comparatively unaffected by this aspect of the industrial modernization of journalism. He writes in an alternatively constructed, perhaps more staidly hierarchical, public sphere, without concessions to the exigencies of popularity. Could one have expected anything else from a dutiful subject of the Prussian king? His political restraint, his refusal of sensationalism, and his relative restriction (more or less) to sober facts is then, at least in part, not only a matter of a putatively scientific stance but also a consequence of a predemocratic social and cultural context.

Stanley's account foregrounds the masses; Rohlfs's narrative avoids masses and presents his own isolation. This difference is nowhere clearer than at the outset. Listen to Stanley's epic sweep, the paradigmatic "stirring scene":

> A most extraordinary and novel sight presented itself to me as I landed upon the bunder at Zoalla. Thousands of half-naked coolies were shouting and chanting a barbaric song while they worked under as hot a sun as ever blazed in the tropics, and hundreds of uniformed superintendents, armed with long *courbaches*, were coercing their labourers under their charge to work. The braying of hundreds of donkeys, the neighing of horses, the whinnying of mules, the lowing of thirsty kine, the

shrill shriek of two anomalous locomotives, the noisy roll of rickety cars as they thundered to and fro, caused the scene to appear at the first impression as if a whole nation had immigrated here, and were about to plant a great city on the fervid beach of Annesley Bay. The mountainous piles of stores covered with tarpaulins, the long warehouses, with their roofs of brushwood, filled to the utmost with the materiel of war, and the noble bay crowded with majestic transports, steamers, men-of-war, great sailing-packets, tiny tugboats, elegant little yachts, and innumerable Turkish kanjeahs from Mocha, Jeddah, Souakim, and Massawa, flitting about with their swallow-winged sails, only served to heighten the illusion.[37]

One can hardly imagine a passage of prose better suited to demonstrate literature's artifactual character. The accumulation of material detail; the panoramic perspectivism; the tropes of violence, technology, and exoticism; the spatiality nearly bursting with stuff: these sentences are themselves imperialism, or at least one particularly heroic account of it.

Of course, Stanley's text is far from devoid of factual interest. Considerable information is provided regarding ship tonnage, supplies of coal and water, troops, animals, and casualties, although it is, characteristically enough, marginalized in a statistical appendix. Furthermore, it is Stanley and not Rohlfs who treats the cause of the conflict, not however as material for critical scrutiny (even though the international press had indeed subjected the British expedition to sometimes hefty critique). Stanley's interest in the background of the campaign has more to do with the seductive drama of the rise and fall of Tewodros than with rational public debate. That is, he includes politics for the same reasons that he marginalizes statistics: to heighten the sensationalism of the material, so evident in the opening passage, which was written as if it were the commencement of national saga. Under a cruel sun, cruel masters command innumerable slaves, bent beneath the lashes of the *courbaches*, whips of hippopotamus hide, and introduce a story about immense quantity: quantities of animals, supplies, boats, and so forth, a fitting outset for an epic campaign. It is a world bursting with material, and it will take the strong arm of a hero or the steady hand of the writer to conquer it.

None of this fervor marks Rohlfs's text. "It was the end of November, 1867," he begins, "when I boarded the Péluse, a steamer of the Messagerie impériale, at Marseille, in order to travel to Egypt. As cold as the weather had been in France in the previous days, when even Marseille had seen some frost, it was a lovely, summer-lit day when we went on board."[38] Although it might certainly appear that Rohlfs hereby commences a personal narrative, in contrast to Stanley's wider, objective scope, such a conclusion would be far from accurate. Both travelers record their own experiences and observations, but they do so in extraordinarily different ways. Rohlfs abjures Stanley's proclivity for self-heroization, and he does so because his text lacks any masses who could provide the backdrop for heroic figures: no masses, no heroes. This distinguishing feature characterizes an overriding tendency in German colonial discourse that, in contrast to British or French material, is often a literature of isolation, emptiness, and void. The *Sonderweg* of German colonialism, the German difference vis-à-vis England and France is this: in place of threatening multiplicity, the confrontation with barbarian hordes, its primal scene involves a self-assertion in a vacuum, emptied of any potential threat, an enforced singularity and a return to an origin. Local culture is either rational (as with Forster) or it is absent, but it is rarely overpowering. Of course, we also saw Cook empty the world as part of a project of geometric mapping; the local population was simply dismissed. In the German tradition, there is a conventional assumption of the viability of local culture, hence, Forster on the dance; but we will find similar phenomena in other writers as well. For ideological and perhaps personal and psychological reasons, Rohlfs could not achieve a similar capacity for interpretive appreciation. He therefore does not end up dwelling on hostile masses (as does Stanley) but presents an emptied space. Mary Louise Pratt has found a similar emptying in Alexander von Humboldt's account of South America.[39]

When, in 1884, Rohlfs enters into the explicitly colonial discussion around the establishment of a German protectorate in Southwestern Africa, it is also in the name of private property, which requires the defense of a nation-state. Rohlfs applauds the Reich's coming to the aid of Adolf Lüderitz, the merchant who pioneered the settlement. No longer the Anglophile of the 1860s, he attacks British claims in the region, not as a critic of colonialism in general, but in the specifically German mode of an anticolonial colonialism, the invocation of equality as the principle according to which European nations should divide up the world among themselves. Because the British could not be trusted to tolerate Lüderitz's presence—Rohlfs's formulation is extraordinarily aggressive: "Internationalist foolishness [*Internationalitätsduselei*] is unknown in the business world. Especially in England."—the intervention by the German state was necessary to provide protection.[40] Protection is after all the ultimate guarantee for the writer who envisions himself constantly surrounded by threatening forces: "Permit me to note that the author of these lines was ambushed by Bedouins in 1842, close to the French southern border of Algeria, and was nearly mortally wounded. Any satisfaction or compensation was out of the question. Yet when the same victim was attacked and robbed in 1880, in the middle of the Sahara, all that was needed was a word from Prince Bismarck in Berlin to bring those otherwise allegedly so unreachable Bedouins to justice. Compensation was received for all damages."[41] Yet when the Reich stepped in to protect explorers, merchants, and settlers, the context for Rohlfs's sort of adventurism had come to an end. The itinerant geographer had escaped Germany by fleeing to Africa, only to prepare the way for Germany to enter Africa. Travel literature, describing the unknown, participates in the erosion of its own preconditions.

3

HENRY STERN AND
MISSIONARY SPACE

The writings of Gerhard Rohlfs provided an opportunity
to examine the character of travel literature at a historical moment of transition from scientific description to
colonialist agitation. There was, however, another nomadic
figure at Magdala whose narrative strategy derived less from
the paranoia of descriptivism than from the euphoria of faith.
Moreover, the study of another all too neglected genre bearing
on extraterritorial expansion—missionary accounts—can
raise questions about types of religiosity, ideological enfigurements, and literary forms. The writings of Henry Aaron Stern
offer a strong contrast to Rohlfs's—instead of natural facts,
Christian faith—while simultaneously allowing us to discover
a further and potent constellation of ideological factors that
contributed to the colonial enterprise. Stern is in many ways an
exceptional, perhaps even eccentric, case, but it is precisely the
examination of such exceptions that do not fit easily into established categories that can generate new insights, which ought
to be the task of a contemporary cultural studies. There is indeed no reason to assume that cultural studies should be restricted to the typical or the ordinary; such a stance would be
oddly conformist. On the contrary, it is in the atypical figure or
the extraordinary achievement that meanings, values, and
goals may become clearest. Furthermore, I here present Stern's
exceptionalism in constellation with Rohlfs, paired figures
whose contrast is intended to foreground a range of problems
as in my discussion of Cook and Forster.

Born in 1820 in Unterreichenbach, near Gelnhausen, into an orthodox Jewish family, Stern grew up in the Frankfurt ghetto. Like Rohlfs he was expected to enter into a medical career but instead received some commercial training in Hamburg, until he traveled to London at the age of nineteen (the same age as Forster when he left London with Cook) to serve as an apprentice in a business firm. But the firm suddenly failed, and the young Stern found himself left to his wits in the foreign metropolis. In Hamburg he had apparently already had some contact with the London Society for the Promotion of Christianity amongst the Jews, a missionary organization founded in 1809. He pursued this connection in London and was baptized on 15 March 1840.

Of the substance of the conversion, the nature of his religious or psychological crisis, we know next to nothing, although it presumably represented a response to a situation that was doubly problematic: the cultural and political pressures on German Jewry in the context of both post-Enlightenment secularization and restorationist conservatism as well as the existential difficulties of the twenty-year-old in a foreign country, suddenly out of luck. The conversion was, in any case, decisive for Stern's career: he had found his calling. He traveled as a convert to Jerusalem where he was ordained a deacon by the Anglican bishop in 1844 and set out on a mission to the Jews of Iraq and Iran. Ordained as a priest in 1849 in London, he undertook a second three-year mission, recorded in his 1854 narrative *Dawnings of Light in the East with Biblical, Historical, and Statistical Notices of Persons and Places Visited during a Mission to the Jews in Persia, Coordistan, and Mesopotamia* (another case, after Forster, of German travel literature being written in English). In 1859, the London Society sent him to Africa to explore the viability of a mission to the Falashas, the Ethiopian Jews. On the basis of his positive report, the society sent him out again in 1862, now with the approval of Tewodros, to convert the Falashas to the Christianity of the Ethiopian Orthodox Church. A year later, in October 1863, Stern, the British consul Cameron, and other European missionaries were arrested on royal command, and they were not released until Magdala fell to the British invasion in 1868. Stern recounted his tribulations in *The Captive Missionary: Being an Account of the Country and People of Abyssinia, Embracing a Narrative of King Theodore's Life, and His Treatment of Political and Religious Missions* (1868). When he returned to England, he undertook a triumphant lecture tour; again like Rohlfs, Africa as Dorado turned him into a celebrity.

The plot is thickening quickly now: a German-Jew who should have become a doctor ends up instead a Christian missionary to the Jews of Ethiopia and is imprisoned by a monarch who claimed descent from Solomon and Sheba. To complicate matters, the army that liberated the prisoners served a government whose prime minister was Benjamin Disraeli. When he replaced Lord Derby, who had resigned for health reasons late in February 1868, the British press expressed astonishment that the aristocratic Tory Party would cede leadership to the offspring of Jewish immigrants from Venice. (Disraeli was of course baptized; religious restrictions on political positions were not abolished until 1890). This complicated network of resonances and reflections suggests that the Abyssinian campaign, the narratives it produced, and the associated, incipient emergence of imperialist fantasies—reconstructed visions of the relationship between Europe and the rest of the globe—may have something to do with shifts in the ideological status of what was then called the "Jewish Question." But what? Not surprisingly, the answer lies in Jerusalem.

The joint Anglican-Prussian bishopric in Jerusalem was established in 1841; the first bishop, Michael Solomon Alexander, another German-Jew, arrived in England in 1820, served as cantor in Norwich, Nottingham, and Plymouth until converting to Christianity in 1825. Professor of Hebrew and rabbinics at King's College during the 1830s, he also played an active role in the London Society for the Promotion of Christianity amongst the Jews until he left for Jerusalem in 1841. It was he who ordained Deacon Stern in 1844. Yet to understand the underlying issue, one has to look beyond the symbolism of a Jewish convert as bishop of Jerusalem. Nor does one get very far by pointing out political developments, such as the increasingly complex international interests in the eastern Mediterranean. Although such points are certainly relevant, their significance depends on a cultural analysis and eclipses the important ideological transformation going on, which is centrally mediated by a revival of the notion of a mission to the Jews. For that mission, a major component of the undertaking in Jerusalem, represented an important change in the self-understanding of European Christianity—for which the relationship to Judaism was always crucial—at a time when Christianity was still very much a state religion in England and Prussia. In other words, a change in the state ideology, in particular, in the religious self-identification of the state, generated the historical novelty of a mission to the Jews and thereby provided the foundation, or at least part of the ideological legitimation, for a new sort of extraterritorial cultural expansion. To be sure, missionary activity had been involved in overseas expansion previously, notably in Latin America. Yet, as we know from Forster, Spanish colonialism could hardly provide a convincingly positive image of a worthwhile undertaking to a sensibility schooled on reason and tolerance. The extension of the Spanish Inquisition into the New World was a world apart from the nearly philosemitic framing of the new mission. Nineteenth-century colonialism, even its religious component, is by no means a direct continuation of the conquistadors, and its cultural self-legitimation derived from a dramatic post-Enlightenment reorganization of the relationship between Christianity and Judaism.

Apostolic directives notwithstanding, throughout most of its history Christianity addressed its missionary activity to gentiles and excluded the Jews. This inability to fulfill half the charge of the Gospel represented an internal inconsistency that derived from the double character of Christianity as a universalizing religion and a state ideology, at least through the eighteenth century and—not only covertly—later. As an ideology functioning to stabilize the structure of political authority in hierarchical societies, it found anti-Semitism useful as a mechanism with which to identify perpetual outsiders in order to produce the illusion of a cohesive Christian community. In other words, its complicity in heteronomous political structures necessarily undercut its universalist religious creed. Jews were thus most useful precisely as representatives of a vilified alterity, and a systematic and sincere conversion effort would have therefore been dysfunctional from the standpoint of a political system based on legitimation through religion and, especially, religious exclusion. Anti-Semitic policies should therefore be regarded as consequences of a politicized and ideological Christianity rather than of Christian religiosity per se. Daniel Jonah Goldhagen misses this distinction in his flawed effort to explain German anti-Semitism as a direct consequence of patristic texts.[1]

This mechanism of traditional anti-Semitism prevailed until the age of Enlightenment and the French Revolution, in the wake of which a gradual emancipation of the Jews began, which entailed a recognition of their potential membership as equal participants in civil society. Of course, this development proceeded at different paces in the various nation-states. Although emancipation may have been understood as an idealistic enthusiasm for tolerance of human rights, it in fact followed directly from the reconstruction of the modern state. That is, by emancipating the Jews the political system in effect could emancipate itself from religion and, therefore, separated from the respective local church could pursue its own affairs with greater flexibility and an autonomous rationality. The separation of the state from the church relieves the state of the need to concern itself with issues of dogma but therefore also frees it from a consideration of the religious or moral propriety of its actions.

This separation of church and state was by no means easy, especially in England and Prussia where the monarch was at least nominally *summus episcopus*. Nor could the ideological legitimation traditionally provided by religion be abandoned abruptly, particularly in the context of the romantic piety of the 1840s. In England that piety responded to the rise of social movements and the consequences of the Reform Act of 1832, and it both echoed and resisted the Anglo-Catholicism of the Tractarians at Oxford (Newman converted in 1845). In Prussia the personal piety of Friedrich Wilhelm IV, who came to the throne in 1840, certainly played a role, and his ministers did their best to exclude from academic and cultural life any of the representatives of left Hegelianism. A mission to the Jews, that is, an emancipation of Jews into Christianity, clearly represented a more conservative and less threatening response to secularization than did the one suggested by Marx in his treatment of the Jewish Question. Given the normative status of tolerance in the wake of the Enlightenment, the mission to the Jews would ideally no longer be blocked by an anti-Semitism that had never been genuinely compatible with at least some of the precepts of the apostolic faith.

Thus, it is precisely the Enlightenment, the revolution, and the habits of tolerance that, perhaps surprisingly, allow for a mission to the Jews, who—so it was argued—should no longer be excluded arbitrarily from the Gospel. Yet such a mission simultaneously indicated an increasingly aggressive posture on the part of European Christian culture vis-à-vis other cultures. It therefore set the stage for a general acceleration of missionary work that, at least for Germany, had previously served largely to maintain contact with German emigrant communities but gradually was refashioned as part of an expansionist imperialism. The joint bishopric in Jerusalem, moreover, would permit the two Protestant monarchs to begin to construct an anti-Catholic alliance. Finally, and perhaps most importantly, the mission to the Jews played a not insignificant role in the reconstruction of national representations. The image of Prussian liberalism would finally give way to a religious Prussia with a benevolent, if unctuous, orientation toward Palestine. Such was the ideological background of the pilgrimage of Wilhelm II, the imperialist kaiser, at the end of the century.[2] The parallel derivation of a conservative national narrative with a religious core—from Judaism to Christianity to Britain—was Disraeli's story to tell, especially in *Tancred*.

No longer perpetual strangers and scapegoats, Jews were now instrumentalized on two levels. As objects of missionary activity they rendered the new national ideologies plausible insofar as their inclusion in the body politic tended to demonstrate the universal and nonexclusionary character of the modern nation-state. As targets of missionary activity, they provided an excuse to invigorate moribund overseas religious-cultural expansion insofar as the colonization of the Jews represented a sort of dress rehearsal for the colonization of the rest of the Orient. Alexander McCaul, who had collaborated with Michael Alexander on a translation of the New Testament and Anglican liturgy into Hebrew, held the sermon at the latter's ordination in the chapel of Lambeth Palace on 7 November 1841. Sprinkled with attacks on the Oxford Movement and "Romanism" as well as praise for the liberal cooperation between British and Prussian Protestantism, the text presents the basic argument: the need for a bishop to direct the mission to the Jews; the absence of conflict with the orthodox patriarch of Jerusalem whose task lies with his own congregations; and the particular appropriateness of Anglicanism—with the relative severity of its service—for a mission to the Jews, for whom the major cause for rejecting Christianity, so it was argued, has always been the Catholic veneration of images.

These explicit concerns, however, are framed by two remarks that confirm the main argument regarding a connection between the reorganization of the status of Jews in Christian Europe and the articulation of imperialist ideology. At the beginning of the sermon McCaul's task is to enumerate the most obvious, if ultimately peripheral, reasons for sending a bishop to the Near East, including the presence of some scattered Anglican settlements there: "There are congregations or missionary settlements of the Church of England in Syria and Asia Minor, Egypt and Abyssinia, which desperately need the leadership and blessing of a bishop. . . . The waves of political interest, commercial undertakings, and religious sympathies keep rolling back onto the shores of Asia, bringing with them numerous of our compatriots and brothers. In Europe societies have been formed to promote the settlement of the Holy Lands; peoples and churches in the Orient have turned to England for help; princes have requested instruction."[3] That is, before coming to his main concern, McCaul suggests the desirability of international relations, marked by the expansion of British commercial interests in the Near East. He therefore reveals that the mission to convert the Jews is to be the alibi for the state religion to follow the entrepreneurs.

Thus, in one sense, the conversion of the Jews represents an initial phase of cultural imperialism to the extent that Jewish communities were spread throughout the space of North Africa and the Middle East, precisely the same space into which European commercial and political networks of power were expanding. In a second sense, however, McCaul attempts to point to the internal character of contemporary Judaism, not just its geography, to legitimate the imperialism of conversion efforts. The development of reformist movements within the Jewish community is cited as evidence of a profound lability in the wake of emancipation. Although modern secularists (or left Hegelians) might applaud such developments as evidence of cultural progress or the diminishment of archaic ritualist elements—incompatible with the scientific spirit of the age—McCaul treats them as signs that the Jewish community is preparing to break down the barriers that surround it in order to join, not the body politic of a secular civil society, but the true faith of a positive Christianity. "Even the Jewish people itself finds itself in a state of extraordinary fermentation. In France and Germany, it is calling for a synode to reform the synagogue. In England, every large and influential party has already purged its liturgy of any reference to the Talmud. In many parts of Europe, a large number of Jews, often including not a few of highly learned character, have converted to Christianity."[4]

The reference to such conversions among the educated is meant to suggest that the best Jews convert, for they recognize the superiority of Christianity. The implication is a further indication of the Enlightenment character of the argument, which is so very different from twentieth-century assumptions that conversion among the elite is a consequence of a social assimilation, whereas genuine religiosity is associated, romantically, with the vibrancy of a popular community. Furthermore, McCaul goes on to argue that, in the light of these signs of an internal transformation of Judaism, the Jerusalem bishopric has been established at a time when the "return to grace of Zion" must be near: the conversion of the Jews is an indication of the imminence of the kingdom of Christ. Yet if one does not attribute an apocalyptic character to the reform of Jewish liturgy but treats it, instead, as an aspect of cultural modernization and an effort to coordinate religious ceremony within an increasingly secular society, then the logic of McCaul's defense of the missions takes on a very different character. Instead of his manifest message that the conversion of the Jews, for which the signs are so auspicious, is a precondition of a final resurrection, the text suggests something very different: that the post-Enlightenment reconstitution of European society in terms of a gradual secularization, which reduces the role of traditional anti-Semitism, sets the stage for a new sort of cultural expansionism that could provide ideological support for the increasingly international scope of European political and economic interests. The mission to the Jews, which only becomes possible after the decline of traditional religious prejudices—a result in turn of the Enlightenment—turns out to be the precursor for the so-called civilizing mission that plays a central role in the imperialism of the later nineteenth century.

This hypothesis that Jewish emancipation and European colonialism, tolerance, and imperialism might be linked in some nontrivial way is, to say the least, counterintuitive. Would it not be more reasonable to imagine a profound repulsion between the principles of a secular civil society and the brutal violence typically associated with the establishment of a colonial situation? Yet although the Enlightenment led to a gradual integration and eventually civil rights, it also laid the groundwork for a disappearance through assimilation, a process that was halted only through the decidedly nontraditional genocide of the Holocaust. Meanwhile, the same progress that led to emancipation could also lead to colonialism as an expression of European progress. The colonial violence eventually turned into the proving grounds for new intra-European violence. The German *Vernichtungskrieg*, the war of destruction, against the Hereroes of Southwest Africa provided the destructive temperament and racist vocabulary that would lead to the Holocaust. Hence, Arendt's comment, "It is highly probable that the thinking in terms of race would have disappeared in due time together with other irresponsible opinions of the nineteenth century, if the 'scramble for Africa' and the new era of imperialism had not exposed Western humanity to new and shocking experiences."[5] Key components of Nazi racial thinking had their origin in ethnographic and genealogical studies on race-mixing in Southwest Africa.[6]

Nineteenth-century colonialism was not at all a matter of some simple economic necessity, a heightened stage of capitalism, that might require a superstructural theodicy for a new form of commerce. Nor was it only a matter of a particular language, a colonial discourse. Neither the insistence on the determining role of an economic sphere nor the privileging of language as discourse begins to do justice to the concrete material of human experience. Each isolates a particular logic, economy, or language, and each tends to provide a retroactive justification by suggesting that colonial violence was, by and large, the necessary consequence of an immalleable parameter, whether in economy or language. Each finally provides an alibi for the West by presuming that colonial violence represented a novelty in a somehow otherwise normal history of society or culture. A persuasive study of colonialism cannot proceed from the assumption that extraterritorial mechanisms of domination represented a thoroughly new stage or a new discourse. On the contrary, the point is to demonstrate how extraterritorial violence is a continuation and transformation of the self-alienation of the West, its refusal to fulfill its own universalist promise by choosing instead to universalize violence. In the genre of geographical travel literature, represented here by

Rohlfs, this violence took the form of a ubiquitous threat that generated a prose of paranoid descriptivism. In the genre of the missionary narrative, represented by Stern, the threat is homologous, but the consequences for the texts are considerably different. Still, Rohlfs and Stern share a pivotal position. In the former's case an initially apolitical scientific self-understanding makes the colonialist turn; in the latter's case the universal faith justifies the imperialist intervention.

Long before the battle at Magdala political considerations begin to appear, albeit infrequently, in the missionary text. Stern commences his first travel narrative, *Dawnings of Light in the East*, with a reference to European interest in political developments in the Near East. Although he immediately proceeds to relativize that interest and redirect attention to a religious issue, he carries out this substitution in a way that is congruent with the logic of McCaul's Lambeth Palace sermon: a connection is established between a Christian reinterpretation of the status of Jewry and heightened European interest in overseas development. That is, the mission to the Jews mediates the development of an imperialist practice since the Jews are effectively the domestic foreigners with international connections. Thus, Stern:

> At a moment when the public mind is roused, and public attention is attracted to the threatening and tottering position of the East, it cannot fail to be a matter of the deepest interest to the student of prophecy, to turn his gaze from the clouded firmament of the political world, to the moral and religious horizon of those enigmatical personages, who, in the good providence of God, have already, and will yet, on a day not far off, exert a mighty influence upon the destinies of a large portion of these lands. Few Eastern travellers, in their peregrinations, seldom if ever come in contact, or mix with, a people who are considered the basest of the base, and the vilest of the vile; and consequently, in the numerous narratives which have appeared in print, the Jew is never considered worthy of notice; or, if adverted to at all, judged with impartiality.[7]

To be sure, Stern is ostensibly directing the reader's attention away from politics and to the religious issue. Yet, it is equally sure that he claims the attention by first invoking politics, which can only be pursued adequately by way of the religious inquiry since, as Stern imagines, the oriental Jews are soon to exert "a mighty influence." Churchman Stern presumably envisions that influence in terms of apocalyptic prophecy, the conversion of the Jews being a precondition of the Second Coming. If, however, one turns away from that "clouded firmament" and translates the ideological equation into a more sober language, it becomes evident that the mobilization of the Jewish Question is a component in the construction of a colonialist imagination. A tight connection exists between a political project to control "the agitated and tottering conditions of the East," or, as Stern puts it in another passage, "the heavings and throes of impending troubles and dangers in the West" and "the progress of true religion and gospel-truth in both."[8] The global reorganization of political power is inextricably if mysteriously linked to the spread of Christianity, in Europe and abroad.

This textual connection between religion and politics should not be understood in a reductionist way. The missionary narrative is by no means a direct response to Western "dangers," such as the tribulations of 1848; nor is it a simplistic response to Eastern "heavings," that is, the Crimean War. Rohlfs traversed the Sahara transforming geographical facts into a descriptivist text. Stern travels to Persia distributing texts—religious tracts—about spiritual transformation. Rohlfs adopted the mask of Mustafa Bey and underwent a false conversion. Stern's conversion was presumably genuine but no less a mask, just as in Africa he would assume a disguise by declaring himself a Falasha from across the seas.[9] For Rohlfs we had barely enough evidence about his youth to speculate that the adoption of the mask derived from a sense of danger based more on the threat of authority in Germany than in the North African reality (as the traveler himself claimed). For Stern we have even less biographical material, making a psychological profile im-

possible, although some parallels are rather striking. Two dis-
located German youths, rejecting the medical careers prescribed by patriarchal expectations, undergo conversion (to Islam and Christianity, genuine or not), and consequently spend
decades traveling compulsively far away from home. One cannot help but wonder what constellation of social, cultural, or
political factors produced these forced marches through the
wilderness. Do these cases of wanderlust tell us something
about the mobilization of populations in the middle of the
nineteenth century? Stern's texts, those he distributed and
those he wrote, may help provide an explanation for all this
wandering, by Jews and by Germans, and their relationship to
nineteenth-century imperialism.

After the Persian trips, Stern traveled through Arabia and
later set out on his *Wanderings among the Falashas in Abyssinia*,
the title of the last of his specifically travel narratives, published in 1862. As little as Rohlfs's journeys could be accounted
for with a naive reference to the progress of science, so Stern's
paths cannot be cursorily dismissed as simply a matter of missionary religion. To understand the motivation behind his per-
sistent, perhaps even obsessive, trekking, it is vital to pay attention to the title of the final travelogue in which the
activity—traveling, marching, journeying, visiting—is ultimately formulated as "wandering." What compels him to wander? Did the wandering begin perhaps much earlier, with the
trip to Hamburg or the move to England? Did a pressure in the
European—more specifically, German—context force the
German Jew into a fate of eternal wandering? Certainly, a social historian might reply with a reference to the dislocation of
the small-town Jewish populations within the process of social
modernization. However, a different discursive pressure operates here, part of a symbolic restructuring of the ideology of
the Christian state during the post-Napoleonic restoration.
Commenting on a tract by Constantin Frantz, *Ahasverus oder
die Judenfrage* (1844; Ahasverus or the Jewish question), Michael A. Meyer recalls the relevance

of an age-old myth still very much alive in the nineteenth century. It is the legend of Ahasuerus, the eternally wandering Jew, which Frantz conjures up for his readers. Condemned to roam about the earth for rejecting the messiah, the Jewish people can never find peace. It wants to mingle among the peoples and snuff out its peoplehood, but it cannot—not until the Second Coming of Christ. Thus efforts at Jewish religious reform and cultural integration—no matter how sincere—must always and necessarily be found wanting. They are futile attempts to escape a myth which the Jewish people must live out until the end of days.[10]

Has Stern inherited the tropology of the Wandering Jew (who, we know, served often enough as a figure for premodern travel literature)?[11]

Stern responds to contemporary anti-Semitism with a complex mimesis, internalizing its terms in order to escape its threats. He plays out the fate of the Wandering Jew, a prototypical traveler, but he does so as a missionary with the goal of bringing Judaism, as well as his wanderings, to an end. This dialectic response, which internalizes anti-Semitism in order to subvert it, explains a striking paradox in *Dawnings of Light in the East*. The premise of the text and, as explained in McCaul's sermon, the mission to the Jews in general, was a critique of religious anti-Semitism, which had prevented Christianity from undertaking the sincere conversion efforts it properly required of itself. Stern writes within a context of a nineteenth-century liberalism, with its ideal of human equality, which he unfolds into the imperative of the church to pursue missions to Jew and Gentile with equal vigor. Thus, he complains that "the Church has been unmindful of her duty, and indifferent to the call of thousands of Jews," which he explains with reference to "illiberality and antipathy," "narrow bigotry and inflexible intolerance," "the cold atmosphere of other days," and "former prejudices."[12] Clearly, this is the rhetoric of the Enlightenment, valorizing tolerance and denouncing prejudice, but now retained within a religious project that claims universal validity. "The eye that gazed upon [the Jew], through the thick veil of prejudice, now sees him, through the glowing golden visions of the prophets, and the bright and radiant vista of unborn glories, and unfulfilled promises."[13] What better argument against the Christian anti-Semitism of restorationist Europe than Christianity itself?—certainly not a Christianity tolerant of religious multiplicity or sensitive to the significance of doubt but a self-assured faith proclaiming a universalist gospel whose missionary progress has no room for retrograde prejudices.

This liberalism, if the scope of the term can be stretched this far, is one side of Stern's project. The other side, the paradoxical but ultimately necessary counterpart, is a vicious hostility to Jewish life. An inveterate wanderer can only respond with contempt to the sedentary cultures he encounters in his eternal expeditions, particularly since the travel is motivated by the agenda of conversion. Responding to anti-Semitism with an Enlightenment denunciation of prejudice, he simultaneously reproduces the full range of anti-Semitic prejudices in the descriptions of his travelogue. Consider, for example, his account of the Jews in Baghdad: "they are all strictly rabbinical Jews, superstitious, bigoted, and intolerant; full of zeal for the Talmud and the traditions of their elders; scrupulous in the performance of all external rites of religion; ostentatious in their charity, piety, and devotion; tinctured with all the vices of their Mahommedan oppressors, and the errors of their pharasaical forefathers. . . . Their rabbis are proud, haughty, vain, and capricious men; neither distinguished for their abilities, nor admired for their wisdom."[14] It would be superfluous to elaborate on the stereotypical character of the terms of Stern's anti-Semitism. Jews are presented in a standard denunciatory manner as intolerant, zealous, external, proud, and so forth, but above all as bigoted because of their refusal to accept the universal faith of Christianity. Noteworthy solely perhaps is the suggestion of a metonymic identity between Judaism and Islam, further evidence for the hypothesis that the mission to the Jews lays the groundwork for a larger imperialist mobilization (and reminiscent of Rohlfs's suggestion of the proximity of Judaism, Islam, and Coptic Christianity, which he saw as the failed versions of monotheism because they lacked the Greco-Roman tradition and the fervency it provided to occidental culture).

One cannot help but suspect that Stern's rote repetition of these caricatures functions as a perpetual justification for his own conversion. His remark on the Jews of Ispahan, for example, makes this connection clear enough: "These poor straying sheep really deserve our prayers and intercessions at the throne of grace. Some glimmering of Divine light has indeed broken in upon their long night; but, alas! their hearts have so much vegetated in sin and vice, and luxuriated in every evil passion, that they have become callous in, and indifferent to, everything that cannot be rendered subservient to their temporal interests, and the bent of their corrupt nature."[15] Faced with texts like these (and the full narrative is in effect an extensive concatenation of such invectives), one must conclude that it is missionary Stern who is the actual carrier of "narrow bigotry and inflexible intolerance," the accusation he directs at ecclesiastical anti-Semites whose ideology he has internalized and made his own. The sole difference is that Stern, unlike Frantz, is a convert, and his wanderings entail a serial reenactment of his own conversion: Ispahan is, ultimately, a metaphor for the Frankfurt *Judengasse*.

On the one hand, a liberal denunciation of prejudice; on the other, a liberal dose of bigotry: this paradox replicates the dialectic of anti-Semitism that drives Stern's travels. It is, however, simultaneously more, corresponding to a general feature of missionary prose. The missionary enters a foreign setting as an agent of a culture in the process of establishing its extraterritorial hegemony; hence, the popular image of imperialism as dependent on Bibles as well as rifles. The effort to assert the influence of the missionary religion, with its universalist claims, necessarily implies a denigration of the local culture—its symbols, rites, and gods—for which Stern's dismissal of Persian Judaism is a clear enough example. However, to transmit a new symbolic order effectively the missionary must enter into a process of interpretation and communication with the target population. He must be able to speak their language and understand their religion, if only to subvert it, and these tasks imply skills beyond the power of rifles. Indeed, in the course of imperialist history missionaries occasionally become the advocates of the local population against the proponents of a logic of purely military domination. For the missionary narrative this implies a potentially double structure: the coexistence of hostility, that is, the denunciation of the target group from the standpoint of a universalist faith, and the empathy required for effective missionary work. In chapter 5 we will see Frieda von Bülow exploring aspects of this missionary's paradox, which is one typological variant of colonial discourse. Unlike Rohlfs the geographer, who describes a world of facts, Stern is concerned with culture, which is constructed in terms of a tension between the false religion of the local population and the true faith. Missionary apologetics entails a constant mediation between the two levels.

This two-tiered project structures the narrative of Stern's journey through Persia. Most obviously, it induces an alternation between religious and cultural-geographical passages. The bulk of the narrative, which is composed of exegetical disputations, is punctuated by reports of local economic and social conditions. Yet the emphasis is clearly on the missionary activity itself, and within those accounts the dichotomous nature of the undertaking is especially evident. I want to cite two examples of encounters in Hamadan early in March of 1852.

Stern's wandering was not only driven by texts, it produced them as well, in the sense that he distributed literature along his way, including the tracts of the London Society, the New Testament, and *Pilgrim's Progress*. The last is itself a suggestive paradigm for an understanding of travel literature: the pilgrimage functions as the explanatory metaphor for a voyage, the goal of which is thereby imbued with a redemptive character. Indeed, missionary activity emerges in its characteristic form by way of Stern's perpetual interpretation of texts, as the following incident demonstrates: "Early the next morning, Mullah Eliyahu, Mullah Eliezer, and others, called on me. I showed them the books and tracts which I had brought with me; they glanced over the contents of all, and then asked, why we made use of rabbinical quotations, and at the same time did not admit their authority; I told them that our object was to convince them, from the mouth of their own revered commentators, of those important and sublime truths which are foreshadowed and predicted in the Old, and luminously developed in the New Testament."[16] The purpose of the mission is, ultimately, the enactment of scenes of textual study in order to impose a new code of meaning. Recall that Mill, polemicizing against the character of British rule in Ireland, insisted on the qualitative difference between the reasons of its supporters and opponents, oppressors and oppressed. In Stern's account too, a similar tension is evident between the missionary and his targets, or more precisely between the rabbinical texts and their Christian interpretation. Yet instead of granting to each an at least local validity (which was the thrust of Mill's argument), Stern structures the event so as to rob the rabbinical tradition of its autonomy and to subsume it into the overriding hermeneutics of the new faith. That is, of course, the goal of the missionary project, but it is important to recognize how the project depends both on an initial identification of the local culture—to some extent, Stern knows the Jewish material—and on its integration into an alternative cultural structure. It is a dynamic of cultural imperialism that does without open violence or force: Stern does not burn the rabbinical texts or proscribe a language or otherwise censor the expression of the not-yet-colonized culture. On the contrary, recognizing and in fact reproducing aspects of that culture, he attempts to appropriate it and thereby colonize it. It is granted provisional and local legitimacy, but only to the extent that it is subsumed under an absolute and universal system of belief. For Forster a universalistic deism served as the precondition of a plurality of local cultures. For Stern the situation is reversed: local customs are pretexts for a single universal faith.

The second example from the visit to Hamadan does not involve a specifically missionary moment; there is no immediate conversion scene. It belongs, rather, to the cultural-geographical level of the narrative, in particular, a description of a building, the sort of report that often appears within travel literature, missionary or not. Nevertheless, Stern can also integrate this material into his project with the same facility that permitted his hermeneutic appropriation of the rabbinical texts.

The building in question is purportedly the tomb of Mordecai and Esther, the central figures in the biblical narrative associated with the Jewish festival of Purim. Stern describes the mausoleum's location and architecture and reproduces the Hebrew epitaphs on the two graves. However, for Stern it is neither primarily an artistic object nor a historical curiosity but rather an element of Jewish culture and therefore an object of missionary interest. Before considering any of the other aspects, Stern foregrounds the significance of the monument for his target population: "The Jews, who are the guardians of this shrine, venerate it with all the warmth of affection, and all the fervor of gratitude which the chained slave feels for his generous deliverer. They look upon its preservation quite as a miracle, and revere it as a beacon of hope, and a sign of their future deliverance from the yoke and tyranny of the gentile, by the invincible Messiah, the lion of the tribe of Judah."[17] Although Stern may be correct in insisting on the importance of the monument, his representation of its significance, that is, the reasoning he ascribes to the Jews, is obviously already motivated by the missionary intention insofar as he imputes to them a prefigurative hermeneutics. Whereas their parochial vision and their specific identification of the Messiah are mistaken, the putative method of interpretation is thoroughly compatible with Stern's Christianizing readings of the rabbinical commentaries. Again, Stern's impetus to scrutinize the target culture leads to a deepened identification, which, however, is limited by the ultimate agenda of a colonizing appropriation.

The pattern is repeated again when Stern enters the tomb and he sees how his companions "threw themselves on the glazed pavement, and with all the tenderness of deep devotion and respect kissed the sacred spot."[18] Not unmoved by the scene, Stern "imitated this affecting example of grateful acknowledgment to the goodness and virtue of these courageous and brave Hebrews." Touched by the "affecting example," Stern in effect enters for a moment into the local culture, a participating observer, and mimics the behavior of his informants. Yet for all the emotional authenticity of the moment, he cannot help but gloss the passage with the suggestion that the building may not be the historically authentic tomb; that is, the local culture with which he empathizes through mimicry at one moment is relativized in the next. (One has to recall the ambiguous valence of Cook's embrace, mixing sincere solidarity with crafty design.) In this case, the tension between participation and colonization is decided in favor of the local culture or, at least, it is left unresolved. Although the original building may no longer be standing, Stern is prepared to accept the claim of the Hamadan Jews that the graves themselves are genuine: "They have no written records on the subject, but as an unbroken chain of oral tradition, and the pilgrimages of the Jews from time immemorial, are cogent testimonies in favor of the supposition, I left Hamadan with the persuasion that I had visited the graves of Mordecai and Esther."[19]

The missionary must be closely familiar with local culture, be it with regard to biblical exegesis, dogmatic disputes, or popular history. Interestingly, however, Stern is compelled to subvert the Jewish claims only insofar as they bear on religious questions; otherwise—as in the case of the mausoleum—he is willing to maintain an empathetic identification with local tradition. In other words, cultural material that is deemed to be irrelevant to the conversion project may well be accepted at face value. The missionary is slipping into the role of an anthropologist. To be sure, this historicism, which allows for the circumscribed validity of cultural particularity, is always framed by the master-narrative of Christian conversion. Nev-

ertheless, it is precisely such historicism that renders missionary penetration more flexible and effective than direct military
control in the long run, while permitting missionary narratives
to include in a central way cultural material that geographical
texts may tend to marginalize.

This potential for a significant cultural component in missionary texts is borne out in the 1862 volume, which includes
some extensive ethnographic passages on the Falashas. Although framed by conversion scenes with the obligatory denunciations of their religion, the cultural descriptions are by
and large devoid of the vindictiveness of the accounts of the
Jews of Baghdad and Ispahan. However, Stern expresses considerable contempt for the Ethiopian church and even attributes his own success among the Falashas to his ability to distinguish between his Gospel and the Ethiopian version of
Christianity. Here again, Stern is close to Rohlfs's judgment
on the Coptic Church. Therefore, although the later text
shows somewhat greater sophistication vis-à-vis the immediate target population, Stern maintains a contempt for Ethiopian culture in general. He is still, or perhaps more than ever,
the imperialist missionary. Despite an agreement with Tewodros to restrict his activity to the Falashas, Robert Hess notes
that Stern "also preached in Amhara villages and never hesi-
tated to denounce the ritualistic concept of religion held by the
Ethiopian Church. An outspoken man, he condemned its
priesthood for ignorance, drunkenness, and venality. He had
little respect for his Ethiopian hosts and for the emperor; one
of his fellow missionaries claimed that Stern always referred
derogatorily to Theodore as 'His Black Majesty.'"[20]

Given this contempt, which was shared by Rohlfs and other
missionaries, Hess is judicious to conclude that "when trouble
came with the emperor, it was almost inevitable that Stern
would be in the middle of it."[21] There is no need to recount the
details of Stern's imprisonment and captivity from October
1863 through April 1868. As one might expect, *The Captive Missionary* has a considerably more acrimonious tone than *Wanderings among the Falashas*. An assertion of the "cupidity and li-

centiousness of the Abyssinian people, and the rapacity and corruption of their rulers" is symptomatic of a hostile tone quite foreign to the writings prior to captivity.[22] Stern evidently lacks the generosity to distinguish between a government and the population. If the animosity seems to echo the caricatures of the Persian Jews, it is also explicable in terms of a shift observed between Rohlfs's North African travelogue and his record of the British campaign. In the context of military confrontation, latent prejudices and hostilities are exacerbated and move to center stage. Such a shift is even more plausible in the case of Stern, who was not merely an observer like Rohlfs but one of the hostages in the fortress. This point is particularly important for isolating the essential character of colonial discourse. For if the rhetoric of denunciation emerges primarily in contexts of violent confrontation, then it is better understood as a discursive consequence of war. Colonial discourse, strictly speaking, is about the exploration of borders between cultural systems and their permeability; it is not essentially about the absolutized polarities of alternative identities. Such polarization results from violent confrontations, and it is therefore characteristic of the politicized colonial— and anticolonial—rhetorics associated with British and French imperialism during and after the wars of decolonization. German imperialism underwent a quite different history. Instead of succumbing to violent decolonization, it was dismantled by the Treaty of Versailles, which transferred the colonies to the victors of the First World War. Furthermore, the Manichaean structures that pervade the colonial representations of English and French literature—counterposing European national identities with exotic alterities—makes less sense in the German context where the national identity was always less stable and less rigid.

Given the origin of the Abyssinian conflict in the unanswered letter, a failure of communicative exchange, it is worthwhile to note some not so subtle changes in Stern's understanding of language. This is an interesting issue since the missionary himself was intimately involved in the distribution, interpretation, and of course authorship of texts. Tewodros's initial message and, in particular, the proposal to establish an embassy in London were so important and their disregard led to such catastrophic results because, as all accounts of the events agree, some highly stylized rules of communication prevailed in contemporary Ethiopia, especially around the court. Of course, this is not terribly different from the sort of behavior considered normal in European diplomatic circles, and it is therefore appropriate to listen to Rassam's characterization of one of the specifically Ethiopian conventionalized roles:

> A Baldaraba, which means an Interpreter or Go-between, is quite indispensable in Abyssinia. Neither King nor peasant, bishop nor monk, Christian nor Mohammedan, can hold intercourse with each other, except through a third person—a domestic generally acting in that capacity. The usage, however, only applies to the upper classes, and, where the parties are strangers to one another, the functionary himself is appointed by the superior to be the medium of communication between him and the inferior. Nevertheless, it is not necessary that the Baldaraba should be present on all occasions, or that, being present, the communications should pass through him, since the person who appointed him may dispense with his services, if so disposed. The chief advantage of having a Baldaraba is this: he has free access at all times to the master of the house, or to the person who appointed him, whereas a stranger or guest has no such privilege.[23]

Against this background of a conventionalized mechanism of discourse, Tewodros's anger at Cameron's failure to deliver his message to Victoria in person becomes more understandable.

In *Wanderings among the Falashas*, Stern provides a shorter and somewhat broader definition of the *baldaraba* as "an official instructed with a traveller's safety, and also occasionally with the supply of his wants."[24] To some extent, the difference between the two definitions could be attributed to the alternative perspectives of the diplomat and the missionary in the field; or Stern's blindness to the communicative role of the *baldaraba* might be a reflection of his own disregard for the Ethiopian context. In any case, it is clear that for both Rassam and Stern, the *baldaraba* provides some sort of mediation to the surrounding environment by assisting in the negotiation of particular difficulties. How different then is Stern's treatment of the office in *The Captive Missionary* where he defines *baldaraba* simply as "spy" and complains that his own *baldaraba* had conspired against him and composed letters "dipped in venom."

Of course, by the time he was composing his prison narrative, Stern was understandably bitter and angry about his Ethiopian experiences, and the redefinition has to be treated within this context. Nevertheless, it is indicative of an underlying component of the episode. Not only Tewodros's letter, no messages at all get across; everything is misunderstood. Thus, another missionary, Joseph Flad, reports that when Stern saw his servant beaten at Tewodros's command for a breach of etiquette, he bit his own finger, an expression of shared pain that, however, the king promptly interpreted as an Ethiopian gesture signifying a promise of vengeance. This misunderstanding allegedly prompted Tewodros's anger and was the direct cause of Stern's imprisonment.[25] There was another and equally direct cause as well, however, which also involved a misunderstanding. In *Wanderings among the Falashas*, Stern had touched on Tewodros's family background, noting that his father had "acquired no distinction in life, and awakened no sympathy or regret at his death," and his mother "was driven by want to eke out a miserable subsistence by the sale of *kosso*," a vermicide. For Stern such humble beginnings were integrated into a sort of rags-to-riches narrative presented to magnify Tewodros's achievements: "the eventful and romantic history of the man, who, from a poor boy, in a reed-built convent, became the chief of a few freebooters, and from a chief of freebooters, the conqueror of numerous provinces, and the Sovereign of a great and extensive realm."[26] Unfortunately, Tewodros had little understanding for the interpretive status of authorial intention and attributed a very different meaning to Stern's "romantic history," reading it instead as an insulting humiliation and a subversion of his claim to Solomonic descent.

The sufferings that Stern endured in the wake of the king's discovery of his book (the only copy of *Wanderings* in Ethiopia was Stern's own) led the missionary to radical conclusions about the nature of writing and the ambiguity of texts: "Had I possessed less candour and some duplicity, not a written line in my possession would ever have gratified the sight of the King or his unscrupulous minions. It is true I ought to have remembered Richelieu's aphorism: 'Give me two lines from any man, and his head shall roll on the scaffold.' I was deceived."[27] He goes on to wish that he had destroyed all his papers and notes, suddenly transformed into incriminating evidence. The author of the missionary narrative, who had traveled through Asia and Africa distributing texts and disputing interpretations, suddenly finds himself entrapped by the letter of his own prose. Language clearly had ceased to function as a medium of communication or consensus. The missionary who had hoped that with the Gospel "the lines of darkness were to melt away before the rising beams of the Sun of Righteousness" now had to turn to the British army, which ushered in "that happy day when the flag of freedom and liberty, honour and power, fluttered to the breeze on the most impregnable force in Abyssinia."[28] He dedicates his memoir to General Napier "by one of the victims of King Theodore's Tyranny." Not the Bible, but rifles, not the text, but military force, had carried the day. Here Stern makes his colonial turn, granting the same approval to the expeditionary force that Rohlfs at the end of his career gave to the establishment of German imperial protection for the commercial outpost on the coast of Southwest Africa. Religion and science yield the stage to state power.

The two authors, Rohlfs and Stern, travel across non-European terrain with different interests. One is a lay scientist, the other a converted missionary. One describes and observes, privileging geographic information; the other disputes and interprets, integrating local culture into the claims of a universalist faith. These alternative perspectives of naturalism and historicism, characteristic of European thought during the second half of the nineteenth century, were summed up by Disraeli with characteristic flourish in his speech at Oxford on 24 November 1864: "I am not prepared to say that the lecture-room is more scientific than the Church. What is the question now placed before society with glib assurance the most astounding? The question is this—Is man an ape or an angel? My Lord, I am on the side of the angels. . . . It is between these two contending interpretations of the nature of man, and their consequences, that society will have to decide. Their rivalry is at the bottom of all human affairs."[29] Stern too sided with angels; Rohlfs probably did not, but both Stern and Rohlfs ended up at Magdala, where, for all of Napier's incompetence (Rohlfs presumed that a German commander would have been more efficient), British firepower rendered Disraeli's question obsolete. In the conflict between Europe and Africa what counted was neither idealism nor materialism but the superior production of violence. If the English government was prepared to do without communicative equality with the Irish, then there was little reason to institutionalize it with Tewodros. To be sure, the British did not colonize Ethiopia, but the underlying structure of the event—the disregard for the communication, the contemptuous narrations, and the stupendous military imbalance—anticipates the full-fledged colonialism of the late nineteenth century. Yet if science and religion, naturalism and historicism—each in its isolation an expression of a cultural differentiation within modern society—were prepared to make the colonial turn, one is compelled to ask where an alternative may have lay, one that might have taken seriously the emancipation project, which was a latter-day version of Forster's Enlightenment universalism and subjectivity. Is there any trace of a free community?

There are two. The first is the legacy of Tewodros himself. Despite miscalculations, abuse of power, and ultimately defeat and failure, he was allegedly able to articulate a project that combined the mobilization of an archaic imagery of redemption, policies of social rationalization, and plans for technical modernization. At least according to some recent historians, this achievement contributed significantly to the symbolic construction of Ethiopian identity, perhaps all the more important in the context of Ethiopia's troubled fate in recent decades.

The other trace of an emancipatory community in opposition to the structures of imperialism involves the Falashas. It is a long and complicated story that can only be sketched here in brief. And just as Tewodros ought not to be reduced simplistically to contemporary Ethiopia, so too the vicissitudes of the Falashas should not be read solely from the vantage point of their emigration to Israel. Soon after the commencement of Stern's mission to the Falashas, accounts appeared in Jewish periodicals, including *Halevanon* (Jerusalem) and *Israelit* (Mainz). On the basis of these reports, Rabbi Esriel Hildesheimer, a leader of orthodox German Jewry and at the time rabbi in Eisenstadt, sent a letter dated Purim 5624 (11 March 1864) to influential figures in Germany and England describing the situation of the Falashas and calling for an effort to counteract the missionary influence. In particular, he drew attention to the rhetorical and dogmatic imbalance between the skilled missionaries and the Falashas, who had long ago lost contact with Jewry outside Ethiopia and had no knowledge of traditional Jewish religious literature: "The state of ignorance and confusion regarding the most sacred matters of their faith has not escaped the notice of the penetrating and zealous English missionaries, who now have no other goal but to exploit it as much as possible and to take as much booty as they can. With this in mind, they carried out disputations with several Abyssinian Jews, and armed as they are with all the weapons of seduction, it was not difficult for them to overturn the faith of these people who had such a vague understanding of their own religion."[30] Important here is not only the missionary's greater firepower but Hildesheimer's usage of the term *disputation*, the designation of the form of medieval public debate initiated by the church with a representative of Jewry for the purpose of humiliation and conversion. He thereby suggests a continuity between medieval ecclesiastical anti-Semitism and modern extraterritorial missionary activity, and Hildesheimer's plea is therefore tantamount to a resistance to cultural imperialism.

Hildesheimer's letter led in 1868 to a fact-finding visit to Ethiopia by Joseph Halévy, a Turkish Jew, traveling for the Alliance Israelite Universelle. His unpublished report led to some philanthropic activity on behalf of the Falashas, but little more happened until one of Halévy's students, Jacques Faïtlovich, visited Ethiopia in 1904 and again in 1908–9, when he was received by the Emperor Menelik II. The details of Faïtlovich's travels and his pro-Falasha agitation, including the foundation of Falasha aid committees, need not be recounted here. What is at stake, however, is the nature of his efforts to mobilize an anti-imperialist community, three aspects of which can be delineated. First, in Europe he actively polemicized against apathy within the Jewish community by invoking an archaic imagery of shared biblical origins, a fiction, perhaps, but one certainly as potent as Tewodros's appropriation of the name of the apocalyptic sovereign of the Fikkare Iyesus. The point of this "imagined community," to use Benedict Anderson's phrase, is that a community was constituted through an effectively transcendental reference, which led to new identifications and practices of solidarity.[31]

Second, Faïtlovich not only imagined the community but visited it as well, providing material and instructional aid to the Falashas. This concrete practice represented a counter mission, as envisioned by Hildesheimer forty years earlier, and it was apparently successful in effectively blocking continued conversion activity. Complaints regarding Faïtlovich's influence among the Falashas, who grew increasingly unwilling to accept baptism, start to appear in the missionary journals in 1906.[32]

Finally, and most interesting against the backdrop of the aborted correspondence between Tewodros and Victoria, Faïtlovich acted as a courier carrying Amharic letters from the

Falasha notables to the European rabbis and Hebrew responses back to the Falashas. The equality of exchange that was impossible between the English queen and a distant African ruler was ultimately realized among the representatives of populations marginalized in Europe and Ethiopia, respectively. The Falasha thereby gained a minimal international recognition, and the groundwork was laid for the development of a shared religious culture. The result then was the possibility, at least, of community, particularity, and autonomy as an alternative to the cultural expansion of European hegemony. The preconditions of that anti-imperialist community included a transcendental component, the powerful biblical imagery of faith, technical assistance, and a pragmatics of equality and mutual respect, in other words: religion, science, and ethics.

From Ireland to Ethiopia, from Oxford to Baghdad, from Berlin to Lagos: this chapter and the previous one, though meeting in Magdala, have been all over the map. So too has imperialism, and to explore some of its ideological enfigurements it has been useful to inquire into some of the constitutive elements of travel literature as evidenced in the texts of the two German authors who witnessed the defeat of Tewodros. The generic separation of geographical and missionary writing points to the polarization of science and religion in nineteenth-century European culture—the disassociation of intellectual realms that Forster had, less than a century earlier, still held together. The constellation at Magdala therefore reveals some of the discursive problems within imperialism, in particular, the proximity of colonialism and anti-Semitism. On this final point there is one last piece of evidence from a successor to Tewodros, Menelik II, emperor of Ethiopia, whom Faïtlovich met in the new capital of Addis Ababa and who by then had successfully resisted an Italian invasion. Faïtlovich cites a letter of the emperor to an English missionary, M. Clarke, which was published in *Le Figaro* on 19 March 1896: "It is not only abroad that they [European Christians] are violent; they are violent internally as well, at home, against the Jews who are, after all, Christian souls and to whom we owe our Savior. There are more than three hundred thousand of them in my kingdom, and even though they enjoy nearly complete independence, they are obedient and industrious subjects. . . . If they are worse in Europe, it is because the Christians are worse there too."[33] Menelik may have the numbers wrong, and the conditions of the Falashas were probably less idyllic than he suggests. Nevertheless, the constellation is remarkable: an African sovereign who had withstood an imperialist invasion suggests that European extraterritorial violence is the external continuation of domestic anti-Semitism. Europe gets a lesson in tolerance from Africa. Forty years after the publication of the letter, in 1935, another German-Jew, Walter Benjamin, concluded his essay on the "Work of Art in the Age of Mechanical Reproduction" with a lengthy citation from Filippo Marinetti, glorifying another Italian war in Ethiopia: anti-Semitism and imperialism were again aligned, under the sign of fascism.[34]

4

ENGENDERED COLONIES

If distant travel implies an encounter with another culture, such encounters by no means rely on a single or stable epistemological frame. Forster's curiosity about the foreign sensibility stands in marked contrast to Cook's stolid disregard for cultural alterity. If control was at issue it was the geometric map of space that was Cook's prize, not the specific constellation of meanings, values, and practices on the South Island of New Zealand. Rohlfs is, in some ways, heir to Cook's science, except that science itself has in the course of nearly a century undergone profound changes. The split between lay and professional practitioners had grown enormously between the 1770s and the 1860s, and the erstwhile disregard for the other cultures had been transformed into denigration and contempt. This new hostility explains the colonial turn in the geographic discourse, although it is still territorial control rather than culture—the hearts and minds, so to speak—that concerned Rohlfs. In contrast, the missionary Stern exemplifies the practice of hermeneutic engagement, in which the priorities were reversed: culture rather than territory was foremost, although his colonial animus is quite comparable to Rohlfs's. All this points to a range of possible variation in the traveler's account between physical geography and cultural ethnography, which implies as well a range of genres. Much of this is surely true for colonial writing in general, or rather for any writing about other cultures and places—that is, travel literature. Within colonial discourse, however, German material is of particular interest, not because of the significance of German colonialism per se, but because of Germany's own liminal situation—never quite a full-fledged European nation-state, never indisputably part of the modern West. Moreover, given its particular history, German nationhood has rested more strongly on cultural identifications than has been the case in England or France, where the self-evidence of national power came earlier and became more firmly established. This specific national background can explain why the colonial discourse in German material structures the cultural dimension in a particular way and can lead to rich and by no means hostile engagements with the other culture. Alterity may become the object of a heterophile desire rather than the object of heterophobic displacement by the British "white man's burden" or a francophone mission of civilization.

Such desire has already been evident, for example, in Forster's observation of the dancing islander; she provokes him, after all, to general reflections on relations between men and women. More broadly, however, there is an element of desire in the curiosity of the travelers, in search, somehow or other, for the qualitatively different experience. In the age of high imperialism, and within the texts of colonial discourse, this desire takes on explicitly gendered forms that are thematized as such. This chapter examines two variants of this gendering: the reproductive metaphors that structure the crucial German colonialist tract authored by Ferdinand Fabri and the imagery of Africa within the gender theory of psychoanalysis. In the former case, gender is especially a rhetorical element within a text that is substantively concerned with colonial expansion; in the latter, colonialism is the trope within a theory largely concerned with gender identities. Yet, as the discussion of each case will show, the distinction between trope and topic is at best heuristic and cannot be maintained for long, since both matters—gender and colonies—intermingle promiscuously.

THE SEXUAL ECONOMY OF COLONIALISM

The document in which the connection between overseas expansion and a reorganization of gender relations makes its first, albeit still subtle, appearance is Ferdinand Fabri's *Bedarf Deutschland der*

Colonien? (Does Germany need colonies?) of 1879, the most influential manifesto of the colonialist movement. At the end of the first decade of the new Reich, which was marked by the suppression of the Social Democratic Party, the termination of Bismarck's alliance with the Liberals, and the shift toward protectionist trade policies, the conjunction of militant colonialist propaganda and a gender-linked discourse is by no means accidental. The ideological construction of the nation was undergoing a profound transformation—witness the anti-Catholicism of the Kulturkampf and the anti-Semitism debate of the early 1880s—that paved the way for the establishment of the first German colonial protectorates in 1884. The relationship between the home country and the extraterritorial regions, the soon to be occupied terrains of the nascent colonies, was evidently changing quickly. An earlier model of the occasional individual traveler, be it a matter of adventurer, explorer, or missionary, was rendered obsolete by the perceived exigency of establishing national possessions in the form of permanent settlements capable, presumably, of reproduction. This necessarily entailed a break in the way literary encounters with the overseas world took place. If earlier reports (we have looked at accounts by Forster, Rohlfs, and Stern) provided information or perhaps illusions—Enlightenment or ideology—the new context called for a new sort of text capable of engendering greater permanence than the ephemeral memoir of an itinerant witness.

In other words, precolonialist accounts of travel in the non-European world should not be read solely as colonialism before the fact. The case of Forster, at least, makes clear that other, emancipatory modes of encounter were possible and that, therefore, broad-brush denunciations of Western metaphysics are of little help in distinguishing between scientific exploration and interventionist domination. There is no explanatory value in trying to squeeze the history of colonialism into the frame of a cheap melodrama between an evil Reason and an idealized Other, cast as an innocent victim and tied up on the railway tracks of progress. If it is true that knowledge may be entangled in power, it is not the case that knowledge is solely power, or that power is the consequence of knowledge alone. To lose sight of such alternatives and nuances would lead, ironically, to a resigned justification of domination, as if Western culture could have never resulted in anything other than imperial expansionism. Such a result would imply, strangely enough, a prompt dismissal of oppositional politics or critical theories.

In fact, one can leave it to the colonialist propagandists themselves, such as Fabri, to claim expeditionary literature for their own project. Thus, listing several causes—economic growth, the end of the free trade period, and the expansion of the fleet—for the sudden relevance of the colonial question, he saves the best, literature, for last:

> We can add a fourth perspective relevant to the treatment of the posed question [i.e., whether Germany needs colonies]. The present has certainly been labeled an age of travel and geographical study. In this regard we Germans have recently been admirably active. Compatriots have participated in scientific research expeditions in all parts of the globe. The number of our very prolific geographical journals as well as our geographical societies is steadily growing; the interest in geographical, ethnographic and anthropological studies has been awakened by scientific research and popular presentations; it is much more widespread today than in earlier decades. This is certainly worth applauding.[1]

These cognitive gains are fortunate for Fabri, of course, not as indications of a growth of knowledge in general, the widened horizons of modernity, internationalism, or a genuine human interest in other parts of the globe but as a potential that can be channeled into the colonialist movement. Yet this potential, the accumulated information produced by an older scientific-literary culture, turns out to be a hindrance as well to the extent that its Enlightenment ideals and research practices resist a politicized mobilization in the national interest. German knowledge, burdened with eighteenth-century habits, has remained too disinterested, too much a matter of what today might be called pure research. The colonial movement must consequently colonize the production of knowledge before it can colonize Africa. Fabri therefore continues: "But should we be and remain in these regions solely the theoreticians, collecting and researching for the rest of the world? Should we continue to leave our studies in order to be at home at the four corners of the world without ever finding a national home in the overseas regions?" The question of finding a home overseas is strikingly reminiscent of Rohlfs's wavering between regarding Africa as home or as a Dorado, a site of extractive exploitation. Fabri can thus proceed by asking, "Is this an arrangement that is compatible with—let us not speak of our national interest but with urgent national needs?"[2] Fabri then concludes, logically enough, with a reference to a classical author, Justus Möser, who had suggested the advantage of colonies in his *Patriotische Phantasien* (Patriotic fantasies) of 1768: an anticipation of German literary life becoming practical—out of the clouds and into the streets.

Fabri's complaint that German culture, for all its wealth of insights, ultimately only contributes to the worldly wealth of other nations because cultured Germans refuse to act in a self-interested manner is a variation on a standard theme after 1848. Literary realism rejected the escapist fantasies of romanticism; empiricist philosophy, and Nietzsche as well, rejected otherworldly idealism. This ubiquitous insistence on practical activity, a central component in the reification of bourgeois society in the era of industrial capitalism, generated a materialist stance on which the dialectical materialism of Marx and Engels had no monopoly at all. Indeed, Fabri's critique of expeditionary literature might well be paraphrased as a version of Marx's famous eleventh thesis on Feuerbach: "Germans have only mapped the world; the point however is to colonize it."

This by no means implies the end of geography, literature, or science but their intended reconstruction in the service of a practical, national project. If Forster, the prototype of the itinerant author, explored a multidimensional life world of physical experience, cultural encounter, and religious transcendence, it was the alternative model of his textual competitor, Cook—the reduction of the globe to geometry—that prevailed in nineteenth-century culture. Forster's "philosophical travelogue" has to cede priority to practical activity. Fabri's text marks the point where that geometric reduction, which despite its military value remained by and large scientific, expands into inhabited space, not however as *Lebenswelt*, practical human beings engaged in material practice and speculative theory, but as *Welt*: incommensurably specific cultures and antagonistic national needs. Instead of Forster's Enlightenment vision of a variegated arena of human creativity, cognitive, pragmatic, and aesthetic, colonial discourse steers toward closed spheres of colonial order, dystopic models of control and domination. Geometry too will soon pursue *Weltpolitik*.

Fabri breaks with idealism and autonomous travel literature in another way as well. That literature, like Cook's narrative, privileged the route of the traveler, the motion of a body in space, which was more or less empty: Rohlfs's Sahara, Stern's Mesopotamian plains. The logic of that motion presumed a Galilean physics of cause and effect: such and such a distance between two points, such and such a cause leading to an equal reaction. Even the missionary Stern describes conversion scenes in which a nearly mathematical logic prevails. It is the rational argument on the basis of Scripture and not a qualitatively different religious experience of numinousness that produces the confessional transformation. In his post-Enlightenment understanding, the convert must be convinced of the new faith on the basis of evidence and argument. There is no scene of pentecostal rapture, only the logic of debate.

Fabri's argument, at first reading, appears to depend on a similar logic; he lists four causes of the colonial question and proceeds to unfold a resultant program. Yet on closer examination none of the causes nor even their simple sum provides an adequate explanation. For example, even the surfeit of expeditionary literature is, as already mentioned, as much a resistance as it is a source of colonialism. That is, the foregrounded logic of cause and effect in Fabri's text is solely a rhetorical artifice, a concession perhaps to increasingly outdated liberal conventions, grown nearly obsolete while the driving force of the text lies elsewhere. In the opening lines of the preface, Fabri names it vaguely: "We are living in times of emergencies and pressure" [*in Zeiten der Nothstände und des Druckes*]. The text then commences with an assertion of minatory pressure and overflowing excess; the system is too full, and a crisis has ensued. Oversatiated, bursting at the seams, this is no longer the empty space of Cartesian geometry and logic; therefore, the argumentative conventions of causality lose their significance and can only introduce the tract in a more or less perfunctory manner.

Yet it is precisely in its paralogical character, where it ceases to argue and simply performs, that the text does become important for the colonial movement. On the one hand, such indeterminancy allowed for an opportunist reception: "Every German expansion-mongerer and colonial agitator had read 'his Fabri' and varied his arguments according to 'need'; for Fabri offered the total solution to all economic, social, political, national, cultural and mental problems of the day: national completion, economic crisis therapy and social pacification domestically through overseas expansion as a 'mission of culture.'"[3] On the other hand, paralogical rhetoric, the disregard for legitimate argumentative borders, itself stages the colonial practice of illegitimate incursion and invasion: the logical transgression is the model of territorial annexation. The obsolescence of the logic of causality and geometric space, which represents the prerequisite for Fabri's colonialist paralogy, results from the central anxiety of the text. Space is no longer empty, excess abounds, the system is pregnant, there are too many bodies. The text displays colonialism as a strategy to control and channel masses of bodies and their reproduction. It responds to a perceived crisis, when the authority of the putative origin, the nation, is threatened by the accumulation of copies.

Although Fabri makes early reference to the numerical growth of the German population, he ostensibly hides it as only one factor among many.[4] One should not, however, measure the text against nineteenth-century demographic statistics but recognize instead its internal dependence on a reproductive anxiety. The "emergencies and pressure" of the preface are, ultimately, an obstetric metaphor, and the task of the text is to control this reduplication. Fabri's argument is better understood if it is moved away from Malthus and juxtaposed to Benjamin's "Work of Art in the Age of Mechanical Reproduction," treated as an analysis of originality subverted by duplication. For Fabri it is clear that power and reproductive force go hand in hand: "Any powerful political state requires room for expansion during its period of blossoming, in which it will not only siphon off its excessive forces; it will also retrieve their productive achievements through a constant flow-back into the motherland; and then be able to increase them through a new flowing forth in an organic reciprocation. No state that refused this law of expansion and repulsion could retain its power and welfare for long." Fabri suggests an economy of excess, driven not by scarcity, not by a compulsion to eke out a living in a parsimonious nature, but by a metastatic plentitude that, if denied the space for expansion, threatens to flood the generative structure.

This structure, furthermore, is emphatically gendered; throughout the text, Fabri refers to the "motherland," the reproductive dynamo. (The few references to a "fatherland" have to do with the legislative entity of the state rather than with a locus of creative fertility.)[5] Indeed, this gendered personification is extended into the pairing of "motherland" with "daughter states," and the gender code is maintained even in the proximity of citations that invoke a fatherland, despite the stylistic awkwardness.[6] Evidently, the female identity of the national territory is not at all arbitrary for Fabri, nor is this surprising given the concentration on reproductive capacity, in particular, the reproduction of bodies. This capacity, finally, is associated with a cyclical motion, the ebb and flow between the motherland and the colonies, a closed circle that, nevertheless, is somehow able to expand to accommodate a perpetual growth of wealth.

The image of an economy of excess, maternity, and a reproductive cycle underlies the purportedly more economistic arguments that Fabri occasionally foregrounds, and that are themselves of curiously little interest. Reading the text against the grain, one recognizes instead that the obstetric scene implies two key strategies with which Fabri hopes to curtail the emancipation of the same excess that he regards as necessary for the flourishing of the motherland. One of his first and most powerfully presented arguments for the establishment of German overseas colonies involves the recognition of de facto overseas emigration, notably to the United States. This emigration results, he argues, from the high growth rate of the German population, apparently assuming a sort of zero-sum game within the German economy of Europe. It nevertheless represents a loss to Germany and a gain for a major economic competitor: "The necessarily growing German emigration will continue to contrib-

ute to the economic impoverishment of Germany, unless it is organized and rechanneled into our own agricultural colonies."[7]

Behind the demographic argument, the rhetorical structure indicates an anxiety about the potential loss of offspring, the children
leaving home. The establishment of colonies would bind the mean-
dering excess to the stable origin, just as it is only the unlimited reproductive capacity of the mother that can support a successful colonial enterprise. Hence, Fabri's claims that colonialism is a proper
project only for the prolific "German race," in contrast to the
French with their declining birth rate (which he attributes to their
national immorality).[8] In this light colonialism appears to be an an-
tioedipal strategy, the tenacious attaching of the otherwise way-
ward offspring to the parent, enforced from above like German nationhood itself. The child is not lost to empty space; it is never
independent, and it remains within the nurturing circle of the maternal economy forever. This connection presumably explains
Fabri's emphasis on agricultural colonies, antimodern utopias, ma-
triarchal and mythic in their circularity and valued considerably
more than the relatively marginal commercial colonies of bourgeois
traders, which are implicitly ascribed to a bad modernity of mercantile rationality.

Fabri imagines a further sort of colony as well, the penal colony,
the site of the second antiemancipatory strategy. Here, however,
the politics are perfectly explicit. Despite "repressive laws"—Fabri
means the prohibition of the socialists—"subversive propaganda"
of the "anarchists" continues to threaten the social stability of the
empire; it has spread through the "masses of the working class" and
receives support from an international movement. Writing only
seven years after the Paris Commune, Fabri conjures up the image
of a German revolution:

> Let us consider that, when the moment appeared to be ripe, an
> attempt at violent overthrow were to be undertaken here too;
> and that, after perhaps bloody fighting, thousands and tens of
> thousands were brought to justice: such a sad possibility
> would certainly present the imperial government with the em-
> barrassment of an unsolvable problem! Where could the thou-
> sands of criminals be housed, especially since our jails are al-

ready inadequate and overfilled? There would simply be no other route than the one chosen by France to deport them to New Caledonia. With benign liberalism one might give the communards an appropriate island—named perhaps utopia—to administer themselves, in order to force them to try out their experiment of improving the world. But to undertake such a step, Germany would simply have to have acquired colonial possessions somewhere. After all, the ever practical English responded to Irish Fenian activity with deportations and thereby quickly suppressed the movement.[9]

Penal colonies are hardly utopian, and Fabri's cynicism on this point is good evidence of the depth of his humanitarian compassion. In fact, for many years he played a leading role in Protestant missionary activity, until he shifted his attention to full-time involvement in the colonialist lobby. No German commune provided a rationale for colonial projects. Nor, for that matter, did agricultural colonies play the central role that Fabri emphatically predicted; on the contrary, commercial enterprises were the leading force during Germany's colonial years. The point, however, is not that Fabri, anticipating the colonial establishments, presented arguments and predictions that were not subsequently borne out. On the contrary, the agitational text was evidently successful—not as prediction but as a strategic mobilization of the colonial enterprise itself. This success had less to do with its logical credibility (the opposite was probably the case given the paralogical character of the discourse) than with an underlying concern with reproduction and control. Agricultural colonies promised to enclose the offspring in the maternal economy; penal colonies provided a device to control subversion. In both cases, colonialism could gain credibility as part of a broader policing strategy. Furthermore, in both cases the colony promised to maintain order and stabilize the established world by blocking the independent trajectories of the excessive masses. The body, in the age of its mass reproduction—too much folk, too little room—endangers the original and induces, as a counterreaction, a strategy of control: the territorialization of the colonies and the establishment of closed circles of flow. Hans Grimm's colonial novel, *Volk ohne Raum* (1926; A people without space), is the later continuation of this argument in the postcolonial Weimar Republic, after Germany had lost its overseas possessions.[10]

The control of the emigrants or the anarchists, the recalcitrant progeny, depends on enclosing them in a circular process, the mythic alternative figure to a linear trajectory of progress. Thus, Fabri repeats images of a "constant cycle" [*stetiger Kreislauf*] or reciprocity [*Wechsel-Verkehr*], and this circularity is implicitly linked to a kinship relation: "Where in England,"—and in the late 1870s England is still regarded as a model to emulate rather than as an imperial rival—"is there a larger family group that does not have one of its members in some position somewhere in the British colonies that circle the globe!"[11] Colonialism is evidently that institution that, in a setting marked by atomization and distancing, holds the family world together, just as it restructures the once private family by incorporating it into a national mission.

This institution can only operate, however, on the basis of the assumption that the colonial terrain is initially empty and therefore available for settlement:

> If we ignore Central Asia, Japan, and Northern China, which already entail closed, to some extent very old political units, then the remaining possibilities for agricultural colonies include North America, part of the southern half of South America, South Africa, Australia, New Zealand, and perhaps some of the island groups in the Pacific. Thanks to a providential order in the economy of historical development, these large, extensive territories have been preserved during millennia for the white race. The aboriginal populations, mainly members of the so-called red race, are without an exception hunters and herders, and therefore numerically very sparsely developed, predestined to be placeholders until the white man arrives and drives back their decreasing numbers into ever smaller regions. The geological and climatic conditions, as well as the resulting quality of the soil in these extensive land masses make agriculture the natural basis of their proper development. Thus, it was first the white man who, turning to the plow rather than the hunt, initiated the cultural development of these areas.[12]

The empty terrain of the colony, a space mistakenly described as without people, becomes the home for the surplus bodies, the people without space, a second womb in the reproductive cycle between motherland and daughter-state.

This emptiness has a history that, despite Fabri, depends less on providential order than on a transformation of a figure of European thought. Compared to Forster's rich texture of a globe populated by experiential subjects, Cook's cartography already seemed relatively empty. Yet Cook himself was hardly eager to suppress populations, even if he suppressed his own responses and has, by and large, a solely logistical interest in the inhabitants of the South Pacific islands. The disappearance of the silent man in the 1799 account of the meeting at Dusky Bay is more ominous; the protocolonial text in effect erases the presence of one of the formerly main actors in the event. Nevertheless, the disenchanted void of Enlightenment travel through Cartesian space has little in common with the beckoning emptiness of the colonialist imagination—a seductive space waiting to be filled and capable of infinite expansion. It is not the transparent space that an itinerant observer might traverse but a fertile expanse in which a community, the colony, might be implanted and grow into an enclosed world.

PSYCHOANALYSIS AND THE COLONIAL MAP

There is certainly an enormous difference between the emptiness of Cook's world and Fabri's imagined empty continents. In the first case the void is a function of a mathematical project; in the latter, it is a seductive mystery and the object of desire. The white paper becomes the "dark continent," a vortex in the fantasy of turn-of-the-century Europe; hence, the prominence of the sexualized metaphor within psychoanalysis. Although Fabri's text betrays how ultimately inadequate arguments for colonization drew on an underlying rhetoric of birth and motherhood, Freud's theoretical elaborations rely at crucial points on metaphoric maps that are implicated in aspects of colonial discourse. Through a close reading of these passages, one can see, however, how Freud operates with colonial tropes that are already gendered to suggest a dismantling of the colonial project. In other words, colonies are gendered for both Fabri and Freud, but although this provides the ultimate rationale for Fabri, in Freud the psychoanalytic dynamic grounded in gender identification points toward an explosion of the colonial system of images, an explosion that is ultimately part of a comprehensive project of emancipation. By pulling colonial discourse into the texts of psychoanalysis, Freud undermines the politics of colonialism, transforming its metaphors into their opposites. Psychoanalysis becomes the anticolonialism of the soul.

To assert an anticolonial component within psychoanalysis is of course quite audacious, and it is important to circumscribe the claim: particular moves that Freud makes point toward a destabilization of colonial discourse. Nevertheless, even in this limited form, the contention will face considerable counterevidence, in particular, Freud's use of the metaphor of the dark continent as a designation of the sexuality of the adult woman. Indeed, in addition to the apparent reliance on a central term of imperialism, it would appear to indicate the gender limitations of psychoanalysis itself. At the very least, the image seems to indicate Freud's own admission that female sexuality lies beyond the scope of knowledge, a dark continent in which the light of science has not yet begun to shine. Is this not tantamount to a concession that psychoanalysis is a primarily male theory that treats women as deficient, signifiers of a lack? Indeed, the metaphor is followed nearly immediately by a recapitulation of the notion of penis envy. Yet Freud's choice of words—he uses the English term in italics in his German text—could be pursued even further; the dark continent is not solely the unknown but the unknown awaiting penetration and exploration, colonialism and control. Freud's apparent misogyny seemingly slides into the language of imperialism, as his own prose appears to draw attention to the character of psychoanalysis as a project of domination and authority.

Such a reading of the passage would not be without appeal in the current antipsychoanalytic climate. What more damning evidence than his equation of female sexuality and the dark continent? However, such a reading would be as false as it would be misplaced. It is crucial to take a closer look at the text to understand the significance of the phrase, which links analysis and colonialism, in the fourth section of *The Question of Lay Analysis* (1926). For the metaphor not only clarifies the implicit political self-understanding of psychoanalytic theory. It also points out a line of investigation regarding sexual fantasies and gender relations within colonialism—Fabri's tract was one example—that in turn lead back to psychoanalysis and its construction around a literary enfigurement of Africa. Psychoanalysis does indeed have very much to do with the "dark continent," but the connection is considerably more complicated than expected. Equally surprising, colonialism, presumably a world of male adventurers and military machismo, has much to do with female sexuality, feminism, and emancipation, as the next chapter will demonstrate.

The 1926 text is a dialogue between Freud—or rather a narrator—and a fictional interlocutor to whom Freud explains central aspects of psychoanalysis in order to demonstrate the legitimacy of lay analysis. Of course, so Freud's argument goes, the analyst needs specialized training. Freud's point, however, is that this preparation is not identical to medical training. Freud is attempting to resist the professional occupation—or colonization—of psychoanalysis by the medical establishment. In the fourth section of the text, two other distinctions come into play. The previous descriptions of mental life are now designated as merely psychology, and the text proceeds to address specifically psychoanalytic, that is, nonpsychological, theorems. These include theories of sexuality, especially infantile sexuality, and Freud underscores the additional difference between psychoanalytic discourse and modes of scientific debate, which emphatically proscribe references to sexual material. In this argumentative context, where psychoanalysis is counterposed to medicine, psychology, and antisexual science, some further differentiations, now within psychoanalytic theory, become relevant. Notable among these is the anatomical gender difference and the presumably differential mental response, that is, alternative self-interpretations of the individual's body.

Freud introduces the topic of infantile sexuality by referring to its absence in the prepubescent latency period, which consequently shifts attention to the early childhood. He proceeds to the substance of early sexuality but first underscores its counterintuitive character. "There is much to be told, for which our expectations have not prepared us, about the contents, manifestations, and achievements of this early period of sexuality."[13] Thus, he suggests that his interlocutor will be astonished to learn that young boys are afraid that their fathers will eat them and that this fear has something to do with sexuality. Freud responds to this imputed astonishment with a didactic reference to the myth of Chronos, that is, myth operates as Enlightenment and clarifies a connection between sexuality and intergenerational violence. Indeed, the passage has a complicated rhetorical structure, insofar as the ostensible message, an explicit description of the castration anxiety and—between the lines—of the oedipal constellation in general, is accompanied by a metacritical exploration of the relationship between psychoanalysis and myth, the "imaginative activities of primitive man, of which myths and fairy tales are the precipitate."[14] At one point, presumably out of regard for his skeptical addressee, Freud collapses the two levels with the suggestion of a developmentalist equation, borrowed from embryology, between children and primitive culture: ontogeny recapitulates phylogeny. The equation, however, obscures the more complex operation of the passage in which psychoanalysis, as a theory of sexuality, reflects on itself as a mode of investigation that employs myth more as a tool of Enlightenment—phylogeny clarifies ontogeny—than as anthropological evidence of premodern society.

This argumentative context is crucial to an understanding of the dark continent metaphor, for it indicates that one of Freud's concerns in the passage is the specific relationship of psychoanalysis to primitive material. The problem involves the possibility of a counterintuitive dependency of a presumably advanced science—psychoanalysis—on the archaic, prescientific contents of myth. The discussion now shifts away from castration to the female genitalia or, rather, to the state of diminished significance of female genitals in infantile sexual interest, at least in Freud's version. An infantile ignorance introduces the inadequate scientific understanding of female sexuality—Freud certainly does concede that psychoanalysis, so far, has been able to explore the sexual life of boys better than that of girls. Does this then not imply that female sexuality is truly the "dark continent," a sphinxlike riddle, unexplored and unknown? As the passage shows, at the last moment Freud deflects this conclusion by mobilizing the overriding argumentative distinction of the section. If female sexuality is a dark continent, then it is precisely not this for psychoanalysis. In Freud's words:

> Another characteristic of early infantile sexuality is that the female sexual organ proper as yet plays no part in it: the child has not yet discovered it. Stress falls entirely on the male organ, all the child's interest is directed towards the question of whether it is present or not. We know less about the sexual life of little girls than of boys. But we need not feel ashamed of this distinction; after all, the sexual life of adult women is a "dark continent" for psychology. But we have learnt that girls feel deeply their lack of a sexual organ that is equal in value to the male one; they regard themselves on that account as inferior, and this "envy for the penis" is the origin of a whole number of characteristic feminine reactions.[15]

Thus, Freud concedes that a cognitive lacuna does indeed exist in the infantile misunderstanding of the anatomical distinction, and this misunderstanding stands in some implied but not elaborated relationship to the impasse in the scientific comprehension of female sexuality. It is arguably the case that the psychoanalytic theory of sexuality has a male bias. At least, Freud himself admits as much, and it is by no means controversial to suggest—with Freud—that Freud's own progress in the study of female sexuality is limited. Yet it is surely no argument against the psychoanalytic project in general to assert that it has been elaborated incompletely. Of greater interest here, however, is the characterization of the impasse and the different forms it assumes in competing disciplines. For psychology the unknown is the "dark continent"—this is Freud's allegation and the sense of his usage of the controversial image—whereas psychoanalysis, so he claims, in contrast and opposed to psychology has achieved at least minimal progress, despite the relativizing admission that it knows more about boys than about girls. Moreover, this putative progress, the notion of penis envy, is obviously linked directly to the topic of castration anxiety, treated in the previous paragraph of Freud's text and clarified with the aid of mythic material designated as primitive fantasy.

At this point, one does well to bracket any doubts regarding the plausibility of Freud's claims to reconstruct the logic of the internal argument and the interdisciplinary competition it stages. As underdeveloped as all scientific comprehension of female sexuality may be, psychoanalysis is suggested to have been more successful than psychology. To what can one attribute the relative cognitive advantage of psychoanalysis? Both disciplines locate the topic in a conceptual terrain laden with primitivist connotations—and we must, of course, remember that it is Freud, an interested party, who is describing the metacritical scenario—but in very different ways, with divergent rhetorics and ramifications. Psychoanalysis attempts a clarification of the material with the help of myth as Enlightenment, whereas it is psychology, the competitor denigrated by Freud, that adopts the imperialist stance that labels the object as a "dark continent" in order eventually to transform the mystery into a victim. The scientific politics of this historically overdetermined metaphor entails constructing its referent, female sexuality, as first beyond cognition—the essentially unknown—and then as a targeted object of colonial conquest. The assertion of the radical alterity of a dark continent, the practice that Freud imputes to psychology, prepares the way for its violent occupation.

In contrast, Freud tries to assert that psychoanalysis proceeds by demonstrating how the same apparently exotic material, which presumably astonished the fictional addressee of the text, is simultaneously extraordinarily close, indeed, is a constitutive element in the socialization processes and mental life of even those cultures that boast of their own distance from the primitive world. Writing in a context in which a conventional distinction between primitive culture and modern civilization is a standard assumption—one permutation of which is to point to the other as a "dark continent" and thereby diminish it—Freud undertakes a theoretical elaboration of an alternative encounter with the unknown. This argument is strengthened by observing that Freud uses the English-language term *dark continent* in the midst of his German-language text. The bilingual problem repeats *in nuce* the German-English configuration observed in different forms in Forster and Cook, Rohlfs and Stern, as well as in Fabri's anxiety regarding emigration to the Anglo-American world. For Freud the bad colonial discourse, which is attributed to psychology, takes place naturally in English. In contrast, a genuine appreciation of the rationality of primitive culture, reminiscent of Forster's reading of the Maori dance, is reserved for the Austro-German of psychoanalysis.

Because Freud's point in the text is to characterize psychoanalysis, even when he distinguishes it from psychology he does not elaborate on the latter extensively. Yet it is clearly psychology that is associated with the rhetoric of a dark continent, the metaphor that interests us, and we can therefore approach it only through the self-interested psychoanalytic argument. In addition to the epistemological distinction between psychoanalytic usage of myth and the exoticizing nomenclature of a "dark continent," there is also a political distinction, beyond the obviously imperialist reverberations of the term. If psychoanalysis is counterposed to psychology and psychology is associated with the imperialist vocabulary of a dark continent, is psychoanalysis, then, implicitly an encoded theory of anti-imperialism? The answer must await an examination of the larger metaphoric map that Freud unfolds elsewhere. At this point, however, referring solely to the passage from *The Question of Lay Analysis*, we can deduce that psychoanalysis is intended in Freud's presentation to be an egalitarian project. Does psychology differ from it on this score as well?

Freud presents his rudimentary theory of female sexuality as a critique of a false consciousness that is associated with the construction of an evaluative hierarchy. The crux of the matter is a misreading that treats a genuine anatomical difference as a deficiency, and this misunderstanding has severe consequences for the young girl. If, however, Freud suggests that a subjective sense of inferiority is a consequence of, not anatomy, but a misunderstanding of anatomy, then his theoretical project may evidently include an attempt to subvert the ensuing hierarchy of gender. In this sense, his use of the term *equivalent* [*gleichwertigen*] with reference to the female genitalia is telling. Genuine anatomical equivalency, despite difference,

is obscured by ignorance and, presumably, a lack of sexual education—in other words, Enlightenment. Moreover, the implicit egalitarianism with regard to the genital question echoes the emancipatory substance of Freud's usage of Oedipus. This is suggested in the
foregoing section of *Lay Analysis* when Freud refers to the conflict
between Zeus and Chronos as a revolt against a tyrannical and patriarchal authority. Yet this constellation of equality and emancipation is itself the implied political character of psychoanalysis as contrasted to psychology. One can paraphrase the concluding
sentences of the quoted paragraph in this way: although psychology constructs female sexuality as a dark continent, the object of colonial desire and imperial control, psychoanalysis explores the construction of gender hierarchy, especially its subjective, that is,
mental reverberations—the false consciousness of women is the
myth of male superiority—and denounces it as the consequence of
error and ignorance. Moreover, to the extent that the denunciation
inherent in the label "dark continent" includes a dismissive evaluation of cultural materials that are primitive or mythic (rather than
scientific), Freud has also unsettled that hierarchy by appropriating
mythic narratives into the core of his effort to construct a new science. Not only does psychoanalysis refuse the transformation of female sexuality into an object of colonial administration as a "dark
continent." In addition, it is this refusal that depends on a significantly different construction of nonmodern, primitive culture. Psychoanalysis scandalizes the scientistic logocentricity of institutionalized rationality by demonstrating the actuality of myth at the
very center of civilized, modern life. The premodern is by no means
solely past; the nonmodern is not just elsewhere. In contrast, resisting this dialectic and occluding these connections, Europe itself
turns out to be the dark continent, against whose obscurantism
Freud promotes psychoanalysis as the project of Enlightenment.

If Freud's text entails a critique of psychology and, implicitly, of
colonialism, it is nevertheless produced in the context of a defensive
strategy. Psychoanalysis is threatened by a medical occupation that
Freud understands to be only a minimal moderation of an earlier repression.[16] Hence, his plea to the "objective" interlocutor for the
autonomy of the new discipline. Moreover, even if the text suggests

the epistemological and political inadequacy of a colonialist project that controls its object by treating it as a "dark continent," it is precisely that project—the colonialist occupation of Africa—that remains in force. To be sure, in that occupation much more is at stake than a metaphor, although the metaphor in question, the designation of Africa as the dark continent, contributes to the legitimating ideology of colonialism. And colonialism is ultimately a metaphoric practice, a carrying over, a transference of power to maintain an institutionalized inequality that, like gender inequality, has no anatomical basis—false consciousness and domination. The web of connotations in the passage suggests that it may be useful to consider reading the metaphor backward. Freud critiques the imputed psychological designation of female sexuality as a dark continent, the colonialist designation of Africa. Turned around, that would amount to a construction of colonized Africa, the Africa of colonialism, Africa-as-colonized, as a locus of female sexuality. In fact, sexual—or more specifically gender-related—fantasies pervade various modes of German colonial texts, including Fabri's manifesto, as well as the fictions that will be treated in the next chapter. The sexual metaphors in colonial literature certainly bear out Freud's own accounts: psychoanalysis as the alternative to the colonialist vocabulary of psychology provides an at least partial critique of colonialism and the psychology of the colonizers. Psychoanalysis undermines colonial discourse precisely at its most gendered point.

Both in Rohlfs and in Stern we saw a growing willingness to denigrate the culture of the non-European population. It can surely be argued that a related dismissiveness was evidenced in Cook's judgment on the islanders. This feature of colonial discourse, its negative valorization of alternative cultures, is called into question by the psychoanalytic retrieval of the primitive material of myth. Yet the Freudian intervention into colonial discourse goes one step further. It is not only a matter of the revaluation of the marginalized culture of nonscientific myth that is critical. It also involves the substance of the material that becomes the core of the psychoanalytic paradigm. For the primitive material that Freud rescues from the oblivion of the "dark continent" is nothing other than the oedipal myth as a narrative of emancipation, an attack on patriarchal authority in the name of establishing an autonomy free from domination. Freud's insistence on the centrality of an emancipation is articulated against the power of institutionalized reason as the vehicle of repression: repression of myth, sexuality, and psychoanalysis. Most important, however, is that Freud stages this autonomy project at two crucial junctures, which frame his career, through a specific identification with African material in fantasized battles against European power. In other words, the adversarial construction of psychoanalysis as a critique of repressive power draws considerable sustenance from an anticolonial rhetoric of African resistance to Europe. Freud's engagement with colonialism, therefore, is hardly limited to the destabilization of the dark continent metaphor but involves crucial and emphatically autobiographical frameworks for the whole psychoanalytic project. Freud fuels psychoanalysis by adopting specifically anticolonial identifications in *The Interpretation of Dreams*.

Having long postponed a trip to Rome, Freud, so he reports, often dreamed of that city, which he interpreted as a wish fulfillment of a childhood identification with the African Hannibal, who crosses the Alps but fails to reach Rome. Because of his experiences as a Jew with the anti-Semitism in Roman Catholic Austria, the young Freud admired the Semitic general who could challenge Roman military superiority. The centrality of this connection for *The Interpretation of Dreams* is, as Carl Schorske and others have pointed out, announced by the book's epigraph, taken from the *Aeneid*: "Flectere si nequeo superos, Acheronta movebo" [If I cannot bend the higher powers, I will stir up hell]. This is a lucid statement of the revolutionary impulse in psychoanalysis borrowed from a text centrally concerned with a relationship between the Africa of Dido and the Roman foundations of European power.[17] The magnum opus of psychoanalysis begins with a motto of African resistance to European power.

In *The Interpretation of Dreams*, the African enfigurement, Freud's Hannibalism, appears in an aggressive mode. Three decades later, in the 1936 letter to Romain Rolland describing "A Disturbance of Memory on the Acropolis," the mode is resigned and nearly defeated. To elucidate his own parapraxis and loss of reality at a conventional symbol of Western identity, Freud cites—and thereby implicitly identifies with—a figure from the opposite end of the Mediterranean. Boabdil, the last Moorish king of Spain, refused to believe the news that his last fortress, Alahama, had fallen to the Christians and therefore had the messenger killed. Freud similarly refuses initially to believe that he had actually arrived at the Acropolis and consequently, for a moment, denies its reality. The psychoanalytic text explores the guilt behind that denial—Freud's own ambivalent feelings about having surpassed his own father who never came this far—but for a cultural studies reading the metaphor is the key: it places Freud at the limits of Europe and allows him to slip into the role of the non-European—out of place on the Acropolis—and simultaneously into the incarnation of the North African monarch.[18]

It is important to clarify the status of the material within this discussion. It is certainly not the case that psychoanalysis is constructed or intended primarily as a commentary on European-African relations. On the other hand, these textual incidents—Hannibal in the dream book of 1900, the dark continent metaphor in 1926, and finally Boabdil the African king in 1936—are far more than random accidents of word choice. Freud's psychoanalytic project, as a project of emancipation, evidently permits the critique of familial authority (Oedipus) to slide into a critique of imperial power. Moreover, the central components of the theoretical elaboration are poised within a highly politicized scenario of Europe as Rome contra Africa as Hannibal: the concern with religion, especially Roman Catholicism; the archaeological paradigm, a further link to Rome; and anti-Semitism, both as an occasional issue in the Freudian texts and as the perpetual context for psychoanalysis in Vienna, to which Freud counterposes the Afro-Semitic warrior. To be sure, these connections rely on a metaphoric link, but the material is at the heart of the articulation of psychoanalytic theory.

Africa figures as part of the material that institutionalized reason disregards—dreams, sexuality, primitivism; all the "dark continent"—but that Freud insists on redeeming. For Freud (as for Forster, with whom Freud shares a fundamental orientation toward a project of Enlightenment), no part of human experience is absolutely outside reason, even if it is outside Europe. Photographs of his office show it replete with references to the archaic and exotic. We should not, however, imagine him as the collector bringing home the booty from psychic safaris but rather as an ambassador insisting on the rightful place of the otherwise marginalized material. Psychoanalysis, of course, recognizes the difference between the realm of conventional reason and that of alterity, but its mission includes insisting on their equivalence and overcoming any hierarchy that diminishes the standing of the irrational.

Yet this critical project, including the psychoanalytic subversion of a presumed priority of European civilization—and the assertion of such a priority is vital for colonial discourse—is neither unproblematic nor fully stable. Despite the continuity of the commitment to rescue the repressed and recognize it as a manifestation of rationality, major changes in the understanding of this material and its symbolism take place, and these changes are themselves intricately involved in the political vicissitudes of psychoanalytic theory. The overriding liberalism of the Freudian project, its concentration on individual autonomy, encountered the emergence of a postliberal political culture around the turn of the century, which led to the apparent imperative of developing a corollary postsubjective and postsexual theory of symbolism. The results, which bear directly on the culture of primitivism and exoticism, can be traced through a close reading of some crucial material layered into later editions of *The Interpretation of Dreams* that is indicative of the immanent crisis of the theory. Considering the Freudian theory of symbolism and its transformation, one discovers an additional dimension to the judgment on psychoanalysis. Although it intends to challenge "the higher powers" and emancipate the "dark continent," it also encounters the permanence of power that it cannot overcome. Freud records the failure of the psychoanalytic project through the colonial discourse of an occupying army.

In a laconic introduction to an addendum to the 1919 edition titled "A Dream of Bismarck's" (chapter 6, section E, part II), Freud—and not some Victorian conservative hostile to psychoanalysis—makes a curiously uncharacteristic prudish distinction: "thoughts of a serious kind, far removed from anything sexual."[19]

The passage is in fact an extended citation from a 1913 paper by Hanns Sachs, which commences with a letter of 18 December 1881 (included in *Gedanken und Erinnerungen* [Thoughts and recollections], Bismarck's autobiography), in which Bismarck reports an 1863 dream of his to Kaiser Wilhelm. Freud inserts this material in the section on "Representation by Symbols" because of an obvious phallic symbolism: Bismarck holds a riding whip, which grows "to an endless length" as he beats a rock.[20]

The subsequent commentary by Sachs identifies the masturbatory scene as a constitutive component of the manifest dream content as well as of two other strands: the Mosaic imagery of the leader striking a stone to bring forth water to calm the querulous people and the dream content's contemporary relevance to the dreamer Bismarck who wrote that "the whip grew to an endless length, the rocky wall dropped like a piece of stage scenery and opened out a broad path, with a view over hills and forests, like a landscape in Bohemia; there were Prussian troops with banners, and even in my dream the thought came to me at once that I must report it to your Majesty."[21] Recalling that Bismarck himself had dated the dream "in the Spring of 1863, in the hardest days of the Conflict"—that is, the Prussian constitutional conflict—Sachs makes the topical import of the imagery explicit: "Already at the time of this dream Bismarck desired a victorious war against Austria as the best escape from Prussia's internal conflicts. Thus the dream was representing this wish as fulfilled, just as postulated by Freud, when the dreamer saw the Prussian troops with their banners in Bohemia, that is, in enemy country."[22]

So the "serious matter" that Freud emphatically distances from the realm of sexuality is Bismarck's political desire, the calculation that the domestic liberal opposition might be undermined by a bellicose foreign policy and, moreover, a policy that would include the military occupation of Austria. Freud apparently concurs with Sachs's suggestion that the latent content of the dream, the motivating wish, is the political strategy and not some infantile sexual desire—a curious inversion of the original psychoanalytic tenet that innocuous material from contemporary experience is appropriated by the dream work to provide expression for repressed libidinal goals. In this case, Freud underscores the reverse representational operation: "the dream is an excellent instance of the way in which thoughts of a serious kind, far removed from anything sexual, can come to be represented by infantile sexual material."[23]

This last, briefest of remarks, which Freud uses to introduce the excerpt, is his sole commentary on the dream, and one is struck by the sudden asceticism of the author who is elsewhere always prepared to expand at length on new material. Why has Freud become as speechless as Cook at Dusky Bay? Even more surprising is the very inclusion of the seemingly superfluous example, which illustrates a point already demonstrated sufficiently and about which Freud has nothing new to say. The passage, and Freud's reluctance to comment on it, are troubling given the shift to the whole theory implied by this interpreted dream. What compels Freud to set this monument to Bismarck in the body of *The Interpretation of Dreams*? What fascinates him in the oneiric fantasy of Prussian banners flying over Austrian territory in 1919? And—especially—why does he defer so fully to Sachs? what silences Freud at the sight of Bismarck triumphant?

In our context, the psychic interiority of Bismarck is much less important than the internal history of psychoanalysis as it erupts in the ambiguity of this single passage. For tensions within Freudian theory emerge here in a way that shed light on the relationship between the formation of psychoanalytic theory and the political developments of the twentieth century. However, it is first necessary to note the not yet explicitly political problematic that surrounds Bismarck's dream. Only two paragraphs of section E—involving the priority of early childhood memories in the construction of dreams, that is, an antithetical hypothesis to the one invoked in relationship to Bismarck—were present in the original edition of 1900. In the editions of 1909 and 1911, extensive new material was incorporated into chapter 5, section D, on "Typical Dreams," much of which was later shifted to chapter 6, and section E, which appears for the first time—remarkably late—in 1914 (as already stated, the Bismarck material itself was not added until five years later).

This editorial history of additions and reorganization betrays a subtle transformation of the central interpretive project. At the outset of chapter 2 Freud distinguishes his method from several competing and popular models of dream interpretation, including the so-called decoding, which "treats dreams as a kind of cryptography in which each sign can be translated into another sign having a known meaning, in accordance with a fixed key."[24] Rejecting this mechanical approach and its reliance on putatively objective dream books, Freud advocates a subjective construction of the interpretive process: his technique "imposes the task of interpretation on the dreamer himself. It is not concerned with what occurs to the *interpreter* in connection with a particular element of the dreams, but with what occurs to the *dreamer*."[25] Free association represents the modern alternative to the superstitious codes of antiquity, and such a subjectivist account would seem to preclude any easy equations, any cryptographic rules of thumb, and perhaps even the very notion of typicality in the interpretation of dreams.

Yet in the initial exposition in chapter 6, section E, Freud reluctantly concedes the presence of nonindividual symbolism in dreams and hence the inadequacy of a rigorously applied method of free association: "As a rule the technique of interpreting according to the dreamer's free associations leaves us in the lurch when we come to the symbolic elements in the dream-content."[26] Interpretation henceforth no longer depends solely on what occurs to the dreamer but equally on the facility of the interpreter to recognize collective meanings. Freud therefore proposes a "combined technique," mixing the subjectivism of the original program with a repertoire of symbols associated with the "people" and "found in folklore, and in popular myths, legends, linguistic idioms, proverbial wisdom and current jokes."[27]

This is a profound shift in psychoanalysis that began in the 1890s—and in part always remained—an emancipation project of the autonomous individual coming to speech. Here that liberal substance is relativized by the power of a populist substrate. When Freud proceeds to list some typical symbols (and, once again, such a listing is susceptible to precisely the same critique he himself leveled at the dream books of antiquity in chapter 2), the political substance of the theoretical revision becomes evident, for he begins with the symbols of state power: "The Emperor and the Empress (or the

King and Queen) as a rule really represent the dreamer's parents; and a Prince or Princess represents the dreamer himself or herself. But the same high authority is attributed to great men as to the Emperor; and for that reason Goethe, for instance, appears as a father symbol in some dreams."[28] Although he goes on to enumerate the representations of genitalia—tree trunks and umbrellas, boxes and chests—the crucial discursive association has become clear. The theoretical shift from free association to a typical symbolism corresponds to a revision of the initial liberalism and an acknowledgment of the power of community and authority, emperors and empresses, kings and queens.

The question posed by the apparently unmotivated insertion of Bismarck's dream can now find a preliminary answer. It is certainly what it is ostensibly supposed to be: a textbook illustration of the Freudian understanding of a standard phallic symbol. Yet the very notion of standard symbolism here testifies to an impasse in the original theoretical construction and simultaneously to an attraction to a Caesaristic political model. Instead of the manifest content serving as a camouflage for sexual desire—that would be a classic Freudian model as, for example, in his study of Leonardo—it is the sexual imagery of masturbation that is allegedly the medium for the latent thought of political strategy. Freud not only refuses to question this radical inversion, he generously gives it his approbation by underscoring how that strategy, as a "serious" one, is necessarily far removed from a denigrated realm of sexuality. The insertion into the text of the image of authority, Bismarck, and the theoretical assertion of the authoritarian image—the typical symbol—are evidently joined by an uncharacteristic program of libidinal repression. The price of that denial of sexual energy is the enervation of Freud's theoretical animus and, consequently, his own rhetorical disappearance, the silence vis-à-vis the image of the leader.

The overdetermination of the Bismarck passage as both a political locus and a symptom of a theoretical turn is no exception but rather a consequence of the underlying project of *The Interpretation of Dreams* and of psychoanalysis as a whole. For it is a misunderstanding to treat Freud's work as essentially a theory of interiority that undergoes politicization so to speak, as solely an afterthought in his later cultural-anthropological writings or in the elaborations of his leftist heirs: Otto Gross, Wilhelm Reich, Herbert Marcuse. On the contrary, it is at its core social and political and nowhere more clearly than in this book, which cannot be reduced to a manual for dream interpreters or a formalist description of condensation and displacement. It is a massive collection of material, extraordinary evidence of the state of the European mind at the end of the nineteenth century. Its architecture is organized around the conflict with the father, the oedipal struggle, as the core of all political contestation, and it explores at least two historical instances of political conflict: in Freud's 1848 dream of Count Thun and in the Roman dreams, the significance of which has already been mentioned. Only when one grasps the structural significance of these two points for the organization of the book does Bismarck's dream come into focus as the resolution of the perplexing conundrum in Freud's thought, namely, the perceived inadequacy of the emancipation project—which he refuses to surrender—in the context of apparently untouchable structures of power. In lieu of emancipation, he will be finally drawn to stage—not at all gratuitously but by the logic of the text—Bismarck's victory march.

Although the political argument concludes with this emphatic assertion of power, it began in a very different key with the ultimate dismantling of patriarchal authority. That *The Interpretation of Dreams* was written under the influence of the death of Freud's father is underscored in the preface to the second edition. Yet the text is hardly an unambiguous act of mourning. On the contrary, Freud admits to sentiments of animosity, indeed disdain, for his father, who had related to his young son how he had once responded in what Freud perceived as a cowardly manner to an anti-Semitic affront in his own youth; Hannibal would have acted more courageously. But the struggle to death with the father is given its most radical treatment in one of Freud's earlier elaborations of the oedipal complex. He introduces the problem ostensibly to account for dreams of the death of loved ones, which, according to a central thesis of the book, must represent wish fulfillments, and the argument leads to the seminal literary critical passage, the readings of *Oedipus* and *Hamlet*.

Freud belittles explanations of *Oedipus* as a drama of destiny that derives its strength from an abstract conflict of subjective human will and an objective fate. Instead, he admonishes us to pay attention to the "particular nature of the material," that is, the temptation of parricide and the desire for the mother.[29] Yet the same principle compels us to pay attention to the particular nature of Freud's material: two plays in which the death of the father is simultaneously the death of the king; two cases where the personal struggle is congruent with a political crisis. Therefore, the initial description of such a central component of psychoanalysis as the oedipal complex is already a scene of political thought: how to overcome the seemingly natural authority that impedes the articulation of the social subject.

Even at this outset, the political thinker is not blind to the difficulties of pursuing the project. It is less Oedipus's retribution that troubles Freud than a double movement of repression in Shakespeare's version. First, the son is incapable of carrying out the revolutionary act himself. Rejecting Goethe's ascription of this incapacity to Hamlet's overly contemplative nature, Freud argues in terms of an economy of affect. It would make no sense to take vengeance on the uncle for committing the murder the son himself had always desired. Thus, it is the oedipal dynamic that, turned back on itself, impedes Hamlet's action. Second, and more importantly, Freud notes that although *Oedipus* names the forbidden wish, "in *Hamlet* it remains repressed; and—just as in the case of a neurosis—we only learn of its existence from its inhibiting consequences."[30] Both Hamlet, the prince, and *Hamlet*, the text, are encumbered by a prohibition that precludes the achievement of their immanent impulse, and their distance from their precursors of antiquity is a consequence of a negative cultural progress: "the changed treatment of the same material reveals the whole difference in the mental life of these two widely separated epochs of civilization: the secular advance of repression in the emotional life of mankind."

If Freud is suggesting that the progress of repression induces Hamlet's neurotic oscillations and his failure as a political actor, he has also revealed the Achilles' heel of psychoanalysis. For this central narrative—which pessimistically stages the impossibility of fulfillment—is at odds with the pretense of releasing the subject from compulsive patterns of behavior and dispelling the illusions of religious and political superstition. The dynamic of the theoretical production of psychoanalysis turns out to be a result of the encounter between Freud, liberal proponent of the Enlightenment, and the counter-Enlightenment of bourgeois society. In *The Interpretation of Dreams* he consequently investigates two scenes of political regression, the failure of the Revolution of 1848 and the virulent anti-Semitism of turn-of-the-century Vienna, both political corollaries to Hamlet's resistance to act.

Freud seems strangely eager to downplay the specificity of the material. Certainly, he indicates how the dream of Count Thun "gives one the impression of being in the nature of a phantasy in which the dreamer was carried back to the Revolutionary year 1848," and he accounts for this setting by referring to several sources among which he includes his memories of the recent jubilee celebrations of Franz Joseph's ascent to the throne.[31] Nevertheless, he dismisses this content by treating it solely as the remnant of recent experiences that provides a casing for a more substantive content: "This revolutionary phantasy . . . was like the facade of an Italian church in having no organic relation with the structure lying behind it. But it differed from those facades in being disordered and full of gaps, and in the fact that portions of the interior construction had forced their way through into it at many points."[32] When Freud writes of "this revolutionary phantasy," is he describing the single dream or is he passing judgment on the revolution itself and its adherents? In the latter case, the ensuing interpretation becomes Freud's *Eighteenth Brumaire*, an account of the failure of the revolution, whose fervor is diminished to a mere fantasy that is genuinely unable to transform "the structure lying behind it," the structure of society and power.

The validity of such a reading of the passage—that is, as an inquiry into the inadequacy of the revolutionary movement and, therefore, a sort of denial of the revolution altogether—can be demonstrated by exploring a salient pattern in the report. In addition to the usual two-tiered text—the dream report and the subsequent commentary—this case includes an extensive preface in which Freud recounts how he witnessed Count Thun pass arrogantly by a protesting ticket inspector and enter a first-class train compartment to travel to the kaiser in Ischl. Waiting on the platform, Freud plans to protest should another such case of aristocratic privilege transpire. Suddenly he finds himself humming a provocative tune from *The Marriage of Figaro* while "all kinds of insolent and revolutionary ideas were going through my head."[33] In contrast to this semiconscious reverie, genuinely a "phantasy" of revolution, the dream of the following night casts Freud very differently, as an apparent victim of the revolution fleeing the political assembly and, in the next sequence, the revolutionary city as well.[34] Moreover, this slide from the radical preface to the counterrevolutionary dream continues in the interpretation. There, Freud, as we have seen, proves eager to bypass "the particular nature of the material," which he compares pejoratively to the facade of an Italian church, as he extends the flight of the dream into the argument of the interpretation.

Although the interpretation is staged as a sort of explanatory expedition into a hidden interior behind the manifest material of a revolutionary surface, it constitutes a final stage in Freud's processing of the revolutionary material and ought to be read as encoded political theory. His denial of the significance of the revolutionary context as a fantasy or a facade is therefore in fact an evaluation of the revolution itself, and the substance of the dream interpretation includes three points relevant to that characterization. Freud first discusses an incident from his adolescence, a schoolboy revolt against an unpopular teacher, designated the "school tyrant."[35] However, the youthful conspirators, the actors in the schoolyard uprising, display multifold associations with the aristocracy and not, as one might have expected, with some oppressed stratum—as if history had miscast the agents of emancipation. This is, in any case, the suggestion of the material of the interpretation. Meanwhile, other developments are unfolding, including a rising anti-Semitism, and Freud cites a corresponding incident almost parenthetically as a second source of the dream. Finally, he recalls a third source, an altercation with "someone who was my senior and my superior, someone who has since then shown his ability as a leader of men and an organizer of large groups (and who also, incidentally, bears a name derived from the Animal Kingdom)."[36] That figure is likely Viktor Adler, the Social Democratic leader.[37] As political theory, the dream interpretation evidently juxtaposes three causes of the weakness of the middle-class revolutionary activity: the elitist consciousness of the bourgeois participants; the ideological competition provided by anti-Semitism; and the separation from the socialist movement.

This analysis of failure conflicts with the reading emphasized by Freud, who was compelled to foreground the aspect of wish fulfillment and the priority of infantile material. Thus, he treats the final image—he is holding a glass urinal for an elderly man—as an act of vengeance on his father for the chastising he received as a child for wetting his bed: "I was making fun of him, I had to hand him the urinal because he was blind."[38] The oedipal component as well as the connection to the political sphere are treated in the lengthy footnote to this section: "the whole rebellious content of the dream, with its lèse majesté and its derision of higher authorities, went back to a rebellion against my father. A Prince is known as the father of his country; the father is the oldest, first, and for children the only authority, and from his autocratic power the other social authorities have developed in the course of the history of human civilization—except in so far as the 'matriarchy' calls for a qualification of this assertion."[39]

So for Freud the dream ends happily with the son's assertion of power over his father, old, blind, and exposed, conquered by the youthful hero. But is the final image really that one-sided? Or does the dream tell us more than the interpreter? "I was a sick-nurse and had to give him the urinal because he was blind." To cast the father as Lear (while fleeing the revolution), to adopt as a doctor the role of his nurse, to care for his father's bodily functions—all this suggests more than unnuanced victory. It suggests filial devotion, certainly, and the loyalty of a royalist as well as subservience—indeed, subordination, not only oedipal revolt.[40] It is the same ambiguity that pervades the metaphor of the Italian church; in an equation with the revolution, Freud denounces its apparent architecture until he rescues the church in order to denounce the revolution even more.

This ambivalence regarding the church comes to the fore in the discussion of the Roman dreams. In addition to the dream of Count Thun, it is Freud's Hannibalism that frames the political thinking of *The Interpretation of Dreams*: two references to social conflict, two representations of dramatic challenges to authority, and two dismal failures. Despite the early identification with the Carthaginian warrior, by the time of *Civilization and Its Discontents* (1929) at the very latest, Freud offers arguments for the functionality of religion and, at least in some passages, the need for structures of social authority. To be sure, such claims are juxtaposed with a conflicting commitment to an Enlightenment project, but it is a profound tension, grounded in the ambivalence of the oedipal conflict and evident already in the complicated textual field surrounding Bismarck's dreams.

Does the work suggest this strange concatenation? The cranky bourgeois cannot stop the aristocrat from getting first-class treatment; the unruly schoolboys are self-indulgent and arrogant; Freud never gets close enough to Viktor Adler's socialism, and Hannibal never gets to Rome. Therefore, Bismarck marches through the mountains into Bohemia, occupying territory understood to be Austrian. The success of German colonialism—the invasion of Bohemia—is the failure of Hannibal's resistance. No matter how Freud, identifying with the African warrior, may destabilize colonialist discourse, his own theorizing takes a conservative turn. The inclusion of the Bismarck addendum is not a gratuitous accumulation of more of the same but the conclusion of the immanent line of political thinking: because the emancipation project fails, the conquering hero enters, and Freud's Oedipus-Hamlet, as well as Hannibal-Boabdil, steps aside for Bismarck-Fortinbras. Although psychoanalysis depends on Freud's anticolonial posture, it is simultaneously undermined by the internal ambivalence of its emancipation project.

But Bismarck's entry may have been overdetermined by a further exigency in 1919: the fate of German Austria after the dismantling of the Austro-Hungarian Empire. In the wake of the collapse of the

Hapsburg regime, arguments for the Anschluss were widespread in Austria and underscored the economic fragility of the rump state. The model of a German occupation of Austria might equally be read as a colonial scheme. In any case, the insertion of Bismarck's fantasy within the body of *The Interpretation of Dreams* in the 1919 edition apparently gives expression to annexationist sentiment. However, if the passage does have that political significance, then it becomes all the more crucial to scrutinize its rhetorical setting, especially Freud's silence, his refusal to gloss Sachs's commentary.

The refusal is particularly glaring since Freud, as we know, must swallow a lot. He gives explicit approval to Sachs's revisionist claim that politics is separate from—and presumably superior to—a netherworld of sexuality. He accepts, moreover, the inversion of the theory of symbolic representation. Of course, Sachs does not miss the masturbatory iconography, but he erases it in two layers of cultural overlays. When he casts Bismarck as the biblical hero, his Moses is "the leader, whom the people he sought to free rewarded with rebellion, hatred and ingratitude." That is Moses as the opponent of the Jews, which coincides with Freud's usage of the figure: the authoritarian emancipator facing a revolt against freedom. Meanwhile, according to Sachs, Bismarck the political dreamer is able to repress fully the infantile sexuality and to achieve a wish fulfillment compatible with the agency of censorship, hence the desire at the dream's conclusion to report the vision to the king.

This last point is particularly important since it is argued in a strictly psychoanalytic manner but comes to strongly antipsychoanalytic conclusions: the separation of culture (including politics) from libidinal forces and the disappearance of private interiority in the interest of public service. Hamlet's affective life and the scientific discourse constituted through a reflection on it are suddenly swept into the past. With the figure of Bismarck, as constructed by Sachs and as inserted into *The Interpretation of Dreams*, classical psychoanalysis discovers the authoritarian personality. It is a subjectivity thoroughly occupied by state power, both an outcome of the earlier political considerations—Count Thun and Rome, the failures of nineteenth-century liberalism—and a theoretical turning point that marks the obsolescence of a liberal psychoanalysis. Yet the rise of modernized authority is pursuant not only on the demise of liberalism but on the decline of Africa as well, since Hannibal has failed and Boabdil has been crushed. In other words, the two African tropes framing psychoanalysis are both marked by failure or defeat, with which Freud identifies, but it is precisely the fact of these defeats that perpetually threatens to destabilize his own project.

The obsolescence of the liberal precepts of psychoanalysis evokes Freud's reticence, an absence of commentary wavering tentatively between refusal and acquiescence. As the original project shatters on its material, psychoanalysis surrenders some of its critical capacity. Interpolating Bismarck's dream, Freud loses his voice, much like the "attentive man" from Dusky Bay. The two-dimensionality of the first preface, mediating between the scientific public and individual privacy, collapses into the ubiquity of political authority. The subjective theory of symbolic representation gives way to the self-evidence of collectivist allegories, and the oedipal revolt of young Germany against old Austria concludes with Bismarck's gesture of renewed submission to his patriarchal majesty. Psychoanalysis as political theory pursued emancipation but discovered structural permanence and, at that moment, the limits of its own critical potential. But it is this problem that runs like a fissure through Freud's late cultural theory, and it is this problem that splits the subsequent psychoanalytic tradition: the attempt to redeem the critical impetus of the emancipatory moment or a conformist transformation of psychoanalysis into techniques of adaptation to a therapeutic society.

Yet if the emancipation of the individual subject as the genuine goal of early psychoanalysis is attenuated by the failure of liberalism and the amplification of authority, the status of mythic and primitive material also subtly shifts. Initially, it is integrated into the Enlightenment project; it is precisely not a "dark continent," a radical other to reason or to the subject. On the contrary, myth appears first as an integral part of Enlightenment itself, since Oedipus becomes aligned with science. To the extent, however, that Freud, at his most Jungian moments, deemphasizes the role of the subject, as in free associations, and must accept ready-made, standard symbols, symbols become archetypes, culturally specific enfigurements of the irrational. This transformation produces the exotic, amplifying a potential within the Enlightenment since Cook but otherwise outweighed by presumptions of a universal rationality. The extensive itinerary through the metaphors and materials of *The Interpretation of Dreams* demonstrates how liberal psychoanalysis attempted to retrieve the denigrated realm of the colonized and to win it for reason. Yet as psychoanalysis in the course of Freud's career shifts toward models of typical symbolism and authoritarian figures, it implicitly relegitimates the most exoticizing readings of alterity. To the extent that I have demonstrated that this shift results from an internalization of political defeat, then we can understand that the exoticization of the other is little more than the distorted external projection of an emancipation denied because of the continued immobility of real social structures. Psychoanalysis, the grand interpretive scheme of modernism, records within itself the invention of the primitive, initially as a source of scientific clarification but eventually as the stereotypical archetype of irrationality, the very opposite of Enlightenment.

In an initial phase, psychoanalysis scandalized the scientific establishment by claiming that purportedly irrational material—dreams, parapraxis, and myth—might be construed as decipherable expressions of rational meaning. The pursuit of such meaning through the interpretive labor of analysis was a late heir to the Enlightenment elevation of reason and quite consistent with traditions of liberalism. However, the resistance to psychoanalysis derived not only from a conventional science, as represented by the interlocutor in *Lay Analysis*, who is unaccustomed to hermeneutic bravado. It also followed from the experience of the limits of reason and liberalism, driven back by various political forces after the 1870s, and the history of psychoanalysis is marked by a constant revision to keep up with this opposition. Dido's defiance and Hannibal's prowess enfigure the heroism of revolt against imperialist power. As late as the dark continent metaphor, Freud externalizes domination, locating it in the competitor discipline and in the other language. Nevertheless, Bismarck's dream of German occupation makes its way into *The Interpretation of Dreams*, and with it comes a signal reversal in psychoanalytic assumptions regarding symbols and cultural theory. Boabdil's defeat puts an end to the revolution associated with the meta-phor of Hannibal. The other ceases to be a location of reason—such was Freud's initial approach to myth—and becomes instead the outside to reason, the absolutized other fully foreign to the concep-tual thinking that contemporary critics denounce as Western. Trac-ing this invention of exoticism is crucial, for it allows us, first, to re-call how the Enlightenment legacy once envisioned a shared foundation of reason; here Forster concurs with Freud. Second, by understanding how the exoticization of the non-Western world is a consequence of historical forces, we can see how the postmodern celebration of the other—the mythic, the primitive, the non-West-ern—is deeply implicated in a system of global segregation.

5

COLONIAL LITERATURE AND
THE EMANCIPATION OF WOMEN

The establishment of colonial space implied both the control of domestic masses, as Fabri envisioned in his sexual economy of empire, and the suppression of the colonized population. Yet these repressive functions were frequently drowned out by emancipatory reverberations within colonial discourse. In other words, the ideological defense of colonialism could be successfully persuasive only to the extent that it could present—or misrepresent—colonialism as a vehicle of progress and liberation, that is, as part of the Enlightenment. Ten years after the publication of *Bedarf Deutschland der Kolonien?*, Fabri played a leading role in the antislavery movement of 1888. Bringing together representatives of both Catholicism and Protestantism and thereby contributing to a healing of the deep national rift of the Kulturkampf, the movement mobilized public sentiment against the Arab slave traders in East Africa: colonial discourse proceeds with strong humanitarian credentials. (Yet recall how American abolitionism was often interspersed with visions of the freed slaves recolonizing Africa.) Fabri, typically, compared the antislavery movement to the Crusades, suggesting that German confessional unity could be achieved through a violent confrontation with an external, Islamic enemy.[1] In fact, the movement was immediately instrumentalized by the colonialist lobby: European expansion in the region was defended as a mechanism to free the Africans from Arab slavery. Nevertheless, even in the liberal context of this imagined emancipation, the African population is nowhere recognized as a legitimate community in its own right. Africa remains the place where Europeans—not Africans—are called upon to act and to act out the fundamental forms of their identity structures. Forster's curiosity and eagerness to see the islanders has given way to a disregard of local populations altogether.

The emancipatory character of colonialism with regard to slavery may have been largely a sham, although it anticipates various twentieth-century issues regarding the appropriateness of Western values in the Third World. Do norms derived from the Western European Enlightenment apply in different contexts because of their universal validity or are they intrinsically culturally specific? How should we think about Western ideals of gender equality in non-Western contexts? The configuration of emancipation, Enlightenment, and colonialism is in fact particularly intriguing with regard to the case of the German women in the colonies for whom colonialism might appear to offer an attractive alternative to the rigid hierarchy and patriarchy of the Reich. Our contemporary concern with the vicissitudes of issues of race and gender were already played out in intriguing ways in the age of colonialism. It is, for example, interesting to note that the military journal *Überall: Zeitschrift für Armee und Marine* (Everywhere: A journal for army and navy), an important organ of colonialist propaganda, very quickly developed a women's section, edited by the popular novelist Emma Vely. In a related vein the political activity of women's organizations in support of the colonialist project has been the topic of an intriguing recent study.[2] However, it is in the writings of Frieda von Bülow, the first significant author of *Kolonialliteratur*—indeed, she is arguably the founder of the genre of colonial fiction in Germany—that the connection between colonial expansion and gender is explored most effectively, and it is there that one can trace the engendered character of colonialism. Fabri's pamphlet displays a reproductive fantasy as the primal scene of colonialism; von Bülow's fiction proposes the consequent reorganization of gender relations.

As Joachim Warmbold has shown in his valuable studies, von Bülow well deserves prominent attention in the literary and cultural history of the period.[3] Active in some East African settlement enterprises and closely involved with Carl Peters, the premier colonialist agitator, she produced in addition to travel reports an extensive corpus of fictional treatments of German colonialism. Despite some predecessors, it is she who establishes during the 1890s a type of literature whose vicissitudes can be traced through better-known authors such as Gustav Frenssen and Hans Grimm. Here, however, neither an exhaustive treatment of this tradition nor a complete profile of von Bülow is at stake but rather the unique characteristic of her fiction, the simultaneous investigation of gender relations and the colonialist project. In her novels, *Ludwig von Rosen* (1892), *Tropenkoller* (1896; Tropical fever), *Im Lande der Verheissung* (1899; In the land of promise), and especially in the *Deutsch-Ostafrikanische Novellen* (1892; German East African novellas), the colonies appear as the privileged site of a reorganization of male and female identities. Nor is this choice of site arbitrary; it is by no means the case that von Bülow merely uses the African setting to stage her critique of Wilhelmine patriarchy. On the contrary, her analysis of colonialism and her analysis of gender relations are mutually constitutive, indicating the complexity of the relations between colonial discourse and emancipation. Surely, colonialism is understood, conventionally, as domination; in this chapter, I will explore its congruence with the emancipation of women in some specific texts. The previous chapter showed how psychoanalysis, counterintuitively, operated with a rhetoric of anticolonialism; now we turn to the equally unexpected alliance of colonialism and feminism.

Colonial discourse includes an invocation of an erotic crisis and promises to allow for a new sort of man and a new sort of woman or, to put it more strongly and provocatively, for men to become women and women to become men. To the extent that such transformations fail to transpire, von Bülow suggests it is because of the inadequate and still too Wilhelmine administration of the colonies. Von Bülow writes from the position of the colonist who claims to understand the colonized population well enough to rule it but for the disruptive interventions of an insensitive and intrusive state bureaucracy based in the metropolitan center and blind to local cultures. In this sense she is indeed capable of a critique of colonialism. But it is a critique from the right, since she accepts the colonialist premise while measuring its de facto realization against an idealized notion of its genuine mission, and only therein finds it wanting. Anticolonial colonialism? In any case, for von Bülow, colonialism has the potential to overcome the deficiencies of patriarchal and Prussian hierarchy through a reorganization of gender relations, including the emancipation of women, now challenged by new tasks and freed from the strictures of imperial Germany. In addition, colonialism harbors the potential feminization of men, for whom a successful colonialism would depend on less, not more, machismo. Ultimately, for von Bülow the colony promises a radical queerness, a perpetual transgression of gender and, perhaps, racial separations, and this hybridizing utopia is thwarted only by the conservative resistance and the authoritarian imperiousness of the German bureaucracy.

Her novel *Ludwig von Rosen* is dedicated to "the founder of our German–East African Colony, Dr. Carl Peters" and is prefaced with an epigraph, a statement by Konrad Küster cited from the *Allgemeine deutsche Universitätszeitung* of 1 October 1891: "The German character has always shown itself by thriving mightily in need and danger and exhausting work, while fantasies [*Schlaraffenland*] have been pure poison for it more than for others. But our colonies offer so much work and danger, that any German who is afraid of neither can satisfy his need for activity. Through work and danger even the most jaded and foppish [*gigerlhafte*] person can again become a character, a hero." The suggestion that Germans are particularly susceptible to fantasies with presumably enervating consequences echoes Fabri's complaint that German expeditionary literature had remained solely scientific. What is at stake is the enfigurement of the familiar contrast between an otherworldly lack of realism on the one hand and, on the other, the imperative of practical activity. German idealism is declared obsolete again, whereas German realism (like German nation-hood) is deemed to be belated and, therefore, all the more ur-gent. Yet this standard estimation appears in a new permuta-tion in the motto that von Bülow has chosen for her novel. For Fabri the necessity of work was directly linked to national eco-nomic concerns. Germans should, so he suggested, no longer engage in a pure science from which others profit but should instead turn themselves to reaping the material harvest of their own cognitive explorations: why should German geographers map Africa for the benefit of French or English empires? The same link between labor and a national commonweal figures, of course, in the model of an epigraphic invocation of German work—Julian Schmidt's dictum at the outset of Gustav Freytag's *Soll und Haben* (1855; Debit and credit): "The novel should seek out the German people where, in its industrious-ness, it is to be found, namely, at work."[4] Despite Küster's im-plied differentiation between German and other national char-acters, the accent in his statement lies elsewhere, between deficient personalities and their possible transformation through achievement. Labor, no longer a matter of the pro-duction of wealth in a national interest, takes on a primarily therapeutic significance. In the colonies at least it is prescribed as a sort of psychological cure, a treatment that, unlike the "pure poison" of fantasies, could heal the corrupt and deca-dent individual, the most jaded and foppish, and transform him into a hero.

It is appealing to read von Bülow's choice of the epigraph as a relativization of the dedication. At first she sets Peters on a pedestal but, then, with the help of Küster's statement sub-verts the initial praise by suggesting that the activity in which he is engaged may be the result of a personality disorder, that colonialism entails the acting out of a neurosis, and that—this is the best case from von Bülow's standpoint—colonialism might also prove to be the means by which the neurosis could be overcome. In other words, the whole paratextual commencement, the dedication and the epigraph, may constitute a critique of Peters and, by extension, von Bülow's critique of a particular masculinist version of colonialism. Evidence for this reading includes von Bülow's subsequent disappointment with Peters as well as evaluations of his pathological character in the scholarly literature on German imperialism.[5] Von Bülow's goal is a correction of this masculinist colonialism through a reorganization of gender codes. In this text Küster's statement anticipates the course of the novel and its effective sequel, *Tropenkoller*. Ludwig von Rosen, an impoverished aristocrat in imperial Berlin, is entangled in the corruption and erotic decadence of the wealthy; reduced to the tolerated lover of the wife of a wealthy businessman, he understands himself to be her "slave." Colonialism presents itself as the alternative, a possibility for vigorous activity and unlimited opportunities unhindered by the musty limitations of the Old World. If the account of colonialism in the ensuing narrative is by no means uncritical (in the sense already discussed—a critique of the colonial administration from the standpoint of the colonist), von Rosen has nevertheless been cured: colonialism provides an answer to the cultural crisis of the Wilhelmine bourgeoisie. He has escaped the incapacitating decadence of the capital and, in the penultimate sequence, the former "slave" is himself engaged in a battle against an Arab slave trader: colonialism becomes the site of freedom. By the conclusion his relationship to the heroine, the "emancipated" Sophie Biron—emancipated, that is, in the sense of the conventions of gender—appears to be sealed. The emancipation of women, erotic emancipation, and a victory over the slave trade are combined through the colonial project. How much clearer could the legacy of the Enlightenment become?

Therefore, an obvious reading of Küster's epigraph as a map of a trajectory from an effeminate figure, blasé and foolish, to a masculine hero would be erroneous, at least as far as von Bülow's narrative goes. The sexual politics are precisely the opposite. Von Rosen moves from the patriarchal hierarchy of Berlin where he is, in effect, only a man and only sexually so, to the colonies where he, and not only he, can find freedom: from slavery to abolition, from courtesanship to emancipation, from patriarchy to parity. The plot of escaping decadent sexuality by entering a bourgeois sphere of authentic love is a familiar late-eighteenth-century form; one thinks of Schiller's *Kabale und Liebe* (Cabal and love). Here, however, the emancipation takes place, paradoxically, through colonialism. Von Bülow foregrounds the counterintuitive connection between a democratic discourse—a critique of hierarchy coupled with a Rousseauistic anti-civilizationalism—and the colonialist imagination as if it were ultimately the colonist, and not the colonized, who could play the role of the noble savage. In particular, this constellation of democracy and colonialism is brought to bear directly on the question of gender relations. Thirty years later Hans Grimm's fascist *Volk ohne Raum* would pose colonialism as an undertaking necessary for the emancipation of the German working class; von Bülow explores the potential of colonialism for the emancipation of German women.

Because of the importance of colonialism as an alternative to the patriarchal hierarchy of the Reich, von Bülow does not mince her criticism and pays particular attention to the inadequacies of really-existing colonialism. The complexity of the significance of *Tropenkoller*, in particular, depends on this contradiction between an idealized colonialist agenda and the disappointments of real practice. The novel entails the heroine's search for values in a devalued world. Not surprisingly, Sophie is repeatedly characterized as "too emancipated" for marriage—certainly a critique of the institution of marriage—and it is she, the figure of emancipation, who is the prime carrier of the ideals that allow for a critique of hierarchy.[6] However, not every hierarchy is subject to her criticism. Not, for example, the hierarchy between colonizer and colonized, for she is an adamant proponent of the colonialist project. Within that project, however, she denounces the reproduction of the heteronomous order, needless ranks and titles, imported from the European metropolis. The colonist appears as the anticolonial who resents the codes of the home country and their annoying interference in the life of the settler. Thus, the novel criticizes the perpetuation of a consciousness of vertical social status; parodies an extremist patriotism; and, simultaneously, confirms the colonist's perspective on the excessive and intrusive liberalism of the imperial administrators.[7]

Yet these particular political judgments are, in the final analysis, peripheral to the novel's central concern, the ubiquitous tropical fever of the title, a nervous malaise that makes its way through the colony and severely impairs the efficiency of all the Germans. Von Bülow is, however, not at all concerned with a primarily medical account. The disease is a metaphor for the psychological disorders produced by an inadequately democratic colonialism, and it is, at the same time, her version of fin-de-siècle nervousness transplanted into East Africa. On this point Sophie concurs with von Rosen's diagnosis in a key passage in the text:

> "The glory of command in the land of the savages goes straight to the head of these servant types," he thought; "that's it! They are so unaccustomed to being masters that they lose their poor little bit of common sense and end up with a ridiculous version of megalomania. The subaltern bureaucratic mentality loses control, as soon as he turns into Bana Kubwa.—This is something very different from deleterious effects of this climate for the nervous system, that doesn't spare even the noblest of natures. . . . [It] appears to me to be a form of parvenu behavior, grown malignant due to the climate and other complications."[8]

To be sure, von Rosen, the aristocrat, himself maintains a hierarchical perspective, blaming the noxious nervousness on the psychology of figures with characters and backgrounds less noble than his own. Nevertheless, the psychological disorder he describes is attributed directly to a reproduction of the hierarchical culture of the metropolis. The authoritarian personalities who in Bismarckian Germany apparently occupied subaltern positions and suffered discrimination cannot adjust to the possibility of their freedom, a freedom that, for von Rosen, is no less desirable because it presumes the domination of "savages." The problem with colonialism, for him and apparently for von Bülow, is not that it enslaves the colonized but that the slave mentality of the bulk of the colonizers cannot appreciate the freedom that Africa offers. The former slave von Rosen and the emancipated Sophie are the exceptions; their liaison is proof that the colony can provide a setting for a no longer hierarchical and, therefore, postpatriarchal order of gender relations. The colonies beckon with the opportunity of freedom for the settlers who are capable of seizing it.

In the novel, this colonialist utopia is muffled by the extensive accounts of colonial deficiencies, attributable primarily to the excessive influences from Germany: meddling bureaucrats or servile colonizers. It is in the *Deutsch-Ostafrikanische Novellen*, however, that von Bülow can concentrate on the alternative, the *unerhörte Begebenheit*—the unique event central to the poetics of the novella—and the strange metamorphosis of the colony into a feminist *locus amoenus*. Throughout the three novellas the African population is characterized in derogatory terms, as ludicrous or treacherous, indolent or bloodthirsty. The establishment of political authority required military force and the vilification of the opponent. No matter which particular denigration prevails at a given moment, the Africans are never central to the plot, however, which always unfolds among Europeans. Nevertheless, the Africans are not merely the backdrop for events that might as well transpire elsewhere; they are the colonized, the objects of strategies of control. Von Bülow's texts attempt to reconcile two reformist projects in the colonies: a reform of the colonial administration to make it more effective and a reform of Wilhelmine gender relations to modify their patriarchal character. The modernizing result is the double suggestion that colonialism—the set of practices associated with the establishment of a permanent German settlement in Africa—would benefit from a feminization of its administration and that the institution of marriage, fraught with all the problems that sensibility in the age of Ibsen could easily recognize, could perhaps best be revitalized precisely in the colonial setting. The *Deutsch-Ostafrikanische Novellen* explore these possibilities in three different permutations: a critique of patriarchal behavior on the part of the male colonial administration; a critique of the internalization of patriarchal norms by the female spouse; and a characterization of the utopian potential of a feminization of the male colonist. These three stages, which correspond to the order of the anthology, are evidently intended to suggest a process. The analysis of male failings and the subsequent treatment of female failing both involve a major sacrifice: the death of a woman and the renunciation of love. The concluding text, entitled *Das Kind*, in contrast concerns the prevention of a sacrifice and the rescue of a child by the male colonist who learns to be a mother. The border transgressions inherent in colonialism are apparently also transsexual.

In the first novella, *Der Heilige von Kialmasi* (The saint of Kialmasi), von Bülow ostensibly explores the tension between colonial administration and missionary activity. The structural conflict between loyalty to state authority and devotion to religious faith is announced with far from subtle onomastic indicators. The new arrival, Reginald Witmann, has come to rule, and the saint of the title, Christian Forstner, preaches the gospel in the jungle: Caesar versus Christ. The substance of the conflict is elaborated explicitly in several conversations that suggest the sort of contradictions that were operative within colonialist discourse. For example, Witmann can comprehend the mission solely in terms of an expansive nationalist agenda, as the following statement makes clear: "[I am beginning to believe] that the missionary and the colonist can really cooperate and thereby become truly and lastingly effective. Basically, both want the same thing; they just choose different starting points. A pious Christian is, as such, a loyal subject and citizen. He won't disregard the welfare of his nation. Meanwhile, the patriot has the duty to defend the religion of his people everywhere and to support its spread."⁹

Although Witmann intends his remark as sort of concilia-
tory gesture, Forstner cannot help but regard it as supercilious
and presumptuous—the administrator's effort to colonize religion. To be sure, the missionary is not immune to the nationalist appeal, but he resists the strategic appropriation of the religious undertaking: "It is a special grace of God that I am
permitted to work on German soil and for my nation, something my brothers have not been allowed to do for centuries.
Yet I would carry out my tasks in a foreign sphere of interests
with the same love as I have shown here. Neither a mission of
culture nor national interest is decisive for us: we are only following the directive of our Lord and Savior to preach the gospel to the heathens."[10] The exchange suggests the possibility of
a link between von Bülow and the late-nineteenth-century
critics of the established cultural Protestantism in Wilhelmine
Germany, associated with Albrecht Ritschl and Adolph von
Harnack.[11] In the chemistry of the story the distinction is, however, crucial for the theme that colonialism cannot rule by the
sword of the administrator alone. It depends, on the contrary,
on the establishment of a new sort of community, charismatic
and, as will be seen in a moment, feminized. If the administrative paradigm of rationalized domination derives from Cook's
cartographic project, the substantive practice of colonialism—
at least as envisioned by von Bülow—depends on the engen-
derment of irrational loyalties that go beyond the limits of a
merely instrumental power. Therefore, at least some versions
of a critique of instrumental reason, of science and technology,
turn out to be very compatible with strategies of domination.
In this case, moreover, it is clear that it is in the colonies that
the cultural revolution can commence. They are the first German territory "in centuries" where missionary activity can take
place because these are the first colonies (acquired much later
than those of Spain, France, and England) and, especially, because the religious wars in the age of the Reformation quickly
linked territorial religion to dynastic identity, effectively pre-
cluding missionary work. That early modern solution is abro-
gated in the colonies where, moreover, after the Kulturkampf,

Protestant and Catholic Germans can coexist in a shared mission.

That community depends on the sacrifice of the third figure in the novella, Forstner's wife, Hedwig. In fact, the manifest content, the debate between representatives of state and church, knowledge and faith, reason and its critic, is little more than a pretext for the staging of an erotic triangle. The cited exchange, in which Witmann even argues as a rationalist skeptic, critical of the "infallible dogmas" of faith, takes place at the missionary's home, and Witmann catches himself committing adultery in his mind: "he envied the missionary for his possession of this charming woman."[12] It is against the background of this desire that the conversation ensues, and it is this desire, the subsequent seduction scenario, and Hedwig's de facto suicide that constitute the core of the plot.

The novella is then less the locus of tendentious considerations on the character of colonial policy than a contrast between two modes of masculinist behavior vis-à-vis the colonial woman. Forstner has brought her to the colony and involves her in his work while respecting her independence. Witmann is astonished that a German woman has any place in the colonies. When he addresses her as "gnädige Frau," she laughs and expresses preference for a simpler, more democratic designation.[13] Colonial literature derides the excessive formality and polish of Europe, to which it counterposes a more rough-and-ready egalitarianism that, however, excludes the local population. Instead of displaying nostalgia for a distant homeland, colonial literature generates an incipient anti-Eurocentrism. When Witmann suggests that he would guard his future wife like Argus, thereby criticizing Forstner's liberal reluctance to supervise Hedwig, she expresses her disapproval, evidencing a modernist sensibility. That is, the Forstner marriage stands clearly for the potential emancipation in the colonial setting, which permits the woman to shed the conventions of polite society and engage in a challenging *vita activa*. The settler woman on the frontier lays claim to an equality deemed unlikely in the metropolitan center. Correspondingly, Witmann is the clear case of the colonist who, at least initially, brings to the egalitarian colonies all the baggage, the hierarchical distinctions and patriarchal biases, of the civilized capital. The anticolonialism of the colonists represents a permutation of a Rousseauistic hostility to civilization as the colonial setting becomes the state of nature for the white race.

It therefore comes as no surprise that Witmann, with his civilized polish, is also a scoundrel, the dashing playboy who, set off from the listless missionary, pursues Hedwig and seduces her. Attempting to avoid a subsequent encounter, she runs into the wilds, overexerts herself, and contracts a fatal fever. To add to the melodrama, it is her death—and her deathbed confession to her husband—that resolves the conflict between the men and between church and state. Witmann rapidly becomes much less of a martinet and tacitly accepts the leadership of the missionary: "Without realizing it, he began to reduce the demands he placed on his servants, and only very rarely would he allow himself to be provoked to utter an angry word. 'He has become a good master,' the blacks concluded. They didn't notice that he would send them to the Padiri [the missionary] in case of arguments or that he would occasionally send them to Kialmasi for church on Sunday."[14] Is it then the sacrifice of women that grounds the male solidarity in the colony? Not at all; such a conventional reading—treating the woman's death as the vehicle for the male reconciliation—would take the melodrama at face value. Although sorrow follows Hedwig's death, there is no shared mourning; Witmann and Forstner remain estranged for quite some time. More important, however, is the profound change in Witmann's character, the disappearance of his authoritarian machismo. That is, although the fictional figure Hedwig certainly dies, woman—understood as the set of antipatriarchal characteristics that Hedwig enfigures—does not perish but lives on instead, now in the persona of a feminized Witmann. No doubt the death is intended to be the traumatic event that might explain such a psychosexual transfiguration, but it is the transformation, not the death, that reconciles the colonist and the missionary, the transsexual and the widower. The novella closes then with a new couple. Forstner accepts Witmann's invitation to spend the night in his home, and ebullient expressions of admiration follow: a beautiful friendship as barely sublimated homoeroticism begins.

From this standpoint, the conflict in the novella takes on a very different light. It is from the start Forstner, not Hedwig, whom Witmann desires: witness the erotic tension of their debates and their verbal embraces. Witness, moreover, the opening incident in which Forstner comes to the aid of Witmann, cast as the classic damsel in distress. Hedwig then turns out to be a device for Witmann to reach his unresponsive beloved and to get to him as well. The hidden story of colonialism, in this text, is the metamorphosis of the Prussian officer into a female companion. The social basis of such a narrative must have involved the real history of sexuality in the colonies, where the German population was overwhelmingly male, and with the discriminated status of homosexual practices and miscegenation. Yet it is precisely these discriminations that erupt into the texts and resonate with the overriding ideological paradigms. Fabri's imagination of colonialism and reproduction echoes through von Bülow's concatenation of female emancipation and colonialism, in which the conventional identities of European culture are freed from their limitations.

This concatenation produces the complexity of the texts that combine discussions of colonialist strategy with an analysis of gender relations, linked by a peculiar sexual economy. For this reason a prominent feminist of the stature of Gertrud Bäumer could appreciate von Bülow as a political author, as the comment from an obituary published in *Die Frau* in 1909 demonstrates: "in contrast to the sort of petty, agitated, and girlish subjectivity current in women's literature, frequently pushing private emotions obstinately and embarrassingly into the center of attention, here [in von Bülow's texts] one finds a great, expansive horizon of real interests."[15] The well-known reference to a "wide field" in Theodore Fontane's *Effi Briest* marked an evasion of conflict and a complicity in repressive strategies directed against women's emancipation and toward the defense of the patriarchal marriage. In contrast, Bäumer suggests that von Bülow's "wide horizon," the horizon of colonialism, is the precondition for the emancipation of woman into national and political life. Thus, she proceeds, "Life in the colonies is not merely the background for emotional developments and internal events; it is truly the main issue. It is a matter of the questions and conflicts of colonial politics, and the work out there is clearly understood in a magnanimous and courageous spirit, a service to the nation, to Germany's duties in the global economy. We feel that the author is fighting, alongside these pioneers of German power and culture, through all the unspeakable difficulties caused by pettiness and bureaucracy at home and the hardships of the conditions out there."[16] Thus, the voice of feminism on the value of empire. Colonialism is clearly not only an opportunity for the patriarchal masculinity of Wilhelmine culture to discover effeminate qualities, mediated by a subliminal homoeroticism. In Bäumer's eyes, and in von Bülow's as well, it is a challenge presented to the German woman to escape her marginalization, indeed, to escape any lingering "girlish subjectivity" or femininity and to enter public life, like a man. In the second of the East African novellas, *Mlinga Goni*, the central figure fails to live up to this challenge, and the text directs attention to the deleterious consequences of the internalized patriarchal value system of her psychology.

Mlinga Goni also presents a balance of public and private matters. The colonial-political theme involves the tension between the entrepreneurial colonist and the cumbersome administrative apparatus. Gerhard Rüdiger, the sole colonial officer at the tiny outpost of Embe Sa Doso on the coast of the Indian Ocean, oversteps his charge by initiating the cultivation of a particularly fertile plot of land that otherwise was lying fallow. Although the representative of the local chieftain had seemingly approved the project, backdoor politics—an example of "native treachery"—leads to the palace of the Sultan of Zanzibar and thence to the colonial office, which reprimands Rüdiger and forces him to abandon the enterprise. The tendentious message is obvious: the colonist could do well with less bureaucratic meddling.

This political material is entwined with gender matters, again structured in a triangle, although with some important differences from the first novella. Rüdiger's friend, Felix Landolf, makes only a cameo appearance. He is the macho adventurer about to rush off onto a perilous expedition into the interior and has come only to request that his wife, Sophie, be allowed to stay at the station for the duration. Landolf disappears before Sophie's arrival, the three points of the triangle are never simultaneously present, and the novella is centrally concerned with the latent attraction between Rüdiger and his guest. Sophie's resignation, largely a result of the disappointing marriage with Landolf, is highlighted by her proximity to Rüdiger, who comes to appear as both the better colonist and the better husband. On both scores he is taken to be capable of the serious commitment that Landolf regularly evades: a good colonist should be a good husband and not a reckless adventurer. Although Landolf is off on another wild escapade in the jungle, Rüdiger nurtures the agricultural development and nearly makes the outpost profitable. Still, the bureaucracy does not support him. Similarly, although Landolf effectively ignores Sophie and despite the fact that Rüdiger appreciates her, she leaves the latter when their friendship threatens to become intimate. In both public and private dimensions, the novella suggests a better option and criticizes the structures that resist it: bureaucratic administration and patriarchal values. The imperial government and the conventions of marriage stand tragically in the way of effective colonization.

If the liaison fails to come to pass, it is not necessarily because of prudishness on von Bülow's part. Elsewhere, in other texts, she was certainly prepared to put adultery in a positive light as a defensible alternative to an inadequate marriage, as for example in *Die stilisierte Frau* (The stylized woman). (This text appeared ten years later, in 1902, and shifting social mores may partially explain the more tolerant treatment.) Moreover, internal textual evidence indicates that Sophie's flight from

Rüdiger is intended to be a failure, not a moral victory. Each partner has a companion: Rüdiger's gardener, Böhne, and Sophie's Goanese servant, Ines. The servants' romance, which parallels their masters', leads to a wedding engagement devoid of complications. Even the topic of miscegenation is avoided fully. Against the background of this utopian union, the failed couple—Sophie's failure to remain with the better husband as a pioneer woman—appears all the more dismal.

Sophie's choice depends neither on a hidden loyalty to Landolf nor especially on a principled loyalty to marriage in general. In other words, the text presents no conventional justification of her refusal of adultery. The point rather is that, for all her attraction to Rüdiger and his colonial undertakings, she misunderstands the emancipatory promise of the colonial setting. At those moments when she most seems to prefer life in Embe Sa Doso to the metropolis, she interprets it in the wrong terms: as a return to "patriarchy"—her term—meant in the sense of personal, familylike relations, a *Gemeinschaft* rather than the alienated *Gesellschaft* of Berlin.[17] That is, the sole alternative she can imagine to Wilhelmine patriarchy is a better, more traditionalist patriarchy, which, however, is not different enough to induce her to leave her husband. From the start rather morbid and attracted to thoughts of death, Sophie comes to the colony fleeing civilization—and the world of her swashbuckling husband—but she arrives as an already broken person. In Embe Sa Doso she encounters a life that would have been better, and she feels its power, but she misunderstands it. She envisions Rüdiger, who might have nurtured her like a mother, as a friendly patriarch. She is, ultimately, the representative of the narrow-minded female subjectivity that the feminist Bäumer criticized for hesitating to step out into the "wider horizons."

In *Der Heilige von Kialmasi* von Bülow presents colonialism as the context for a male effeminization and, implicitly, for homoeroticism as the basis of colonial solidarity. In *Mlinga Goni* colonialism beckons to the woman trapped in a repressive marriage to participate in dimensions of society previously reserved for men. Rüdiger's lack of machismo mirrors Sophie's underscored masculine qualities. Such implicit transsexualism conjoins with the inklings of miscegenation, not only with respect to Böhne and Ines but Sophie as well, whose background is demonstrably obscure. When we finally learn her lineage, it is almost as if von Bülow goes out of her way to ward off the suspicion that she might be a tragic mulatto. Crossing genders, crossing races, crossing borders: the widening horizons of imperialism initiate processes of hybridization that tend to subvert traditional structures of identity. Colonial discourse explores borders and undermines them at the same time.

In *Das Kind*, the last of the East African novellas, the triangle that structured the two previous texts disappears. Instead, the story investigates the metamorphosis of the male colonist into a figure of motherhood, a startling if socially overdetermined transgendering with profoundly beneficial consequences both for his own self-understanding and for the colonial undertaking. Unlike the coastal narratives of the first two novellas, which were concerned with the lability of a liminal presence on the African continent, *Das Kind* is set in the interior on a tobacco plantation, an agrarian world of immense productivity and reproductivity—Fabri's agricultural colony. Instead of the labile settlings on the coast, here Africa has been penetrated and brings forth new life. Lieutenant von Derendorff, overseeing the plantation, rescues a newborn African child about to be sacrificed by his tribe because the complications during labor were interpreted as signs of demonic possession. A deep bonding ensues, and the infant becomes von Derendorff's child. Later, when the plantation is stormed during an anticolonial uprising, von Derendorff rushes to whisk the child Musa out of the line of fire, which so impresses the rebel leader that he magnanimously spares the lives of both.

The clear message of the text is spoken at the conclusion by a Catholic missionary, who is consoling the Protestant von Derendorff for the loss of the plantation. "Dear friend, of what significance is that plantation that the enemy destroyed, now that the much more noble seed that you planted in the hearts of these simpletons has sprouted forth! Keep your head high, Herr von Derendorff! I say to you today: the love that you have planted in the hearts of this poor and forgotten people will someday bring a blessing to you and yours."[18] Exemplary and nurturing behavior as part of a role-modeling cultural imperialism, von Bülow suggests, is more important than holding territory through the power of arms, and only on the basis of such behavior may a long-term colonial success be established. She is not necessarily siding with missionaries against the state, but she is certainly insisting that the stability of the colonies depends on more than the masculinism of military prowess. That increment, however, is by no means primarily a matter of the religious indoctrination that one might expect from a missionary. In *Das Kind* it involves the hermaphroditic reconstruction of von Derendorff. He is both mother and—as the imagery of seed reconfirms—also father; colonialism necessitates a profound modification of the gender codes of Wilhelmine patriarchy and the revaluation of traditionally female qualities. Fabri's obstetric anxiety turns into von Bülow's male mother.

This sort of transformation involves a radical reconstruction of the body as well, and the text effectively begins with alternative typologies of corporeal organization. Von Derendorff's African servant Moritz appears as the thoroughly colonized body: "Moritz wore a sort of servant's uniform, of which he was very proud. It was an Arabian shirt of striped cotton and a broad red wrap for a belt. The black of his face and arms completed the national colors." White shirt, red belt, and black face compose the imperial German flag. The servant is nothing but servant, his body is fully part of his colonized servitude. In contrast, von Derendorff is introduced at a distance from his own body, on which he fixes his vain gaze in a mirror: "Lieutenant von Derendorff was not immune to the charm of his own image in the mirror. 'Too bad that all my admirers here are blacks,' he thought with a self-satisfied smile; 'the tiny details that make up the distinguished man are beyond the grasp of these poor fools.'"[19] To be sure, von Bülow is parodying the preservation of standards of European fashion in the African interior, a standard gesture of *Kolonialliteratur*. Moreover, von Derendorff's racism will be subverted by the course of the text; his illusion that Africans do not appreciate his appearance will be disproved by consequences of his own exemplary behavior, as interpreted in the concluding passage discussed earlier. Most important, however, is the status of his body within von Bülow's master-slave dialectic. Moritz is fully integrated into the colonial project; the color of his face is only part of the colonizer's flag. Von Derendorff still stands at a distance, which is his weakness, for he is dependent on the gaze of another, and it will be the child who will eventually allow him to overcome the melancholy of his mirror-bound narcissism. The male colonist, so it seems, is not complete until he gives birth, and the course of the plot—the ripening fields, the bloody battle, and von Derendorff's awakening from delirium at the mission, as if in a hospital bed—is vivid enough surely to indicate a symbolic rendition of pregnancy and labor.

This reading is confirmed by the account of von Derendorff at the outset. The mirror scene is followed by the foil, Moritz's emblematic body, which in turn introduces von Derendorff's reverie at breakfast:

"A kingdom for a piece of black bread," he sighed, and then he imagined how nice it must be to have a cute little wife, all for himself: a wife who knew how to cook and could bake bread and cake. I would love her enough to eat her up, and she'd of course love me even more. What a life that would be! In the morning she would sit across from me at breakfast, and I could look at her sweet smile, instead of Kyölfen's ugly face [his companion at the plantation]. She puts the best, tastiest pieces of her homemade cake on my plate and coos, "Dearest, try one more!" The fantasy became sharper and all the more seductive. He put his head in his hand and began to think seriously about realizing his dream. But then the other side of the coin came into focus: fanatical cleaning, feverish order, laundry, darning socks! These were the dark points in the heavens

of the feminine. Yet for von Derendorff the horror of hor-
rors was named by the word *nursery*! The thought alone
made him quiver. Babies in diapers with their never-ending crying and complaining and, and . . . he ceased his
considerations.[20]

The passage is worth considering in its entirety because it
describes precisely the problematic psychology that von
Bülow expects to be transfigured in the colonies. The oral fixa-
tion, which conjoins with the narcissism of self-reflection, implies at best the imagination of commitment—he only dreams
of a wife—and resists the threat of genuine physical presence,
the new body of a child. In a sense it is von Derendorff himself
who is the child of the title until he finds fulfillment in the er-
satz childbirth. Not until he renounces his narcissistic fantasies, loses his distance to reality, and begins to nurture (here an
echo of Fabri's anti-idealism as the foundation of colonialism)
does he come into his own as a colonist. The transformation
begins at the moment he rescues the infant; because the rescue
takes place on a river bank where the infant was to be drowned,
von Derendorff, with his conservative Prussian familiarity
with the Bible, makes an allusion to Moses in the bulrushes.
"'That's the way it goes,' he thought, 'I'll just follow the example of the Egyptian princess.'"[21] The child is named Moses, or
Musa, while, in the colonial context, the Prussian officer becomes the African queen.

For von Bülow, this maternalization of the colonist is obviously an imperative of progress within the colonial undertaking: the vain lieutenant grows up only by giving birth. This
fantasy is part of the colonial imagination that conjoins neatly
with Fabri's visions. The colony capable of reproduction is im-
mensely superior to an ad hoc military settlement. In *Das Kind*,
however, this representation of colonialist progress is simultaneously undercut by a parameter that runs counter to von
Bülow's evident intention and subtly denounces it. When he
surveys the plantation, von Derendorff's identification with
the Egyptian princess follows on an earlier reference to the
Mosaic narrative: "He found the view charming again today.

Glowing in the sun and full of promise, the stretch of African earth that he planned to conquer for German culture smiled at him. The fields of the promised land must have once appeared this way at Nebo to the yearning eyes of Moses, the shepherd of his people."[22] That is, the text describes a motion from an initial identification of von Derendorff with the adult Moses to a subsequent identification of Moses as the child Musa, a trajectory of infantilization. This regression leads to the final scene where we find von Derendorff in his sickbed, imagining himself a child again. The encounter of the bedridden lieutenant with the missionary inverts an earlier scene in which a healthy von Derendorff visited a convalescent Kyölfen. Thus, despite the foregrounded message of progress from narcissism to motherhood, the text simultaneously stages a regression from masculine maturity to infantile dependency. The superficial attainment of colonial maturity is undercut by an infantilizing regression: adulthood is the real immaturity.

Yet this regression is a constitutive part of the colonial project. The colonizer too will be colonized, as von Derendorff's distance from his body in the mirror stage is ultimately displaced by the model enfigured by Moritz's corporeal colonization. The text stages a master-slave dialectic in reverse, in that the slave is denied emancipation but the master loses his distance to physical presence, undergoing a parallel degradation. A telltale slip sheds lights on the subsequent universalization of servitude. Naming the child Musa/Moses, von Derendorff remarks, "Have not I too retrieved the child from the river, to which it had been given over, according to the law of its people?" Of course, it was not the law of Moses's "people" that condemned the infant to death but rather the law of the oppressor. Von Derendorff ignores oppression and social difference in general, as in the course of his regression all differences and borders begin to dissolve. The endpoint of this development would be the absolute reduction represented by Moritz, whose body is his master's flag. The colony is consequently also the setting in which religious differences were obscured. Not only do we find a staged reconciliation between the Protestant lieutenant and his Catholic companion—colonialism as the ideological conclusion of the Kulturkampf—but also the envisioned reconciliation of Christians and Moslems, that is, the Islamic rebels around the figure of the infant rather than the man Moses.[23] This too is a deeply Enlightenment motif—the reconciliation of religions in the colony as the site of tolerance.

Von Bülow's investigations into the relationship between gender roles and colonial politics are far from stable or monovocal. Extremely varied results appear: the effeminate colonist, homoeroticism, the critique of patriarchal marriage, the masculinization of women, and the male mother. Despite the three-stage organization of the novella collection, it appears to be less the conclusive dialectic that it was likely meant to be than a laboratory exploration of a monstrous colonial sexuality, a playing through of competing permutations. Ten years later, after her retreat from the colonial undertaking and her turn to "Frauenliteratur"—fiction targeted to a female audience—she nevertheless continued to insist on the connection between the two topical areas. In the novella *Sie und Er* (1902; She and he), von Bülow treats the possibility of a decidedly postpatriarchal modern marriage. Maria is an established photographer and a successful, slightly masculine businesswoman: "How clear her voice, how precise her expressions, how concise and reasonable her directives."[24] Yet her professional obligations prevent her from maintaining her home well, that is, from managing her servants adequately. Jano is a poet, somewhat despondent because he has betrayed his genuine talents by producing more and more for the culture industry. (Indeed, the commercialization of culture, both visual and verbal, is a central concern of the text.) The bonding that eventually ensues is premised on a modern arrangement; Jano will be a "Hausmann," a house husband, so to speak, responsible for domestic affairs to allow Maria to pursue her professional goals.

In our context, however, the key point of interest is Jano's surprising ability to take on his new tasks. He is prepared for the radically modern role of the emancipated male and able to carry out the traditionally female role of commanding domestic servants because he had learned how to run a home of his own in the colonies: "He caught himself imagining an ideal home under his command. He was talented on precisely this score. During a year that he had spent on the southern African coast, he had had a chance to try it out. He had done very well running the house with his blacks and even given small dinner parties. And a very famous German woman who lived there with her husband and who had much less luck keeping house with her niggers often said: 'Herr Jano, you are such an excellent housewife; whenever I eat here, I always think that we women are really superfluous after all.'"[25] In this late text the sexual transformations of the colonial setting are more or less frozen into a stable, nearly mechanistic relationship. Where male colonizers live without women, they learn to command domestic servants. Here too a certain amount of transsexualism is still evident—Jano enjoys remembering himself as a "Hausfrau"—but the reorganization of eroticism and reproductive fantasies of the earlier, colonial novellas has disappeared. Nevertheless, even in this reduced form, the characteristic aspect of von Bülow's texts remains evident. For her colonialism was inseparable from a restructuring of gender relations, in particular, a critique of patriarchal institutions, in a setting far away from the repressive social roles and traditionalist hierarchies of Europe. Colonialism was a project of modernization, not for the colonized, but for the colonists and, especially, for women. That the emancipation of settler women could go hand in hand with hostility toward African women has been ably discussed in a recent study by Marcia Klotz, and it is to settler texts that I now turn.[26]

SETTLER TEXTS

That the colony might be the site of a feminist utopia for settler women—though surely not for colonized women—is certainly counterintuitive. Yet von Bülow's suggestion is an extreme case of an evident congruence of sexual or gendered imaginations within colonial discourse. I have been able to describe some of the consequences of this overlap both in the major agitational text, Fabri's brochure, and in the prose fiction that established *Kolonialliteratur* as a genre. Given this connection, one has good reason to listen closely to Freud's usage of the term *dark continent*, just at the moment when he introduces his theory of sexuality. Indeed, I have tried to show how a set of African images appears at crucial points in his elaboration of the psychoanalytic agenda, as if there, too, Africa was a site of a destabilization of European gender codes. In fact, vernacular records of colonialism confirm the link between sexual anxieties and colonialism. Two of them are poems (the author of one is probably a man; the other is anonymous) found in the state archives in Windhoek, the capital of Namibia and the erstwhile capital of German Southwest Africa. The other two are narratives of female colonists, "pioneer women." These are vernacular texts in the sense that their authors were not primarily literary professionals but rather direct participants in colonial practices, unlike the professional lobbyist Fabri or the once well-received author von Bülow. However, these additional texts reproduce some of the same sexual imagery of established colonial discourse, thereby confirming the hypothesis of a connection between the apparently public and private spheres of colonial politics and sexual fantasy.

Appended to a typed autobiographical narrative, "Humoristic Memoirs from Southwest Africa as a Trooper 1893," one finds a twenty-eight-stanza poem, a ballad entitled "Des Reiters Fluch" (The curse of the rider). A note indicates that the text was either written in or refers to events of May 1894 regarding the establishment of a small outpost during the first campaign against the rebel Hendrik Wittboi. Three German "riders" set up camp near the farm of a wealthy "bastard," that is, a mulatto, and promptly begin to court his daughter, the "Bastardmädchen." Gottfried, who succeeds in seducing her, is ambushed by the father and brother, who castrate him; the ballad concludes with the rider's curse.

The verse is rough, the images hackneyed, the narrative crude. The point, however, is not to judge this vernacular text in terms of belletristic sophistication but to examine its testimony regarding the sexual construction of colonial discourse. Part of this is empirical social history: the overwhelmingly male composition of the colonizing population, the option of miscegenation, tensions between colonizers and colonized on the level of erotic relations and sexual rivalry. (In 1897, Carl Peters—colonial propagandist and Frieda von Bülow's lover—

was expelled from colonial service in the wake of the so-called Kilimanjaro Affair when he murdered an African man for sleeping with his own African lover.) In this text, however, it is the extreme violence of the encounter that is so striking. Succumbing to the seductiveness of Africa is punished by emasculation—hardly the same as the effeminization imagined by von Bülow but adjacent, at least, in defining colonial settlement in sexualized terms.

The second poem is entitled "Bittleid der Windhuker Gemeinde an die Hereros zu den gelungenen Viehdiebstählen am 14. Juli (400 St. Kleinvieh), 17. Juli 1904 (30 St. Grossvieh bei Sperlingslust)" (Plea of the Windhoek community to the Hereros regarding the successful cattle rustling on 14 July [400 small animals], 17 July 1904 [30 large animals near Sperlingslust]). The seven-stanza text registers in a humorous tone a complaint over the loss of cattle, describes the settlers' depleted rations, warns that short-term victories on the part of the Hereros will be punished by German reinforcements, and ends with a plea to leave the remaining cattle alone. The *Gelegenheitsgedicht* in doggerel complements the former poem well. Now the colonist speaks as a mistreated lover, beseeching the "dear, dear Herero" not to be so brutal and to refrain from frightening the community; otherwise, the military will persecute them, that is, play the role of the vengeful father and brother of the *Bastardmädchen*. However, it is in the final stanza, which caps the humor with a punch line, that the underlying anxiety comes to the fore:

> Drum bitten wir Dich jetzt bei Zeit,
> Lieb Herero, sei doch gescheit!
> Gönn Winduk doch die letzte Kuh,
> Und ein paar Hammel noch dazu!
>
> [So we are now asking you,
> Dear Herero, please be smart!
> Please leave Windhoek the last cow,
> And a couple of sheep as well!][27]

The comic effect derives, of course, from the silliness of the rhyme and the exaggerated deference of the request, but it also depends on the tension between *Kuh* and *Hammel*, especially the connotations of the latter term. On one level, it is simply a matter of a rhetorical diminution, a sudden decrease in quantitative value between cow and lamb, beef and mutton. That is, the humor is a consequence of extending the major item into an appended request for small change. On a second level, however, the humor derives precisely from the multivalence of *Hammel*, particularly within the agrarian context of the colonial economy: a wether, that is, a neutered ram, but also, metaphorically, a fool, simpleton, or boor.

The speaker, who has adopted the position of a beleaguered victim making a desperate plea, concludes with the implication that should the Hereros enter into the requested negotiations, it is they who would be fooled and turned into mutton. The *Bittlied* appears then as an attempt to trick what is perceived to be an overpowering force and render it a wether. Yet, if it is the rebels who would be the mutton should they concede to desist, then the precise economic meaning of the term (which is presumably the basis of the connotative reverberations) becomes important. If the Herero is taking away the community's meat, the text conjures up the imminence of castration: the Herero as wether. Simultaneously, it is ostensibly on the contrary the colonist who is threatened and therefore adds his signature to the poem, as wether, in the final verse.

The poem provides an indication of anxiety and nervousness in a besieged settlement of the German colonial wars, and the attempt to master that anxiety with trivial humor proves the point. For the economy of the closing joke depends, at least in part, on sexual imagery that reveals the colony to be the site of a sexual threat or, more precisely, a threat to the gender identity of the colonists. The same transsexualism that was celebrated in von Bülow's prose now takes on the character of a danger from the perspective of a presumably male author. The manifest thematization of military operations—indeed, the full text invokes the inevitable incursion of the German army—gives expression to other anxieties involving the proscribed practices of homosexuality and sexual relations between the colonizing and colonized populations, enfigured as the possibility of castration. Simultaneously, the same anxiety subverts the clear opposition of the drama since the polarization of the Windhoek community and the Hereros tends to disappear in the ambivalence of the wether: is the castration directed at the colonized, as a sort of retribution for their crimes, or at the colonists in the transsexual scenario or is the ultimate subtext altogether different? The blurring of differences in the final words betrays the real experience of the difficulty of maintaining the ideological separation of colonizers and colonized in a context in which mixing is the constant practice despite conventional denials. The rhetorical proximity of an image of race-mixing is particularly noteworthy given the exceptional brutality of the Herero campaign, which was prosecuted by the Germans as a *Vernichtungskrieg*, a war of destruction, with the goal not of subduing the Hereros but of eliminating them.

Similar concatenations of colonialism and castration anxiety are evident in the autobiographical narratives of the female colonists. These are rich documents with detailed if, certainly, biased records of the colonial experience; they are without a doubt chronicles of Wilhelmine culture in an extreme form. In this context, however, the key point of interest is the participation of these female chroniclers in the gendering of the colonial drama. Thus, in Helene von Falkenhausens's *Ansiedlerschicksale: Elf Jahre in Deutsch-Südwestafrika 1893–1904* (1905; Settler experiences: Eleven years in German Southwest Africa 1893–1904), the author insists on the privileged role of women in the Herero uprising that drove her to leave. She portrays African women as diabolical and vicious, with threatening, Fury-like faces. Her accounts of male Hereros are, of course, far from flattering, but she reserves particular venom for the description of the women.

This frightened misogyny is even more constitutive of Elsa Sonnenberg's *Wie es am Waterberg Zuging: Ein Beitrag zur Geschichte des Hereroaufstands* (1905; What happened on the Waterberg: A contribution to the history of the Herero uprising). From her arrival in the colony, Sonnenberg appears to have been traumatized by the encounter with the Herero women:

> I was terrified by the women. My husband left me alone in the wagon at Okanjande because he wanted to visit a settler; then a couple of frightening figures of women came up to me slowly, gesturing vigorously with their hands and berated me rather shamelessly. Every sentence seemed to be a question and generally ended with "Eh?" Their shiny brown oily bodies were

barely covered with a thin and dirty piece of brown leather; they had heavy, coarse iron rings on their weak feet. Beneath their peculiar three-pointed hats, their hair hung down in thin little braids tied with twine. "See that you get away!" I cried fearfully. They laughed, spoke with our boy, called out "morro" to me and slowly limped away to the water.[28]

The contrast with the encounter at Dusky Bay could not be greater: in the place of Cook's Enlightenment invitation, "friend, come hither," Sonnenberg's imperative to depart is blunt. That difference is an indication of the distance between Enlightenment and empire, even if a tendentious criticism would prefer to confuse them today. The key point here, however, is that within colonialism, especially in this set of vernacular texts, a male castration anxiety is complemented by female misogyny. Even the German woman foregrounds the threat stemming from the colonized women. Race appears to be thicker than gender.

Part of this hostility is evidently jealousy and sexual competition. Sonnenberg understands that given the disproportionately male makeup of the German population, African women represented an indisputably erotic attraction. Thus, she complains, "The dearth of white women has extremely negative consequences for the conditions. During my stay in Southwest Africa I unfortunately had to see more of that than I wanted to."[29] This translates initially into physical repugnance at the "disgusting smell of the heathen Herero women."[30] It culminates in an emphasis on the viciousness of women in the rebellion. They are allegedly particularly aggressive: "women in heathen costume" play a central role in the uprising, and later she hears "the terrible howling of women. . . , part of the heathen custom of mourning for the dead."[31] Apparently, even when they mourn, these women are judged by Sonnenberg as incapable of human expressivity, only an animal-like *Geheul*.

Like the poems, these texts are introduced here only as documentations of the gendered character of the colonialist imagination, not as objects for closer literary study or interpretive acrobatics. For the settlers as for the propagandist and the novelist, the colonies were a location of sexual metamorphosis, with one important distinction, however. For Fabri this represented a desirable opportunity to overcome residual idealism, while von Bülow valued the escape from traditional gendered hierarchy—in both cases a sort of cultural progress. In contrast, for the settlers, the metamorphosis represented a mortal threat. The single discourse takes on a different character when viewed from different structural positions; indeed, discourse theory always remains inadequate to the extent that it excludes an analysis of social structure. In particular, colonial discourse would seem to be fraught with an internal division, a class struggle among reactionaries. On the one hand are the propagandists of colonialism, writing largely from the metropolis and arguing with the national interest of the metropolis in mind. On the other are the colonists themselves, funneled into this peculiar form of emigration and confronting both the power of the hegemonic discourse and the real experience of travel into the colonized territories. With this conflicted situation in mind, one can account for the ambivalence in the conclusion of the Windhoek poem as being an expression of the double bind of the colonist, compelled to uphold a metropolitan identity—always a weak metaphor, for the settler in Africa is only by quite liberal extension still a "German"—while placed in a metonymic proximity to the African population.

The experience of threat by the "pioneer women" is particularly interesting since it demonstrates that the gendering of colonialism is not a solely male enterprise. Female colonists also fear the female mass. Despite his presentation of crucial material for the ideological history of fascism, Klaus Theweleit's *Male Phantasies* is flawed on just this point. The construction of the rebellious crowd as somehow female is neither solely a male prerogative nor is it without a prehistory.[32] The appearance of the same material in colonial texts suggests the wide-ranging sexual anxiety behind the political developments in early-twentieth-century Germany. The connection between colonial fantasies and fascist fantasies is, moreover, hardly accidental. The administrative strategies and dehumanizing ideologies of the colonies were part of the origins of totalitarianism, as Hannah Arendt has argued.[33] The connection is extremely tight for the material discussed in this chapter: as mentioned, the suppression of the Herero uprising was waged as a *Vernichtungskrieg*, a war of annihilation, and by its conclusion the population had dwindled—from death in battle as well as starvation and disease—to less than one quarter its original size. Furthermore, Eugen Fischer, head of the Institute for Racial Hygiene in Berlin during the Third Reich, began his "scientific" career with a study of the "bastards" in Southwest Africa.[34] The colonial anxiety about miscegenation would seem to be the genuine precursor of the Nürnberg laws. If sexual fantasies in colonial discourse appear to anticipate the gynophobia of the fascists, it is in part because colonialism represented the proving ground for fascism more broadly. The connection is particularly compelling when—as with the material presented in this chapter—the colonial enterprise is set off from Enlightenment rationality and presented instead as an organic world of mythic fertility. Colonialist ideology generates this notion of a self-enclosed world, which is the precondition for encountering outsiders as exotic, radically different, and, ultimately, incompatible and menacing.

A radical reorganization of spatiality has taken place, and it is useful to retrace the process with reference to some of the texts treated thus far. The itinerant rationality of the Enlightenment explores a transparent space whereby a dialectic commences that has been associated with the alternative models of Forster and Cook. For the transparency of space in the two models differs considerably. For Forster it implies a universal rationality, grounded in religious faith and indicating the fundamental comprehensibility of all human endeavors. These are understood to be richly diverse—diverse in the sense of reflecting a multiplicity of particular cultures and diverse in that each particular locale is the locus of a multidimensional life world encompassing physical experience, ethical and cultural pragmatics, aesthetic interiority, and transcendence. Cook's geometric rationality, in contrast, evacuates the world: it is transparent because it is empty and flat, a surface to be charted and, certainly, eventually controlled. This evacuation, the production of empty space by a truncated Enlightenment, is the context for the subsequent expeditions. The travelers pass through an empty expanse according to the laws of a Galilean physics, isolated bodies in frictionless space, where every action produces a reaction: Tewodros's hostage taking and Napier's response. Yet it is there that an inversion begins to take place. Although Rohlfs, the paranoid descriptivist, commences his Abyssinian narrative with an account of isolation in the passage to Africa, Stanley, the brash American journalist, staged a world bursting at its seams, full of things if not of subjects. Colonialism entails, first, an initial purge to produce an empty space—in 1799 the "attentive man" of Dusky Bay had mysteriously disappeared in the context of a decidedly patriarchal rationality. Second, it entails its subsequent occupation by a specifically colonial world, a repopulation that sets itself off from the patriarchal Cartesianism (its own prerequisite) in order to produce a world of cyclical reproduction, a settler colony. Within this world borders dissolve and transgressive practices are constant. Yet the same world in fact presumes the establishment of a new border with which it is closed off, round and full, and outside of which material exists that is, by definition, extraworldly: exotic, primitive, a threatening nature, and an irrational numinousness. For Forster the friends at Dusky Bay were strange at first but by no means beyond the scope of a cosmopolitan reason. A century later, from within the colonial world the external—Tewodros the barbarian or the Herero women with their undisciplined questioning and threatening gestures—is necessarily and by definition beyond reason. It is at this point that colonialism produces, as an effect of its own constitution, the exoticism of alterity.

6

THE MYTH OF ANTICOLONIALISM

E mpire and Enlightenment were intertwined from the start. We have seen how Captain Cook, mapping out the oceans for the British Crown, was accompanied by Georg Forster and his father, generating a scientific record, just as we can trace the complicity of science and discourses of progress—and by no means only scientific or technological progress—in the penetration of Africa in the nineteenth century. The mobilization of German public support for colonial engagement through the antislavery movement was couched in terms as humanitarian as those familiar from contemporary, postcolonial, and post–Cold War debates over West European reengagement in Africa and elsewhere. From the age of discovery to the counterinsurgency at the end of the colonial era, European expansion has relied on the collaboration of intellectuals, the carriers of Enlightenment, just as modern, post-Enlightenment intellectuality has presupposed a universalized space in which a transcendental reason could claim global validity. Does this complicity indicate a tight and univocal linkage? Can we equate Enlightenment—the faith in reason, the validity of science, and the labor of intellectuals—with empire?

This is, of course, the claim of much contemporary cultural theory derived from poststructuralism, ranging from the work of Jacques Derrida to that of Michel Foucault (as different as their visions are), both of whom lay blame at the doorstep of reason. In that case logocentricity and imperialism become indistinguishable, the rejection of Western metaphysics is a sine qua non for dismantling colonialism, and the postcolonial setting is properly understood as subsequent to established structures of Western thought—postintellectual. If Enlightenment and Enlightenment intellectuals make colonialism, then colonialism can only be undone by doing away with Enlightenment rationality and its cerebral purveyors: off with the heads.

There are, however, obviously some extraordinary problems with this line of thought that would imply, for instance, the impossibility of the notion of a postcolonial intellectual, surely an unacceptable result that forces a reexamination of the legitimacy of the polemically tight linkage between colonialism and Enlightenment. If Enlightenment qua intellectuality can survive colonialism, then the relationship between Enlightenment and colonialism must be more complex than initially assumed: complicitous often enough, but perhaps not always, and definitely not identical. Knowledge is not only power. Forster's sailing with Cook does not mean that we cannot tell them apart or that the difference between them is irrelevant; and Cook's service does not make him the same as Cecil Rhodes, who in turn is not the same as Jean-Marie Le Pen. This series is certainly not intended to indicate something like gradations of evil but rather the need for a complex and differentiated understanding of politics, including the dynamic processes of imperial politics.

Broad-brush attacks on colonialism or on the role of intellectuals, Eurocentrism, or Enlightenment in it are less than useful. There may or may not be sound philosophical grounds for an attack on logocentrism, taken as the legacy of the Enlightenment; to politicize such attacks opportunistically makes for imprecise philosophy and even more obtuse politics. Recall Derrida's flaccid treatment of apartheid. Beginning with an obviously Heideggerian move, he focuses on the etymology of the term, specifically, the capacity of Western language to form generalizing substantives in *-heid*. These are derived, so he suggests, from underlying philosophical assumptions—the assumptions of post-Socratic theory—

about the relationship between concepts and the real that are, he goes on to argue, the root causes of South African racial politics. He writes, "the glaring harshness of abstract essence (*heid*) seems to speculate in another regime of abstraction, that of confined separation. The word concentrates separation, raises it to another power and sets separation itself *apart*: 'apartitionality,' something like that. By isolating being apart in some sort of essence of hypostasis, the word corrupts it into a quasi-ontological segregation."[1] Therefore, if we follow his line of reasoning, there could have been no genuine change in the apartheid system until there was a radical change in the language, by which he must mean much more than a new set of campaign slogans—more like a complete overhaul of a grammar based on a subject-object paradigm. Otherwise, one remains in the fallen world of logocentricity.[2] The advantage to such an account is that it provides deconstruction with an opportune political spin and one, moreover, that distracts from the embarrassing proximity between deconstruction's antiuniversalist theorization of difference and apartheid's own antiuniversalist ideology of separate development. Deconstruction's celebration of difference, like de Man's attacks on equality, sounds uncannily close to the former politics of Pretoria.[3] The disadvantage, however, is that this strong linkage between logocentricity and colonialism—blaming apartheid on Western metaphysics—is fully incapable of accounting for the real political process through which apartheid is being dismantled.

Yet the problem is hardly restricted to poststructuralism and deconstruction. When Derrida forces the connection between apartheid and reason—clearly, a particular instance of colonialism and Enlightenment—he is effectively undertaking a rhetorical linkage that concatenates two distinct tropes in order to redirect the moral authority derived from the critique of apartheid into an attack on the intellectual. To explore the hidden agenda behind this move, one must, however, move beyond Derrida. If the strict identification of Enlightenment with colonialism suggests a corollary equation of anticolonialism and the critique of the Enlightenment—to attack colonialism it appears imperative to attack Enlightenment and Enlightenment intellectuals—then when does the critique of colonialism begin to become a vehicle for, perhaps even only a pretext for, attacks on intellectuals. Indeed, when is anticolonialism just an alibi for anti-intellectualism? If the intellectual, as the agent of Enlightenment, is presumed guilty for colonialism (since colonialism is allegedly generated by intellectuals engaging in Western metaphysics), then an occasion for anticolonialism is as fine an opportunity as any to go after the intellectual. If, however, the strict connection between intellectuals and colonialism proves untenable, then, mutatis mutandis, so does the politicized critique of Western metaphysics, which becomes a one-dimensional identification of Enlightenment and power, and so forth. What is the relationship between Western culture and Western colonies? The locus classicus for this discussion is Jean-Paul Sartre's 1961 introduction to Frantz Fanon's *The Wretched of the Earth*. A close examination of the representation of colonialism within the rhetoric of Sartre's anticolonialism will eventually allow us to further clarify the features of colonial discourse. The attack on the Enlightenment ends up as a turn to myth, the myth of anticolonialism.

It is not the real practice of anticolonialism in the political culture of the Algerian revolution nor the substance of Fanon's argument that is at stake here but anticolonialism as an aspect of Sartre's position and its relevance to a judgment on intellectuals and European thought. Sartre makes this distinction himself, indicating that Fanon is addressing his African compatriots without regard for a European readership, to which Sartre, by way of contrast, directs his own remarks. The articulation of anticolonialism, in other words, proceeds on the basis of a rigorous separation of the two readerships, and I will return soon to this capacity of anticolonialism to engage in the same segregationist strategies of which it accuses the colonialist regime.

Sartre unfolds his argument, so he suggests, because he sees Europe facing an impending catastrophe—"She's done for," he writes in 1961, as if the catastrophe of fascism and the Holocaust had not already taken place—and to convince his readers (as distinct from Fanon's) to support and join the anticolonial revolution.[4] The grounds for European solidarity are, from the start, fully distinct from whatever may be the motivation of the Algerian fighters. Sartre's argument reproduces this distinction internally, as he relies on two separate but related themes: the complicity of humanism in colonialism and the insufficiency of idealism in politics.

"Not so very long ago," so the text begins, "the earth numbered two thousand million inhabitants: five hundred million men, and one thousand five hundred million natives. The former had the Word; the others had the use of it."[5] Sartre's map invokes, to use Abdul JanMohamed's term, a Manichean distinction: word and deed, theory and practice, illusion and reality.[6] Yet despite the surplus materiality ascribed to the second, colonized position, the narrative of colonialism presented by Sartre does not, surprisingly enough, begin with brute force or brutal instrumentalization but rather with "the Word" and the role of cultural imperialism in the institutionalization of colonialism. Instead of beginning the story with the military occupation of territory or economic penetration, Sartre locates the fall into colonialism in the educational sector. Power does not grow out of the barrel of a gun; it comes from matriculation: "The European elite undertook to manufacture a native elite. They picked out promising adolescents; they branded them, as with a red-hot iron, with the principles of Western culture; they stuffed their mouths full with high-sounding phrases, grand glutinous words that stuck to their teeth. After a short stay in the mother country they were sent home, whitewashed. These walking lies had nothing left to say to their brothers; they only echoed. From Paris, from London, from Amsterdam we would utter words 'Parthenon! Brotherhood!' and somewhere in Africa or Asia lips would open '. . . thenon! . . . therhood!' It was the golden age."[7] Sartre thus dismisses education, especially the humanistic education of Western culture, as simply a vehicle of Western power. He must denounce as delusional the positive engagement of nonwhite intellectuals with the cultural legacy of Europe, such as W. E. B. Du Bois's insistence in *The Souls of Black Folk* that "I sit with Shakespeare and he winces not. Across the color line I move arm in arm with Balzac and Dumas, where smiling men and welcoming women glide in gilded halls. From out the caves of evening that swing between the strong-limbed earth and the tracery of the stars, I summon Aristotle and Aurelius and what soul I will, and they come all graciously with no scorn nor condescension."[8] For Sartre, Du Bois's appreciation of European culture is a delusion and a result of colonialism.

In the course of the essay, Sartre suggests a history of colonialism: starting from this golden age through an awakening of the colonized population to consciousness and then to resistance, violence, and emancipation. And there is evidently much in the narrative that derives from Hegelian phenomenology and its narrative of emancipation. In this history, however, it is noteworthy that it is culture that stands at the beginning rather than, say, invasion and subjugation or commerce and exploitation. In classic nineteenth-century debates, some, and by no means only Marxists, saw the economy as the root of society, whereas others, ranging from conservatives to anarchists, pointed to violence and political power. The altercation between Friedrich Engels and Eugen Dühring is only one of the better-known sites of this controversy.[9] It is, by way of contrast, a feature of twentieth-century intellectual life that intellectuals see themselves as the center, rather than violence or economics. Thus, the animus of Sartre's argument, in other words, is directed precisely against culture and idealism—the Parthenon and Brotherhood—where he locates the root of all evil, thereby betraying a philosophical provenance very different from the idealist Hegel and one that is fundamentally antihumanistic. For now Sartre is asserting that the problem is not really a matter of the imposed humanism, violently forced onto the "native elite" of the colonies. Nor is it a result of a false humanism, sometimes dismayingly hypocritical despite genuinely sterling intentions. It is rather a question of humanistic idealism all together, which in its purest form is for Sartre necessarily and essentially mendacious and ineluctably guilty. Thus, Sartre:

> With us, to be a man is to be an accomplice of colonialism, since all of us without exception have profited by colonial exploitation. This fat, pale continent ends by falling into what Fanon rightly calls narcissism. Cocteau became irritated with Paris—"that city which talks about itself the whole time." Is Europe any different? And that super-European monstrosity, North America? Chatter, chatter: liberty, equality, fraternity, love, honor, patriotism, and what have you. All this did not prevent us from making anti-racial speeches about dirty niggers, dirty Jews, and dirty Arabs . . . with us there is nothing more consistent than a racist humanism since the European has only been able to become a man through creating slaves and monsters.[10]

Sartre's "chatter, chatter" is of course nothing other than the "idle talk" of Heidegger's *Gerede*, the devalued speech of the trivial experience in a leveled society, cut off from authenticity.[11] The discourse of intellectuals is equivalent to empty gossip. Humanism is false not because it fails on exceptional occasions to live up to its ideals (a possible liberal criticism of specific instances) but because it is constitutively implicated in a degraded existence that separates the word from its use and the colonizer from the colonized. Enlightenment, with its insistence on logical speech and the validity of reason, is equated with imperialism. The alternative to colonialism is therefore not amelioration through humanism and egalitarianism—say, social reforms, free elections, or political independence—but only the qualitatively new, the radical alterity beyond European discourse and beyond intellectuals. Something like freedom could only begin when Europe comes to an end.

The inadequacy of Sartrean anticolonialism is evident in its simultaneous denunciation of Enlightenment categories, such as egalitarianism, and its constant reliance on a model of emancipation. Here, however, one point is particularly urgent. Drawing on a Heideggerian and, ultimately, deeply romantic figure of absolute difference, Sartre sets non-European existence at an infinitely exoticized distance from the Western metaphysics that the colonizer presumes as normalcy. Leaving aside the logical and highly political consequence that such distance undercuts any claim to equality or normative principles, one can identify the gesture as a Rousseauian allegiance to a noble savage, which, however, is an extraordinary fiction to find at the heart of a militant anticolonialism. Moreover, in earlier chapters, I have identified exoticism and, in general, an insistence on absolute alterity as themselves artifacts of colonial discourse and hardly as some "outside" or "other" to colonialism. In other words, Sartre's anticolonial rage is trapped from the start in a logical error within the discourse of colonialism itself. By insisting on the absolute incompatibility—the difference—of colonizer and colonized, it reproduces the segregation it pretends to oppose. By jettisoning universalism anticolonial rhetoric magnifies the myths of its opponents and lays the groundwork for postcolonial states as violent as the colonies. This process is nevertheless worthy of some closer examination, precisely because it will allow us to focus on the status of colonial discourse and its critics.

This is how Sartre describes a new beginning, stripped of the presumed dogmas of Western culture:

> Europeans, you must open this book and enter into it. After a few steps in the darkness you will see strangers gathered around a fire; come close, and listen, for they are talking of the destiny they will mete out to your trading centers and to the hired soldiers who defend them. They will see you, perhaps, but they will go on talking among themselves, without even lowering their voices. This indifference strikes home: their fathers, shadowy creatures, *your* creatures, were but dead souls; you it was who al-

lowed them glimpses of light, to you only did they dare speak, and you did not bother to reply to such zombies. Their sons ignore you; a fire warms them and sheds light around them, and you have not lit it. Now, at a respectful distance, it is you who will feel furtive, nightbound, and perished with cold. Turn and turn about; in these shadows from whence a new dawn will break, it is you who are the zombies.[12]

An original scene of existentialist politics as the grounds for anticolonialism: for Sartre, colonizer and colonized have nothing in common. No "friend, come hither" might draw them together; they are separated by a gulf of absolute difference. In Sartre's view it is not, for example, injustice that drives the struggle, for that might imply a universal notion of justice or at least international law—mere chatter for liberal lawyers. Nor is it economic calculation, profit and loss, or the politics of the working-class movement—trivial materialism, so very close to European "narcissism." What is at stake is instead the eruption of radical alterity. In the darkness of being there is a clearing of *Dasein* dimly glowing, where a new destiny, a new discourse, and a new language take place, fully indifferent to European legacies and therefore fully incommensurable. To judge it in terms of humanism could only mean to police it and denounce it, but, in any case, such a judgment would necessarily be incongruous, for the new language is absolutely different. It is Sartre's restaging of Heidegger's *Origin of the Work of Art*, an original leap to a new language, for Europe absolutely unspeakable. Therefore, his European reader fades into a ghostlike silence.

In fact, Sartre's account has a hybrid character, for the Heideggerian originality is still located within a prior history, the Hegelian master-slave struggle between colonizer and colonized. If the colonizer is excluded from participation, barred by the limits of European culture, he is still invited to read and watch. Existentialist politics still leave some room for agitprop as an operative vehicle to surpass the past and enter the alterity of postcolonialism. Yet for Sartre that will require more than just the renunciation of the old culture and European hegemony. It will require the new deed, the act of violence that makes the renunciation real: a nonviolent revolution is none at all. "When the peasant takes a gun in his hands, the old myths grow dim and the prohibitions are one by one forgotten. The rebel's weapon is the proof of his humanity. For in the first days of the revolt you must kill: to shoot down a European is to kill two birds with one stone, to destroy an oppressor and the man he oppresses at the same time: there remain a dead man, and a free man: the survivor, for the first time, feels a *national* soil under his feet."[13] Liberation, in other words, does not derive—or does not derive solely—from the post-European discourse, that is, it is not the production of anticolonial intellectuals. On the contrary, it derives from the radical deed, whereby deed is the radical other to intellectuality. It is not a different "Word" that the anticolonial fighter mobilizes in the act of violence but something very different from "Word" altogether: the post-logocentric bullet. The discursive critique of a Eurocentric culture remains insufficient, so Sartre argues, as long as it remains merely cultural criticism and does not enter a postintellectual realm of action.

Before proceeding further with the critique of anticolonialism, attention has to be directed to this particular point, Sartre's characterization of the surpassing of the word as a constitutive gesture in the liberation struggle of the colonized. In this argument, antilogocentricity takes a particularly activist turn, that is, it is not the idealist insistence on coherence nor the structure of logical sequentiality that is at stake but the distinction between conceptual thinking as ideal and a materialism of action, and Sartre codes the latter as anticolonialist. Yet it is precisely this coding that is untenable, since it derives from a long tradition that has itself been implicated in colonial discourse. The exhortation to transcend impractical cultural dimensions and to bring an end to the figure of the intellectual—a conclusion to which Sartre must come if he equates colonialism and Enlightenment culture—is surely archaic and itself grounded in civilizational structures of repression. Recall the animosity directed to Socrates for resisting Alcibiades's charms in *The Symposion*. Like the end of art or the end of philosophy, the end of the intellectual—and the critique of the Enlightenment—is a highly cultured fiction that gives expression to the discontents in civilization in a sophisticated way. It is, however, not unrelated to standard anti-intellectualism as a resistance to expressions of the same discontent one experiences. The critical intellectual who names suffering may be attacked, as if by silencing the messenger the problem itself would disappear (a key subtext in Freud's discussion of Boabdil, the fall of Alhama, and his own disturbance of memory at the Acropolis). In the more specific context of this discussion, it is important to remember how early-nineteenth-century idealism was constantly tempted and haunted by its own outside, its successor or opposite: "die Tat zu Deinem Gedanken." It was this deed subsequent to thought that Heine encounters with prudent trepidation in his *Wintermärchen*, that underlies the fateful urgency of action in Marx's eleventh thesis on Feuerbach, or—a perhaps unexpected corollary but nonetheless homologous—that explains Bismarck's master trope of iron and blood as an alternative to the infinite and inconsequential debates of parliamentary language.[14]

The historical discourse of colonialism participates in precisely the same rhetoric. Overseas possessions become the real opportunity to end philosophy, to escape idealism, and finally to undertake action in the real world. Indeed, the activist gesture that Sartre posited as the alternative to the isolated word, with its greater existentialist authenticity and its anticolonialist potential, was precisely the same gesture that colonialist publicists invoked to mobilize potential settlers. They were to go to the colonies not as indolent idealists but rather to escape the immobility and inactivity of the Old World. The priority of existence over essence explains the attraction of the colonies as an alternative to the inauthenticity of the metropolitan home. Friedrich Fabri's master text of German colonialist propaganda, *Bedarf Deutschland der Colonien?* (1879), in fact commences by complaining that German scholarship has heretofore been too idealist—compelling in its capacity for knowledge and unsurpassed in academic quality but hopelessly uninterested in the consequences of its work, which is why Britain and France could benefit from the labor of German geographers while Germany stood on the sidelines without a colonial empire.[15] Similarly, Frieda von Bülow can suggest that colonialism offers a possibility to escape the vacuity and enervation of a rarefied European society—a chance, finally, to act, to meet real challenges, and to engage in physical labor, understood as a cultural therapy in a land of unlimited opportunity. In other words, both Fabri and von Bülow, prime exponents of nineteenth-century German colonial discourse, ground the colonial mission in an effort to surpass idealism that is hardly different from the activism that Sartre propounded. On this score at least then, colonialism is just as postintellectual as existentialist anticolonialism, which in turn points to the political inappropriateness of Sartre's attack on Enlightenment idealism. Although he and subsequent thinkers blame "the Word," that is, conceptual thinking, and the Enlightenment for colonialism, it is perfectly clear that colonialism depended on precisely the same anticonceptualism and anti-idealism as does Sartre.

Thus far, the point has been to inquire into the status of the intellectual and the Enlightenment within the critique of colonialism. We have seen that anticolonialism, at least for Sartre, entailed a denunciation of intellectuals quite similar to Derrida's attacks on logocentricity, which would tend to confirm the strong linkage between colonialism and Enlightenment posited at the outset. Yet it is precisely this linkage that is challenged by the discovery that the same gesture of surpassing idealism, Enlightenment, and intellectuality is part and parcel of an earlier rhetoric in support of colonialism. Perhaps the tight linkage is beginning to snap. Indeed, it appears to be the case that the specifically French discourse of anticolonialism has less to do with the realities or history of colonialism than with a critique of European culture, and the moral authority of the intellectuals' anticolonialism derives in part from an asynchronicity. That is, the opposition to colonialism is so great because the prior inability—at least in Sartre's case—to resist the German occupation was so embarrassing, whereas for Derrida a generation later the association with Heidegger itself became a political liability that could only be corrected with the emphatic stance on apartheid. French anticolonialism, in other words, became a myth, displacing the myth of the Résistance, which had itself been occupied by the political establishment. The attack on colonialism or on apartheid was merely a political trapping to disguise an underlying hostility to a particular formation of intellectuality.

In light of his activist imperative—the urgency of action— one can argue that Sartre's account is at odds with itself, blurring the difference between, on the one hand, the productivist activism derived from Fichte by way of Hegel and Marx (the need to act) and, on the other, Heidegger's focus on language (the priority of culture). Is the point to abandon the intellectual contents of European culture, such as humanism, or is it a matter of surpassing culture—the autonomy of "the Word"— altogether," in order to carry out the deed? What is the complex nature of the anticolonial process? How will the character of the struggle affect the outcome? Sartre ignores these difficult questions. Once colonialism and intellectuality (read, power and culture) are neatly collapsed into each other, anticolonialism can be giddily free of intellectual reflection. For Sartre, violence is not a *via dolorosa*, chosen reluctantly; it is the royal road to freedom, celebrated as both means and ends: "The war, by merely settling the question of command and responsibility, institutes new structures which will become the first institutions of peace. Here, then, is man even now established in new traditions, the future children of a horrible present; here then we see him legitimized by a law which will be born or is born each day under fire: once the last settler is killed, shipped home, or assimilated, the minority breed disappears, to be replaced by socialism."[16] That is one way, certainly, to address multiculturalism and the viability of minorities in society. Indeed, Sartre's celebration of violence clearly anticipates postcolonial intolerance: that "the minority breed disappears" turns out to be quite predictive for parts of francophone Africa.

Yet aside from the question of whether minorities could have ever survived socialism, the passage highlights a crucial point in the activist turn away from philosophy and toward violence. Sartre could not be clearer in stating and, indeed, applauding the fact that the institutions of the new society would be based precisely on the "question of command and responsiblity"—that is, the obedience structures of military behavior are adopted as the paradigm of emancipation. War or, more generally, violence is therefore not a Clausewitzian extension of politics but the genuine form of all politics, characterized by an instrumentalized activism, which in turn is defined as an alternative to the anemic "Word" of idealism.

This is precisely where Arendt's critique of Sartre set in.[17] Following orders and doing the deed, in particular, the violent deed, is the desideratum for Sartre rather than judging the act or its particular substance. One brings European intellectuality, inculpated in colonialism, to an end when the European intellectual foregoes judgment. Sartre's passing nod to Georges Sorel, juxtaposed to Engels, is resonant enough, just as his celebration of violence is closer to Ernst Jünger than to Clausewitz. Although Sartre does claim the importance of using "every means" to put an end to colonialism, in context he is not concerned with a diversity of means (which might begin with diplomacy, for example) but rather with the readiness to reach immediately for the one and only authentic means, the ultimate means, violence, which becomes an end in itself, the genuine alternative to the chatter of intellectuals.[18]

The dismissal of the degraded speech of the Enlightenment cannot help but call to mind Cook's denigration of the islanders' "chit-chat" and, especially, the loquaciousness of the young woman. The prohibition against the speech of "the subaltern," to follow Gayatri Chakravorty Spivak's cultural theory, is the point at which colonial practice and anticolonial myth converge. The purported resistance against Western structures of individualism is quite compatible with invidious patterns of hierarchy, which depend on codes of both race and gender.[19] Thus, Sartre's dubious equation of anticolonialism and the end of intellectuality inherits a clearly gendered legacy. The conventional metaphor of the colonial relationship is gendered—the metropolitan center is referred to as the "mother country"—and Sartre adopts it uncritically. Or does he not in fact adopt it intentionally and eagerly? "In the colonies the truth stood naked," he writes in the first paragraph, "but the citizens of the mother country preferred it with clothes on: the native had to love them, something in the way mothers are loved."[20] In fact, the translator has made the case for Sartre worse than it might have been. For the French original does not speak of a "mother country" but only of the metropolitans; nevertheless, the invocation of the pejorative love of mothers is purely Sartre's own vicious fantasy: "Aux colonies la vérité se montrait nue; les 'métropoles' la préféraient vêtue; il fallait que l'indigène les aimât. Comme des mères en quelque sorte."[21] But how are mothers loved? Evidently, they are clothed, but that indicates a concealment, whereby a truth authentic enough to satisfy Sartre might be reached only through violation. Clearly, the anticolonial struggle is cast as a rejection of the enveloping vagaries of mother love, which Sartre speaks of with revealing disgust. "Here, the mother country is satisfied to keep some feudal rulers in her pay; there, dividing and ruling she has created a native bourgeoisie, sham from beginning to end; elsewhere she has played a double game."[22] Colonialism as female cunning: no wonder then that when Sartre goes on to personify Europe as a sick woman, he can report that Fanon, as a doctor, "certifies that she is dying, on external evidence, founded on symptoms that he can observe. As to curing her, no; he has other things to think about; he does not give a damn whether she lives or dies."[23] For the real goal is "the new man," and even if we were to grant Sartre the innocent usage of *l'homme* as a generic designation for an ungendered human, it is striking how Sartre frames this man's emergence with misogynist figures of the "massacre of women and children."[24] The socialist metaphor of the revolution as birth pangs has been transformed, and anticolonialism becomes a male fantasy of violence with an unambiguously gendered program for masculinist freedom.

Sartre celebrates anticolonialism as a misogynist undertaking designed to escape the stifling clutches of the mother country. The same gendered metaphor in the background operates differently in the era of high colonialism. For Fabri the underlying concern is the potential loss of parts of the national body, the masses of emigrants who could be bound to the mother through a system of settler colonies. (Indeed, Fabri is driven by his vision of the German population lost to the United States, Canada, and Australia, and it is difficult to dispute that nineteenth-century German social and cultural history is one of emigration. It was less an era of the construction of national identity than a flight from it by Hessians, Saxonians, and Hanoverians who did not want to become Prussian-Germans—but why were those who settled on Cherokee land less colonial than those who occupied Herero territory?) From this perspective, colonial discourse appears to be a conservative effort to preserve the historical organism of the nation, whereas anticolonialism envisions the radically new through ultimate disruptions—breaking with the mother, killing the settler, the new man born in violence (but strangely motherless). Both operate within the gendered terms set up by the same master metaphor, and each is obsessed with the question of separation— Fabri's fear of loss of members of the nation, Sartre's compulsion to separate in order to achieve manhood. If the implicit psychoanalytic imagery is similar, the Manichean distinction between colonial and anticolonial discourse begins to become destabilized precisely because of the shared structures, even though the explicit political positions are far apart.

It is, however, von Bülow who initiates a tectonic shift in the gender code of colonialism by bypassing the master metaphor and exploring the subtleties of gender construction within colonial practice. The key text, as we have seen, is *Das Kind*, which sheds light on the full constellation of intellectuality, colonialism, and gender.[25] Von Bülow constructs the central fig-

ure, Lieutenant von Derendorff, the colonial manager of a tobacco plantation in the East African highlands, as an intellectual—reflective and introverted, colonial in his constant nostalgia for the homeland—and he is contrasted to the African
servants, posed as absolute corporeality. Here, Sartre's distinction between word and deed appears to hold, or it holds until
the very character of the colonial experience begins to undercut the binary opposition and transform the European intellectual. Like any other semiotic system, colonial discourse or colonial ideology is not immune to the impact of colonial
experience, which is, after all, the experience of a radical alterity. Ideology proclaims the absolute separation of colonizer
and colonized, but all historical accounts point toward a more
complex reality of ongoing and diverse interaction. This complexity is occluded by anticolonial depictions that depend on
tropes borrowed from colonial discourse itself with only a
change of the value sign. In other words, anticolonialism—
one of the grand ideologies of the twentieth century—is dependent on its opponent, colonial discourse, from which it
borrows binary structures and the imaginary of absolute separations. Yet anticolonialism reifies those separations, taking
them at face value, whereas for colonial discourse they were in
fact vehicles to mask the reality of transgression and intermin-
gling. The ideological imperatives of anticolonialism prevent
it from recognizing the hybrid realities of colonialism.

The reality of variegated contact between colonizers and
colonized, including intimate sexual contact, was hardly a se-
cret in the colonial era, and a good deal of conservative moral
pressure was mobilized to agitate against miscegenation. If the
literature of the period is less explicit, conventional prudishness is part of the explanation. Nevertheless, von Bülow's novella is after all about the German man, a Prussian officer, with
an African child. It is, in this safely conventional fiction,
adopted to be sure, so there is no need for an African mother,
but gender politics are destabilized in an extraordinary way.
For when von Derendorff, the intellectual colonizer, rescues
the child from drowning, the text places him explicitly in the

female role as mother, a rather emphatic reversal of the masculinist associations surrounding the figure of a Prussian officer. Consider the difference: Sartre's anticolonial fighter is born without a mother through acts of violence, whereas von Bülow constructs a parentage through a feminizing colonialism. To the extent that the novella can be read as a prescriptive commentary, its author is advocating a particular position within colonialism against the militarized versions that would preserve German territories through force of arms—such as the genocidal Herero war. She is therefore proposing a less instrumentalized, more nuanced relationship that would entail complex human involvements. The anticolonial critic would denounce this as paternalism, with considerable legitimacy, except that the gender of the term is wrong. Yet what anticolonialism thereby misses, of course, is the fact of the diversity of human relations within colonialism, which the ideology of colonialism would prefer to ignore and the opponents of colonialism declare impossible.

In contrast, for von Bülow colonialism is a site of gender ambiguity, an emancipatory alternative to the rigid codes of Europe. Therefore, in other texts it is precisely former colonizers returned to the metropolis that prove more progressive in gender relations. Just as the lieutenant could become a mother, the writer in *Sie und Er*, who had spent time in Africa, is capable of running a household and is therefore ready to support his wife's choice to pursue a career—in 1900! In both cases, furthermore, von Bülow is concerned with intellectuals who through colonial encounters are deeply transformed, gaining new dimensions of affective capacity. Intellectuality, of the inherited, conservative sort, is indeed subjected to criticism—it is masculinist and trivial—but it is transformed and redefined through feminization in the colonies.

In addition to the gender-theoretical implications of this claim (which has striking ramifications for the contemporary issues of race and gender: colonization as a vehicle for women's progress), it is important to note how the colonial site is becoming much more complex than in standard, anticolonial accounts. It is not the clear and direct product of Western meta-physics or Eurocentric culture (as the critics of logocentrism would have it), nor is it absolutely outside familiar experience (as national racists would argue to justify their own hetero-phobia). It is instead a site, indisputably, of conflict and vio-lence but also one of contest, exchange, negotiation, hybrid-ization, and change. Because of this complexity of the colonial setting and its discursive articulations, the crudely Manichean anticolonialism of French existentialism is incapable of pro-viding an adequate description, let alone criticism. German material becomes interesting precisely because of the ambig-uous positionality of German and Austrian culture within Eu-rope, but somehow at its margins or, at least, at a distance from the metropolitan sites of major colonial power in Paris and London. The ambiguous and labile nature of German collec-tive identity allowed for a different sort of approach to the other than did the emphatic character of French nationality, which perhaps explains the brittle form of Sartre's polarized world. Therefore, German colonial discourse of the late nine-teenth and early twentieth centuries tends to lack the Mani-cheanism of the Sartrean account and leaves considerably more room for the complexities of cultural hybridization.

It is intriguing that precisely these complex results—the co-lonial setting as a locus of cultural innovation—are confirmed in the prose fictions of Leopold von Sacher-Masoch, which ex-amine the political, racial, and gender complexities of the East-ern Europe of Galicia, Belorussia, and the Ukraine. In a terrain that was, to use the anachronistic term, profoundly multi-cultural, nationality, power, and sexuality interact for Sacher-Masoch in ways that reveal the archaeological underpinnings of his most frequently read work, *Venus in Furs*, and the phe-nomenon of "masochism." The relation of his fiction to the question of colonial discourse is, however, not at all an anach-ronistic projection of our current concerns and interpretations onto the Hapsburg administration in the Slavic East. It is rather thematized expressly in the ethnic analyses of the texts, and it is, moreover, named explicitly in one of the key works.

Including Sacher-Masoch in this study of colonial discourse in German culture requires a clarification of the scope of German identity. His birthplace is now called Lvov, a city in the Ukraine; it was then part of Austro-Hungary, and it was certainly never an integral part of any state called "Germany." Yet this problem—the ambiguity of German national identity—pertains in various ways to all the authors discussed in this book. No "Germany" existed during Forster's lifetime, and his key text was written in English. Rohlfs wrote primarily as a Prussian subject, and Stern was a German exile, writing in English. Freud was Austrian, Jewish, or Viennese (or some compound of these terms). Nevertheless, his array of cultural referents clearly spanned conventional understandings of "German culture"; his writings are replete with allusions to Goethe and Heine, for example. Yet they are also marked by a plethora of references to a wider European culture—Shakespeare, Leonardo, Michelangelo—but precisely this cosmopolitan openness to the world characterizes intellectual life in the German tradition, which was never genuinely reduced or redefined as strictly national. *German culture* is a term that ought to be comparable to Hispanic culture—suggesting a network of references, meanings, and values that stretch across national borders. This more permeable national identity allows for the greater hermeneutic openness to other systems of meaning. Sacher-Masoch participates in this sensibility, particularly in a text that thematizes colonialism and explores its consequences in the multiethnic world of Eastern Europe.

"We drove out of the provincial capital Kolomea into the countryside." With this beginning of the *Don Juan von Kolomea* (1864), Sacher-Masoch announces the colonial question by attaching a footnote to the name of the city, thereby providing some geographic authenticity for his German and other West European readers, who are presumably not familiar with the map of the expansive East: "A province and a provincial capital in eastern Galicia. Kolomea derives from Colonia because the city is built on the classical ground of a former Roman settlement." The topic of the novella then is the Don Juan of the colonies or Don Juan as colonial—the full constellation of race, gender, and power—and the matter is underscored by the continuation of the opening paragraph. "It was Friday evening. Poles say, 'Friday is a good start,' but my German coachman, a colonist from Mariahilf [a name again footnoted: "A German Suabian colonial village near Kolomea"] claims that Friday is a bad luck day, since this was the day our Lord died on the cross and Christianity began."[26] Again the colonial index, compounded by ethnic dispute, appears, and all this in the wake of an epigraph by Karamzin insisting on the impossibility of authenticity in love and the need for perpetual deception. When the narrator and his coachman are suddenly taken hostage by Belorussian peasants acting as a sort of national guard in opposition to the Polish revolutionary movement of 1863, the stage is set for a narration within the frame, a story entailing a critique of the institution of marriage, obsessive seduction, and a reorganization of domestic power. Political revolution and gender revolution are placed in an implicit constellation, not despite, but precisely because of, the colonial setting.

Part of this extraordinary constellation of materials derives no doubt from the fact that colonial literature is also a kind of frontier literature, literature in the extremes of the periphery where, with a Rousseauistic imagination, criticism expects to find renewal. This is no less true today, when critical attention is directed toward marginality, than it was in the nineteenth century. The dissatisfaction with the center implied a search at the edges, which therefore allowed colonial discourse to be regarded as a site of cultural progress. Thus, Ferdinand Kürnberger in his 1870 introduction to *Don Juan von Kolomea*:

> What if in Austria, which has so far so inadequately fulfilled its mission of Germanization; what if, in these times when the nationalities in Austria are in open rebellion against Germanness, a Slavic-born author from the banks of the Prut sent an excellent German novella to the banks of the Main and the Neckar? . . . That fact could mean that German literature had conquered fully new Eastern longitudes and had annexed fully new and fresh primitive peo-

ples [*Naturvölker*], which had not yet written in German but which, in the course of time, have begun to do so more and more. We would see a great, fertilizing stream of sensualism set in motion toward the old Germany, so covered with books. We would see German poets emerging from the prairies of the Weichsel and the mountain forests of the Dneister, new earthy men, who make books out of nature, not out of other books. Their "sources" are not empty libraries but real sources in meadows and forests. . . . We could hope for a poetry from a natural country, not from a country of bureaucrats.[27]

The anxiety about the bureaucratization of German culture is characteristic of the period. The notion that an amelioration might come from the East anticipates the arguments both in Max Weber's *The Protestant Ethic and the Spirit of Capitalism* and in Thomas Mann's *Death in Venice*, where Aschenbach dreams of a new God arriving from Asia.[28] In both cases, renewal arrives through the experience of a vital and alien culture.

In Kürnberger's commentary, however, there is more than a prospective map of cultural practice and the East-West divide. One finds quite clearly a rhetoric of inversion, a qualified surrender of colonial power. Of course, anticolonialism would expect an unadulterated politics of cultural hegemony, as announced rather clearly in the suggestion that German would become the dominant language. However, Kürnberger in effect describes how German hegemony submits to the putative subjects and, given its own internal dessication, enters into a relationship of dependency on the periphery. At the very least Kürnberger is suggesting a cultural creolization, a mixed-race constellation, where the borders blur. (Such mixture should remind us of the German Kilimanjaro discussed at the beginning of this book.) Read more emphatically, he is suggesting a degradation of high civilization in the context of an at least rhetorical elevation of the *Naturvölker*, and it is this primitivist inversion that characterizes the predominant trope of German colonial discourse: an inversion of power in the cultural sphere not unlike the symbolic staging of submission in Sacher-Masoch's fictions.

Does the cultural inversion stabilize the political hierarchy? That hypothetical functioning, a sort of affirmative character of primitivism, is itself presumably much too stable in a context in which degradation and desire draw so close to one another. As the parameter of political power, German predominance is located in a field of considerable ethnic diversity, and destabilization does indeed ensue, just as the German relationship to the colonized peoples becomes more complex. This, however, is precisely why the Holocaust, despite its connection to the Namibian legacy of racial science and *Vernichtungskrieg*, the colonial war of destruction, is not a matter of colonial discourse. The point of the Holocaust was absolute and universal eradication, with none of the ambiguity of desire that marks the colonial situation. East European Jewry held little primitivist appeal for Nazi Germany.

Kürnberger appreciates the "Slavic-born" author from the banks of the Prut writing in German both because this indicates a new geographical expanse for German culture but also, and probably more so, because it is from such authors that he expects a revitalization of German culture. *Don Juan von Kolomea* meets those expectations by articulating a critique: German "books" are regarded as empty and far from life, and Schiller in particular is treated with considerable disdain. The institutionalized culture of the metropolis and its reified idealism have little relevance in a setting where they no longer participate in a narrative of national literary history. "Everything is a lie, a lie! By the way, my friend, have you noticed that actually every man is a liar? There are however two kinds, and you can divide everybody into two groups: those who lie to others, they are the materialists you read about in books, and then there are the idealists, as the Germans call them—they lie to themselves."[29] The colony is a site of destabilization where cultural hierarchies and truth values lose their credibility, leading to the possibility of new modes of cognition. Yet it is crucial to note that the metropolitan, intellectual Kürnberger emphatically welcomes this discourse as a vehicle of ferment and change emerging at the periphery. If there is a process of degradation within colonial discourse, it is not merely a denigration of the colonized, as mythic anticolonialism might imagine. Metropolitan culture also undergoes a degradation, losing an initial position of superiority and getting inserted into a process of hybridization. To be sure, one possible response might be to recoil with heterophobic horror. In Kürnberger's case, at least, the opposite is true, which points to a positive function of colonialism as a mechanism of mixing and rejuvenation. In contrast, we have surely seen how Sartrean anticolonialism reveals a profound horror at mixing.

It is particularly significant, however, that the colonial critique of Germanness extends from literary historical matters to specific gender politics as well. Describing his wife's infidelity as a response to his own and therefore no grounds for complaint, the Don Juan of the title comments, "That is the way things are here. Germans treat their wives like subordinates, but we [Ukrainians] negotiate with them on equal footing, like one monarch to another."[30] This too is part of the inversion: just as German cultural goods lose their privilege in the Eastern context, so German marital practices lose their normative validity and, moreover, male privilege is undermined. In this quotation the shift is described as a matter of greater gender equality than in the German West (and this would conform to the vision we have seen articulated in von Bülow's account of colonial gender relations). For Sacher-Masoch, however, it is not a liberal egalitarianism since his figure slips in and out of roles of subordination, which is the real challenge to established codes of patriarchy: "Or she played a game with me. She goes in her room. 'When I return, you are my slave.' Then she dresses like a sultaness, wraps a shawl around her thighs, another around her head like a turban. With my dagger in her belt and wrapped in a white veil, she comes out: a woman!—a goddess of a woman!"[31]

These games of subjugation mimic the social structures of domination and confuse them. The Don Juan becomes the "slave" of a peasant woman as easily as he serves an aristocrat, and the narration takes place, as indicated earlier, in a setting in which the interlocutors are being held prisoner by peasants hostile to the Polish aristocracy. The specific location is an inn, and the central figure is constantly flirting with the wife of the Jewish owner. In a context of a multiplicity of codes—culture, gender, ethnicity, class—Sacher-Masoch displays the options for transgression and flexibility. The greater vitality that Kürnberger tended to attribute to the force of nature—the rivers, mountains, fields—derives instead from the situation of greater semiotic diversity that characterizes any scene of cultural plurality. Sacher-Masoch's East is interesting precisely as a paradigm of the multicultural diversity that necessarily underlies a colonial situation, even if ideological structures—including both hierarchical colonial discourse and anticolonial Manicheanism—offer extensive resistance to the recognition of that diversity and its fluidity.

Von Bülow could construct the East African colony as a vehicle for gender transformation, whereas Sacher-Masoch derived a restructuring of gender relations from the paracolonial setting of Eastern Europe. Kürnberger hoped for a literary regeneration through the colonization of the European East. The expressionist painter Emil Nolde's engagement with the German colonies outside of Europe generated a similarly transformed capacity for aesthetic expressivity and an alternative cultural-theoretical vision. To be sure, one can hardly claim that the components of his specifically postimpressionistic style derived solely from the encounter with material from Africa and the South Pacific, but there can be no doubt that, as with other painters of his generation, the encounter with objects from the colonial world in the ethnographic museums in European capitals greatly clarified and magnified the tendency toward an alternative expressivity. Hence, Nolde's later recollection of his concerns at the turn of the century:

> I regarded the art of the Egyptians and Assyrians as something very special and mystical. I could not treat it, as was the general rule back then, as a merely "historical object,"

for I loved these great works, even if I was not supposed to. But such love is often the most powerful. The next decade brought insight and emancipation: I encountered Indian, Chinese, and Persian art, as well as the strange works of the Mexicans and the primitive peoples. These were, for me, no mere "curiosities," as the specialists called them. No, we elevated them to what they are: the strange and stringent original art of primitive peoples. Yet even today the science of ethnography treats us like annoying poachers, since we love sensuous seeing more than mere knowledge.[32]

Nolde's imperialist culture does not imply a celebration of a European legacy over and against a denigrated realm of the colonized. On the contrary, one finds precisely the opposite of what one might expect a standard policy of cultural imperialism to have entailed. Nolde intends to learn from the so-called primitive cultures, just as Kürnberger insisted that the Germany of the Main and the Neckar, the Germany of the West, learn from the colonized territories in the East. Sartre's myth of anticolonialism and Derrida's equation of logocentricity and domination, Enlightenment and empire, prove sorely inadequate for analyzing the cultural and political complexities of hybridization. Imperialism and the assertion of metropolitan priorities were, of course, part of the picture, but that was precisely the target of Nolde's incipient criticism, which became ever stronger as his immersion in colonial material continued. Indeed, the polemical criticism directed at the contemporary organization of culture applied both to the structural biases of scholarship and to the art establishment, and both involved a reflection on the global division of culture. Thus, Nolde in 1912: "Not long ago, only a few art-historical periods were regarded as proper for museums. Then others were admitted: Coptic and early Christian art, Greek terracottas and vases, Persian and Islamic art. But why are Indian, Chinese, and Javanese art still categorized under science and anthropology? And why is the art of primitive peoples not valued as such?"[33]

Nolde's sensitivity to the hierarchies of taste are very evidently linked to his own program; hence his complaints that the prestigious salons in Berlin, with their francophile predilections, often eschewed the works of German artists, led Nolde to celebrate precisely the primitive in German art as the core of his expressionism. German art is empowered precisely through the anti-European turn, a turn poised ambiguously between nationalism (Germany as opposed to Europe) and a visceral fascination with the artistic forms of non-European peoples. Germany as the primitive site? The discourse of colonial culture has therefore slid gradually from an admiration for and advocacy of the aesthetics of the colonized culture to an identification with and borrowing from that culture and finally to a redefinition of Germany, the colonizing culture, in terms that derive from the identification with the colonized. This is, of course, the exact opposite of the account provided by the anticolonialism of Sartre or Derrida, who imagine the assertion of the absolute predominance of the cultural and philosophical terms of the colonizer. Instead, the borders are much more porous, and the colonial setting becomes a scene of productive promiscuity in which considerable transformation can take place: Nolde's new painting, Sacher-Masoch's inversions, or even the disguises that the traveler Rohlfs would don.

It is worthwhile to note, in this context only in passing, how Nolde's own primitivism underwent a significant change in the course of his trip to the German South Pacific colonies on the eve of the First World War. His most emphatically exoticizing pictures predate the trip and derive from objects in museum collections. It is during the trip that he faces some of the realities of colonial rule, which may explain the decline in specifically primitive iconography in his later work. This does not make him, however, a clear and dogmatic critic of colonialism. "We Europeans," he writes, "are awfully good and loving people! We are Christians, democrats, socialists, or anarchists, but underneath there is the naked human, the mean creature. And behind the creature stands the devil, clever and smirking, sweetly greeting the destruction of the primitive peoples."[34]

Yet at the same time he never calls colonialism in general into question, accepting, albeit with melancholy, a necessary progress of civilization and proclaiming the superiority of German colonial administration over the European competitors. Furthermore, despite his own vaunted indebtedness to colonial art, he develops eccentric theories about the racial origin of an artist's work, theories that, however, did little good in protecting his oeuvre after 1933. We know that the Nazis apparently removed more works by Nolde from German museums than by any other artist, and the grounds for their hostility were made perfectly clear by ideologues like Alfred Rosenberg: although a "definitive ideal of beauty" has prevailed among "Nordic" artists from ancient Greece through the German Middle Ages and the Italian Renaissance to Goethe, Nolde's work is, simply, "negroid."[35]

Without dissecting the inadequacies of Nolde's reminiscences, one can note how the contrast between Nolde and Rosenberg stages alternative versions of cultural identity. For the Nazi propagandist Rosenberg, a race-based triumphant culture of the North maintains its own internal coherence, despite a vision of a geographical expanse in which Germany, as Europe, can lay claim to the rights of inheritance, from Crete to Norway. This is merely a crude transposition of Nazi war aims into a cultural program. For Nolde, it is precisely the contact with the foreign and, in particular, the primitive foreign, that generates a criticism of contemporary modern culture and its insufficient mode of intellectuality—insufficient in the same way that the realist critic Kürnberger denounced German culture for its bureaucratic bookishness, although Nolde's modernist judgment is surely much more harsh. If the ideology of colonialism—the absolute separation of races because of an imagined absolute superiority of the colonizer—lays the groundwork for Nazi racial policy, the real life of colonialism must have also included considerable contact, ambiguity, and transgression: both in miscegenation, which is the subtext for von Bülow's concerns, and in capacities of cultural interpretation, as with Nolde. Since colonialist ideology is primarily about separation and hierarchy, it is not surprising that discourse theory, focused as it is on articulation rather than experience, emphasizes the scene of domination. But the real experience of colonialism surely also included extensive interaction, translation, and mixing. Yet to focus on such mixing and interaction leads to a more nuanced account of colonialism than the Manichean myth of a politicized anticolonialism permits.

For the painter Nolde, the iconographic corollary to colonial discourse includes the diversification and qualitative difference within a process of mixture and transference. This paradigm of hybridization stands at odds with the reified antinomies of anticolonialism and its positing of an absolute difference as the only genuine alternative to Western metaphysics. This constriction of intellectual vision derives from the simplistic collapsing of Enlightenment and empire, which precludes any discussion of alterity within the Enlightenment: difference is, allegedly, only on the outside. It is therefore not colonial discourse (which we have seen can incorporate considerable heterogeneity) but the figures of thought of anti-Enlightenment anticolonialism—Sartre at his most Heideggerian—that set difference as absolute, betraying ultimately a desire to separate and segregate. When difference is celebrated as existentially impervious to any universalist frame, a reverse racism sets in that can only lead to the Manicheanism that anticolonialist ideology imagined it was attacking. In reality, that separatism is a product of the ideology itself and demonstrates a deep-seated fear of contact with that which is qualitatively different.

The frightened recoiling from such contact, the refusal of the intellectual to engage with the otherness of the colonial subjects, is the issue at stake in Kafka's "In the Penal Colony" (1919).[36] The explorer is the prototype of anticolonial Sartre, if not yet as explicitly radical. He is the liberal intellectual and writer, come to judge and denounce the practices—the primitive practices—of the colonial administration. A Kafkaesque twist indeed: the antiprimitivism, presumably a feature of colonial ideology as the vehicle with which to denigrate the colonized population, has been transformed into the prejudice of the Enlightenment against the colonists themselves rather than against the colonized. The real "primitives," to use the term in its most provocatively derogatory sense, are not the "natives" or "noble savages" but the colonizing riffraff who, from the standpoint of the enlightened metropolis, are neither culturally interesting nor morally defensible. Needless to say, there is little in Kafka's narrative that could be construed as a defense of colonialism. The brutality of the machine is quite enough to understand that a fundamental criticism of domination is at stake. Yet it is the text itself and not the explorer that makes the criticism. The text, however, goes much further than a trivial denunciation of colonialism by displaying how even the anticolonialist traveler, prepared from the start to denounce the backward and illiberal practices on the island, is himself deeply implicated in hierarchical notions of culture and—the prototype of the effete liberal—has no practical aid or advice to offer. Indeed, the explorer enfigures a helpless progressivism as he flees from the encounter with all that lies beyond his conceptual universe: tradition, that is, the incomprehensible legacies of the old Commandant, the irrationality of the body, and especially the constitution of community around the epitaphic inscription on the Commandant's grave. There is a deep knowledge in the colonial setting, clearly and inextricably tied to violence and brutality, but simply inaccessible to the cognitive insipidness of the traveler. It is this life world of the island from which the explorer flees, refusing to assist the islanders who would have escaped with him, thereby displaying the shallowness of the humanitarianism that had grounded his earlier criticisms.

For von Bülow, the colony admits to the possibility of a regendering of intellectuality; for Nolde, it is the site of an encounter with an alternative sensibility and symbolic practices; and Kürnbeger looked to the colony at the European periphery as a source of revitalization. Kafka shows the intellectual recoiling from these opportunities, presumably confirmed in his anticolonialist presumption of the absolute incompatibility of primitive life in the colony with the ideals and aspirations of enlightened Europe. By now, however, the situation with which I began, Sartre's extreme either/or, is fully reversed. Colonialism undermines the clear-cut distinctions of cultural hierarchy constantly wearing away at the structures of power, whereas it is the anticolonialist discourse (Sartre's rhetoric) that is committed to maintaining them. The argument that Western metaphysics is constitutively incompatible with other cultures—for example, with Derrida's version of a post-apartheid South Africa or Sartre's liberated Algeria—makes it effectively necessary to maintain a global cultural segregation and lock the other into an enforced exoticism: East is East and West is West. Kafka exposes this hypocrisy in the flight of the traveler: "They could have jumped into the boat," he concludes, referring to the prisoner and the soldier, "but the explorer lifted a heavy knotted rope from the floor boards, threatened them with it and so kept them from attempting the leap."[37] The entwinement of Enlightenment and empire? Certainly, but in an unexpected variant, for it is precisely enlightened anticolonialism that preserves the segregation of the colonial order. The intellectual who assumes an absolute incompatibility of different cultures, Heideggerian incommensurability rather than Husserlian universalism, may choose to heroize the exotic other but evidently does not want to be in the same boat.

At the turn of the century, colonialism had a more complex significance. Clearly, it set up relations of hierarchy and segregation that were extraordinarily violent and destructive, and von Bülow, Nolde, and Kafka show as much. Although each redefines the intellectual—and, by extension, the European culture of the Enlightenment—through the colonial encounter, their apparent political positions on colonialism vary widely. Von Bülow advocates a nonmilitary colonialism, Nolde wavers between anticolonial romanticism and German patriotism, and Kafka makes an anarchist denunciation of the hypocrisy of intellectual progressivism. The link between colonialism and Enlightenment is far from univocal. Simplistic anticolonialism, driven by its own ideological preoccupations, overlooks an aspect of colonialism that anticipated and set much of the stage for contemporary discussions about cultural plurality and difference. Colonialism posed the question of cultural horizons in a new and urgent way: is the horizon a wall that divides the heaven for radically different groups that cannot or should not mix or is it the site where an encounter with alterity and the risk of alteration might take place? In that latter case, Europe would have to evince a capacity to transform the life world because of encounters with modalities of life deemed different, but never so different as to be beyond comprehensible exchange. Indeed, that assumption was precisely the grounds for the plausibility of colonialism at all. If colonialism could lead to the gross violence of wars of annihilation, the *Vernichtungskrieg* against the Hereros, it was probably not because of a fundamental incompatibility of different races (even if some ideologues imagine such incompatibility) or because the Hereros were impervious to conceptual thinking. Much more venal matters were at stake, and the Herero War was presumably not the only possible version of a German foreign policy. There were plenty of critics who envisioned an alternative.

Indeed, foreign policy is itself a pertinent area of inquiry for an exploration of travel, colonialism, and culture. The establishment of the European empires surely required, on the one hand, the accumulation of scientific knowledge—for example, Cook's geography—which was often accompanied by a vision of empty space, a discourse that warmly invited penetration and settlements. On the other hand, the practical needs associated with seizing control of new territories and maintaining a stable and functional administration soon demanded a very different sort of knowledge as well: detailed and empathetic familiarity with the colonized peoples. No matter how ideological this knowledge may have remained, some understanding, beginning with the local language and extending into an anthropological comprehension of customs, must have been crucial, if only for asserting effective control. For the colonial administration, this, however, necessarily implied stepping back from any consistent and abstract universalism in order to ascribe some validity to the specific particularity of local customs. For an imperial foreign policy, the corollary feature is the capacity to recognize the diversity of nations and cultures in order to deploy power more effectively, whether through diplomacy or arms, than it could be if policy were guided solely by blindly universalist precepts.

The choice is not between universalism and localism or universalism and provincialism. It is between two universalisms: one abstract and theoretical, committed to general principles and immune to local differences, indeed, somewhat heterophobic in its refusal of competing perspectives; the other realistic and empirical, finding the principle of rationality in the given materials of particular cultures, all characterized by difference. This is the opposition we first encountered between the scientific navigator Cook and his companion, the young German traveler, Georg Forster. If there is a feature that characterizes the discourse of colonialism in Germany, it is, not exhaustively to be sure but frequently enough, the capacity to recognize and appreciate—appreciate even at the moment of colonial appropriation—the other culture. There are, of course, examples of appreciation denied, and we have seen them in Rohlfs's later writings or Stern's hostility to Tewodros. Yet both had earlier entered into some significant engagements with the non-European world, and we have seen how in the case of Nolde the emphatically colonial fascination with New Guinean culture led to an extraordinary attachment (no matter how constantly coupled with the racism and hierarchical thinking typical of the period). This points to a hypothesis that there is a strain in German culture that allows for the appreciation of difference, and that this strain tempered colonial discourse, directing it more toward primitivism and the possibility of a heterophilic appreciation than, by way of contrast, the more imperiously universalist discourses characteristic of the colonialisms of England and France.

At the outset of this book, I made mention of W. E. B. Du Bois's evaluation of German culture and his surprising identification with both Bismarck and Kaiser Wilhelm II during the 1880s and 1890s. It is arguable that, despite the racism he heard in a lecture by the Prussian historian Heinrich von Treitschke, it was precisely von Treitschke's advocacy of nationalist awakening that contributed to the formation of Du Bois's program of racial activism and decolonization. Does Pan-Africanism inherit Pan-Germanism? The question goes beyond the scope of this project, but it indicates how the colonial world may have replied to the discourses of colonialism, not simply opposing, but also appropriating European legacies. Sartre has Fanon read Hegel's master-slave dialectic as a narrative of absolute polarization; Du Bois presents a quite different Hegelianism that points to the possibility of multiplicity within a human synthesis.[38] He therefore displays none of the crude anti-Europeanism that contemporary culture has inherited from ideological anticolonialism; nor did he ever demonstrate the undifferentiated anti-Germanism that swept the West during the world wars. Hence, I chose his statement from November 1914 as an epigraph for this book. If we take Du Bois and Fanon to be two exponents of decolonization, it is particularly important to see how they inherit Hegel and German idealism in quite distinct ways. Fanon, as a psychoanalyst, focuses on the question of individual consciousness and its formation through the exigency of a mortal struggle between master and slave—the anticolonial war. Du Bois, in contrast, attempts to integrate Africa into the Hegelian structures of world history, whereby the insistence on history and cross-generational inheritance leads him to a positive evaluation of the category of race.

At the beginning of the century, colonialism posed important challenges to European culture, its intellectuals and its artists. Yet the issues bore considerable similarities to our contemporary concerns at the century's end: the imperative to rethink horizons, practices, and structures of thought and to integrate into the ongoing processes of cultural modernization the real experience of engagement with the world beyond Europe. Today, the same question is both narrower and wider: engagement with the world beyond Western Europe—that is, the rediscovery of the other Europe in the formerly socialist states, the postcolonial wake of the Russian Empire—and with the Third World. What are the vicissitudes of European culture as it confronts radically different symbolic systems? And what of the status of culture as a whole in the face of extreme physical impoverishment that would seem to mock any expenditure for "culture"? Can there be intellectuals after Europe? Or does the apprehension that intellectuals have come to an end betray a hidden Eurocentrism? And what of the vicissitudes of the Enlightenment, of reason, and of the narrative of emancipation? As the space of culture becomes as diverse as the space of the globe, the old fear of a universal leveling of cultural difference seems unfounded. Yet universalism was not only a fear; it implied a utopia of equality as well as a heterophile appreciation of diversity. Enlightenment therefore does not at all necessarily imply empire or domination (no matter how much imperialism may have derived from narratives of progress or the material practices of science). It is, however, precisely the proleptic identification of Enlightenment and domination, of logocentricity and colonialism, that has contributed to the ideological excesses of Sartrean anticolonialism and to the trivialization of much of the contemporary cultural discussion in the American academy.

The case of Forster proves how the universalism of Enlightenment is fully compatible with the ethnographic capacity to recognize difference and to attempt to appreciate it on its own terms. In contrast, the celebration of absolute difference that we have seen in Sartre and Derrida and that, through deconstruction, has come to considerable prominence in the American humanities today, leads quite quickly to the legitimation of separations and then to new exclusions. Every assertion of cultural difference rendered absolute implies definitions of membership as well as borders that, sooner or later, will be patrolled. Meanwhile, the subversion of universalist norms in the name of cultural difference can similarly generate an indifference that only cynicism would regard as a tolerance for diversity. Without some universalist frame we lose a capacity to judge, and we fall into a relativism that condones everything because it understands nothing: abusive practices, designated as expressions of an alternative culture, are callously accepted as further evidence of difference. The West's extended refusal to arrive at a judgment on the war in the Balkans, out of a preference for retaining a neutrality toward the different parties, demonstrates the enervation that has ensued from the erosion of a will to the norms of Enlightenment. The price for this relativism includes the tragic evidence that, after Auschwitz and after all the protestations against the possibility of its repetition, world opinion remains tolerant enough to countenance genocide. "Never again" is no longer a prediction but only a wish.

To assert the inadequacy of the contemporary critique of logocentrism inherited from Heidegger by way of Sartre, Foucault, and Derrida does not imply a simplistic celebration of a univocal Enlightenment. The argument in this book began, on the contrary, with the contrast of Forster and Cook, which was intended quite explicitly as an enfigurement of a dialectic within the Enlightenment. The question of colonial discourse is so urgent because it is the framework within which this dialectic and, more generally, the interaction between science and qualitatively new experiences can be examined. The question of German colonial discourse adds a further level of complexity because of the specific German positionality—clearly a European power but equally displaced from the centers of the colonial process. It is that particular tension, within colonizing Europe but also at its border, that contributes to the tradition of articulating a critique of Enlightenment and the ambiguities of universalism—a universalism that has lost much of its credibility. Today, cultural criticism, as well as many other branches of scholarship, therefore suffers from a waning self-confidence and a loss of foundations. One can respond to this crisis of knowledge—Husserl's "European Sciences"—in various ways: by jettisoning logocentrism because of a politically opportunistic equation of Enlightenment and empire or by trying to redefine Europe, science, and culture to accommodate difference within an unapologetically universalist project. In this sense the colonial question of 1900 prefigures the cultural questions of the twenty-first century.

Notes

INTRODUCTION

1. Falkenhorst, *Auf Bergeshöhen Deutsch-Afrikas*, 77. Unless otherwise noted, translations are my own.

2. Falkenhorst, *Auf Bergeshöhen Deutsch-Afrikas*, 5, 21, 57.

3. Falkenhorst, *Auf Bergeshöhen Deutsch-Afrikas*, 53. See the discussion of Ferdinand Fabri in chapter 4.

4. Falkenhorst, *Auf Bergeshöhen Deutsch-Afrikas*, 1.

5. Much recent work has focused, in contrast, on discourses of race and the body. See Adelson, *Making Bodies, Making History*, and Gilman, *Difference and Pathology*.

6. On the disciplinary tensions between cultural studies and cultural history, see the essays collected in *New German Critique* 65 (spring/summer 1995).

7. Lewis, *W. E. B. Du Bois*, 139.

8. Du Bois, *Autobiography*, 169.

9. Du Bois, "World War and the Color Line," 29.

1. THE ENLIGHTENMENT TRAVELOGUE AND THE COLONIAL TEXT

1. For parallel discussions—where, however, the issues involve the foundations of ethnography as discipline—see Obeyesekere, *The Apotheosis of Captain Cook*, and Sahlins, *How "Natives" Think*.

2. Cook, *Journals*, 1:264.

3. Forster, *Werke*, 1:85–86.

4. Forster, *Werke*, 1:10.

5. Forster, *Werke*, 1:86.

6. Forster, *Werke*, 1:89.

7. Forster, *Werke*, 1:90–91.

8. Forster, *Werke*, 1:90.

9. Forster, *Werke*, 1:91.

10. Forster, *Werke*, 1:92.

11. Forster, *Werke*, 1:93.

12. Forster, *Werke*, 1:93.

13. Cook, *Voyage towards the South Pole*, 74.

14. Cook, *Journals*, 116.
15. Forster, *Werke*, 1:94–95.
16. Cook, *Voyage towards the South Pole*, 1:73.
17. Locke, *An Essay Concerning Human Understanding*, 2:104.
18. Cook, *Journals*, 164.
19. Cook, *Voyage towards the South Pole*, 1:74.
20. Cook, *Voyages round the World*, 188.
21. Forster, *Werke*, 1:94.
22. See Dening, *Mr. Bligh's Bad Language*.
23. Forster, *Werke*, 1:9.
24. Forster, *Werke*, 1:9.
25. Forster, *Werke*, 1:9–10.
26. Forster, *Werke*, 1:9–10.
27. Forster, *Werke*, 1:13.
28. Forster, *Werke*, 1:11.
29. Forster, *Werke*, 1:12.
30. Cook, *Voyage towards the South Pole*, 1:ix.
31. Forster, *Werke*, 1:14.
32. Wieland, *Kleine Schriften*, 23.
33. See Jürgen Habermas, *Structural Transformation of the Public Sphere* (Cambridge, MA: MIT Press, 1989).
34. Forster, *Werke*, 1:14.
35. Forster, *Werke*, 1:14.
36. Forster, *Werke*, 1:593.
37. Forster, *Werke*, 1:405.
38. A summary of the discussion of the background is presented in *Werke in vier Bänden*, 4:161–70.
39. Robert L. Kahn, "The History of the Work," in Forster, *Werke*, 1:698.
40. Cook, *Voyage towards the South Pole*, 1:xxxvi.
41. Gerhard Steiner, "Der junge Georg Forster in England: Zu einem bisher unbekannten Briefwechsel," *Weimarer Beiträge* 4 (1959): 530.
42. Cook, *Voyage towards the South Pole*, 1:xxxvi.
43. See the reading of Odysseus and the sirens in Horkheimer and Adorno, *Dialectic of Enlightenment*.
44. Steiner, "Der junge Georg Forster," 533.

2. GERHARD ROHLFS AND GEOGRAPHIC WRITING

1. Mill, *Essays on England*, iii.
2. Mill, *Essays on England*, 511.

3. Mill, *Essays on England*, 511, 512.

4. Arendt, *The Origins of Totalitarianism*, 127.

5. Rassam, *Narrative of the British*, 1:iii.

6. Rubenson, *King of Kings*, 87.

7. Markham, *A History*, 128, 135.

8. Markham, *A History*, 82–83.

9. Rubenson, *King of Kings*, 11.

10. Rubenson, *King of Kings*, 11–12.

11. Rubenson, *King of Kings*, 13.

12. Markham, *A History*, 77.

13. See Banse, *Unsere großen Afrikaner* and Genschorek, *Im Alleingang durch die Wüste*.

14. Rohlfs, *Neue Beiträge*, 57.

15. Rohlfs, *Neue Beiträge*, 58.

16. Rohlfs, *Neue Beiträge*, 8.

17. Rohlfs, *Neue Beiträge*, 12.

18. Rohlfs, *Quer durch Afrika*, 29.

19. Rohlfs, *Quer durch Afrika*, 29–30.

20. Rohlfs, *Quer durch Afrika*, 14.

21. Rohlfs, *Quer durch Afrika*, 49.

22. Essner, *Deutsche Afrikakreisende*, 112.

23. See Rohlfs, *Quer durch Afrika*, 109; and Rohlfs, "Reise durch Nord-Afrika," part 1, 5.

24. Rohlfs, *Quer durch Afrika*, 56, 65, 68, 138.

25. Rohlfs, *In Abessinien*, v–vi; Genschorek, *Im Alleingang durch die Wüste*, 130.

26. Rohlfs, *In Abessinien*, 169.

27. Rohlfs, *In Abessinien*, 5.

28. Rohlfs, *In Abessinien*, 8, 9.

29. Rohlfs, *In Abessinien*, 46–47.

30. Rohlfs, *In Abessinien*, 3.

31. Rohlfs, *In Abessinien*, 102.

32. Rohlfs, *In Abessinien*, 172.

33. Rohlfs, *In Abessinien*, 176.

34. Stanley, *Magdala*, iii.

35. Stanley, *Magdala*, iv.

36. Stanley, *Magdala*, v.

37. Stanley, *Magdala*, 5.

38. Rohlfs, *In Abessinien*, 1.

39. See Pratt, *Imperial Eyes*, 111–43.

40. Rohlfs, *Angra Pequena*, 4.

41. Rohlfs, *Angra Pequena*, 4 n.

3. HENRY STERN AND MISSIONARY SPACE

1. See Goldhagen, *Hitler's Willing Executioners*, 49–52.
2. See Mirbach, *Die Reise des Kaisers und der Kaiserin*.
3. *Stimmen über Jerusalem*, 9.
4. *Stimmen über Jerusalem*, 24.
5. Arendt, *The Origins of Totalitarianism*, 183.
6. See Fischer, *Die Rehobother Bastards*.
7. Stern, *Dawnings of the Light*, iii.
8. Stern, *Dawnings of the Light*, 272.
9. Isaacs, *Biography of the Rev. Henry Aaron Stern*, 198.
10. Meyer, *German Political Pressure*, 8, 25 n.17.
11. See, for example, Giovanni Marana, *Letters Written by a Turkish Spy* (1686) or M. Wilson, *The History of Israel Jobson, the Wandering Jew* (1757). For a review of this literature, see Elisabeth Frenzel, *Stoffe der Weltliteratur: Ein Lexikon dichtungsgeschichtlicher Längsschnitte* (Stuttgart: Alfred Krönder, 1992), 16–22.
12. Stern, *Dawnings of Light*, 272, 276.
13. Stern, *Dawnings of Light*, 273.
14. Isaacs, *Biography of the Rev. Henry Aaron Stern*, 33.
15. Stern, *Dawning of Light*, 57.
16. Stern, *Dawning of Light*, 242.
17. Stern, *Dawning of Light*, 245.
18. Stern, *Dawning of Light*, 246.
19. Stern, *Dawning of Light*, 249.
20. Hess, introduction to Stern, *Wanderings among the Falashas*.
21. Stern, *Wanderings among the Falashas*, xxiii.
22. Stern, *Wanderings among the Falashas*, 2.
23. Rassam, *Narrative of the British Mission*, 271–72.
24. Stern, *Wanderings among the Falashas*, 96.
25. Flad, *Zwölf Jahre in Abessinien*, 131.
26. Stern, *Wanderings among the Falashas*, 62.
27. Stern, *Wanderings among the Falashas*, 80–81.
28. Stern, *Dawning of Light*, 274; Stern, *The Captive Missionary*, xv.
29. Neil, *Anglicanism*, 264.
30. Hildesheimer, *Briefe*, 31.
31. Faïtlovich, *Quer durch Abessinien*, 170–71; and Anderson, *Imagined Communities*.

32. Faïtlovich, *Quer durch Abessinien,* 75 n.

33. Faïtlovich, *Quer durch Abessinien,* 125 n.2.

34. Benjamin, "The Work of Art in the Age of Mechanical Reproduction," in *Illuminations,* 241–42.

4. ENGENDERED COLONIES

1. Fabri, *Bedarf Deutschland,* 11.

2. Fabri, *Bedarf Deutschland,* 11–12.

3. Bade, *Imperialismus und Kolonialmission,* 104.

4. Fabri, *Bedarf Deutschland,* 2–3.

5. Fabri, *Bedarf Deutschland,* 17.

6. Fabri, *Bedarf Deutschland,* 16.

7. Fabri, *Bedarf Deutschland,* 25.

8. Fabri, *Bedarf Deutschland,* 14, 30–31.

9. Fabri, *Bedarf Deutschland,* 50.

10. See Grimm, *Volk ohne Raum.*

11. Grimm, *Volk ohne Raum,* 39, 40.

12. Grimm, *Volk ohne Raum,* 27–28.

13. Freud, *The Question of Lay Analysis,* 211.

14. Freud, *The Question of Lay Analysis,* 212.

15. Freud, *The Question of Lay Analysis,* 212.

16. Freud, *The Question of Lay Analysis,* 210.

17. Freud, *The Interpretation of Dreams (first part),* ix. On Freud's Roman dreams and the identification with Hannibal, see Schorske, *Fin-de-siècle Vienna,* 181–207.

18. See "A Disturbance of Memory on the Acropolis."

19. Freud, *The Interpretation of Dreams (second part),* 377.

20. Freud, *The Interpretation of Dreams (second part),* 378.

21. Freud, *The Interpretation of Dreams (second part),* 378.

22. Freud, *The Interpretation of Dreams (second part),* 378, 379.

23. Freud, *The Interpretation of Dreams (second part),* 377.

24. Freud, *The Interpretation of Dreams (first part),* 97.

25. Freud, *The Interpretation of Dreams (first part),* 98 n.1.

26. Freud, *The Interpretation of Dreams (second part),* 353.

27. Freud, *The Interpretation of Dreams (second part),* 351.

28. Freud, *The Interpretation of Dreams (second part),* 353–54.

29. Freud, *The Interpretation of Dreams (first part),* 262.

30. Freud, *The Interpretation of Dreams (first part),* 264.

31. Freud, *The Interpretation of Dreams (first part),* 211.

32. Freud, *The Interpretation of Dreams (first part),* 211.
33. Freud, *The Interpretation of Dreams (first part),* 209.
34. Freud, *The Interpretation of Dreams (first part),* 211.
35. Freud, *The Interpretation of Dreams (first part),* 212.
36. Freud, *The Interpretation of Dreams (first part),* 212–13.
37. See Schorske, *Fin-de-siècle Vienna,* 195.
38. Freud, *The Interpretation of Dreams (first part),* 217.
39. Freud, *The Interpretation of Dreams (first part),* 217 n.1.
40. Freud, *The Interpretation of Dreams (first part),* 210.

5. COLONIAL LITERATURE AND THE EMANCIPATION OF WOMEN

1. *Wider die Sklaverei!,* 62.
2. See Chickering, "'Casting Their Gaze More Broadly,'" 156–85.
3. Warmbold, "Germania in Afrika," 309–36.
4. Freytag, *Soll und Haben.*
5. See Essner, *Deutsche Afrikareisende,* 89–93.
6. Bülow, *Tropenkoller,* 41, 56.
7. Bülow, *Tropenkoller,* 9, 40, 104.
8. Bülow, *Tropenkoller,* 64.
9. Bülow, *Deutsch-Ostafrikanische Novellen,* 29–30.
10. Bülow, *Deutsch-Ostafrikanische Novellen,* 30.
11. See Harnack, *Entstehung und Entwickelung*; Ritschl, *Die Entstehung*; and Sohm, *Wesen und Ursprung des Katholizismus.*
12. Bülow, *Deutsch-Ostafrikanische Novellen,* 26, 28.
13. Bülow, *Deutsch-Ostafrikanische Novellen,* 23.
14. Bülow, *Deutsch-Ostafrikanische Novellen,* 108.
15. Bäumer, "Frieda von Bülow," 467.
16. Bäumer, "Frieda von Bülow," 408.
17. Bülow, *Deutsch-Ostafrikanische Novellen,* 147, 177.
18. Bäumer, "Frieda von Bülow," 318–19.
19. Bäumer, "Frieda von Bülow," 260.
20. Bäumer, "Frieda von Bülow," 262.
21. Bäumer, "Frieda von Bülow," 276.
22. Bäumer, "Frieda von Bülow," 267.
23. Bäumer, "Frieda von Bülow," 81–82.
24. Bülow, *Die stilisierte Frau,* 116.
25. Bülow, *Die stilisierte Frau,* 150–51.
26. See Klotz, "White Women and the Dark Continent."
27. "Bittleid der Windhuker Gemeinde an die Hereros zu den gelungenen Viehdiebstählen am 14. Juli (400 St. Kleinvieh), 17. Juli 1904 (30 St.

Grossvieh bei Sperlingslust," in Windhoek State Archive, Accessions A136, Collection R. Louchert.

28. Sonnenberg, *Wie es am Waterberg Zuging*, 8.

29. Sonnenberg, *Wie es am Waterberg Zuging*, 17.

30. Sonnenberg, *Wie es am Waterberg Zuging*, 26.

31. Sonnenberg, *Wie es am Waterberg Zuging*, 59, 72, 75.

32. Theweleit, *Male Fantasies*.

33. *The Origins of Totalitarianism*, 185–221.

34. See Fischer, *Das Problem der Rassenkreuzzung*. On Fischer's connection to Martin Heidegger, see Farias, *Heidegger and Nazism*, 70.

6. THE MYTH OF ANTICOLONIALISM

1. Derrida, "Racism's Last Word," 331.

2. Derrida, "Racism's Last Word," 333.

3. de Man, *Allegories of Reading*, 141.

4. Sartre, preface, 9.

5. Sartre, preface, 7.

6. JanMohamed, *A Manichean Aesthetics*.

7. JanMohamed, *A Manichean Aesthetics*, 7.

8. Du Bois, *The Souls of Black Folk*, 139.

9. See Engels, *Herr Eugen Duhring's Revolution*.

10. Sartre, preface, 25–26.

11. Heidegger, *Being and Time*, 211–14.

12. Sartre, preface, 13.

13. Sartre, preface, 22.

14. Heinrich Heine, *Deutschland, ein Wintermärchen* in *Historisch-kritische Gesamtausgabe der Werke*, vol. 4, ed. Winfried Woesner (Hamburg: Hoffmann und Campe, 1985), 105.

15. Fabri, *Bedarf Deutschland der Colonien?*, 11–12.

16. Sartre, preface, 23.

17. See Arendt, *On Violence*, 20–21, 36.

18. Sartre, preface, 21.

19. See Gayatri Chakravorty Spivak, *In Other Worlds: Essays in Cultural Politics* (New York: Methuen, 1987).

20. Sartre, preface, 7.

21. Sartre, preface, 9.

22. Sartre, preface, 10.

23. Sartre, preface, 9–10.

24. Sartre, preface, 23.

25. In Bülow, *Deutsch-Ostafrikanische Novellen.*

26. Sacher-Masoch, *Don Juan von Kolomea*, 19.

27. Sacher-Masoch, *Don Juan von Kolomea*, 191–92.

28. On Weber, Mann, and the trope of bureaucratization in nineteenth-century German culture, see my *Rise of the Modern German Novel: Crisis and Charisma* (Cambridge, MA: Harvard University Press, 1986).

29. Sacher-Masoch, *Don Juan von Kolomea*, 28. On Schiller, see 36.

30. Sacher-Masoch, *Don Juan von Kolomea*, 55.

31. Sacher-Masoch, *Don Juan von Kolomea*, 41.

32. Nolde, *Das Eigene Leben*, 265. For a more complete discussion of the politics of Nolde's primitivism, see my *Cultural Studies of Modern Germany: History, Representation, and Nationhood* (Madison: University of Wisconsin Press, 1993), 112–22.

33. Nolde, *Jahre der Kämpfe*, 177.

34. Nolde, *Welt und Heimat: Die Südseereise* 1913–1918 (Cologne: Verlag M. DuMont Schauberg, 1965), 99.

35. Wulf, *Die bildenden Künste im Dritten Reich*, 50–51.

36. Pan, "Kafka as Populist."

37. Kafka, *The Penal Colony*, 227.

38. On Du Bois and Hegel, see Gooding-Williams, "Philosophy of History and Social Critique"; Williamson, "W. E. B. Du Bois as a Hegelian"; and Zamir, *Dark Voices.*

Selected Bibliography

(Includes works not cited)

Adelson, Leslie A. *Making Bodies, Making History: Feminism and German Identity.* Lincoln: University of Nebraska Press, 1993.

Anderson, Benedict. *Imagined Communities: Reflections on the Origin and Spread of Nationalism.* London: Verso, 1991.

Arendt, Hannah. *The Origins of Totalitarianism.* New York: Harcourt, Brace and World, 1966.

———. *On Violence.* New York: Harcourt, Brace and World, 1969.

Bade, Klaus J., ed. *Imperialismus und Kolonialmission: Kaiserliches Deutschland und koloniales Imperium.* Beiträge zur Kolonial- und Überseegeschichte, ed. Rudolf von Albertini and Heinz Gollwitzer, vol. 22. Wiesbaden: Franz Steiner, 1982.

Banse, Ewald. *Entwicklung und Aufgabe der Geographie: Rückblicke und Ausblicke einer universalen Wissenschaft.* Stuttgart: Humboldt-Verlag, 1957.

———. *Unsere großen Afrikaner: Das Leben deutscher Entdecker und Kolonialpioniere.* Berlin: Haude und Spener, 1940.

Bäumer, Gertrud. "Frieda von Bülow." *Die Frau: Monatsschrift für das gesamte Frauenleben unserer Zeit* [ed. Helene Lange] (1908–9): 407–12.

Beck, Hanno. *Geographie: Europäische Entwicklung: In Texten und Erläuterungen.* Freiburg: Verlag Karl Alber, 1973.

Benjamin, Walter. *Illuminations.* Ed. Hannah Arendt, trans. Harry Zohn. New York: Schocken, 1969.

Bhabha, Homi K. *The Location of Culture.* London: Routledge, 1994.

Bülow, Frieda von. *Deutsch-Ostafrikanische Novellen.* Berlin: F. Fontane, 1892.

———. *Einsame Frauen: Novellen.* Berlin: F. Fontane, 1897.

———. *Im Lande der Verheissung: Ein deutscher Kolonialroman.* Dresden: Verlag von Carl Reißer, 1899.

———. *Ludwig von Rosen: Eine Erzählung aus zwei Welten.* Berlin: F. Fontane, 1892.

———. *Reiseskizzen und Tagebuchblätter aus Deutsch-Ostafrika.* Berlin: Walther und Apolant, 1889.

———. *Die stilisierte Frau. Sie und Er. Zwei Novellen.* Dresden: Verlag von Carl Reissner, 1902.

————. *Tropenkoller: Episode aus dem deutschen Kolonialleben.* 3d ed. Berlin: F. Fontane, 1905.

Chickering, Roger. "'Casting Their Gaze More Broadly': Women's Patriotic Activism in Imperial Germany." *Past and Present*, no. 118 (February 1988): 156–85.

Cook, James. *The Journals of Captain James Cook on His Voyages of Discovery.* Ed. J. C. Beaglehole. 4 vols. in 5. Cambridge: Cambridge University Press, 1955–74.

————. *Voyages Round the World for Making Discoveries towards the North and South Poles.* Manchester, U.K.: Sowler and Russell, 1799.

————. *A Voyage towards the South Pole and round the World. Performed in His Majesty's Ships the Resolution and Adventure, in the Years 1772, 1773, 1774, and 1775.* 2 vols. London: W. Strahan and T. Cadell, 1777.

Crummey, Donald. "Tewodoros as Reformer and Modernizer." *Journal of African History* 10, no. 3 (1969): 457–69.

Czaplicka, John, Andreas Huyssen, and Anson Rabinbach, eds. "Cultural History/Cultural Studies." Special issue of *New German Critique*, no. 65 (spring/summer 1995).

Dawidowicz, Lucy S. *The War against the Jews, 1933–1945.* New York: Holt, Rinehart and Winston, 1975.

de Man, Paul. *Allegories of Reading: Figural Language in Rousseau, Nietzsche, Rilke, and Proust.* New Haven: Yale University Press, 1979.

Dening, Greg. *Mr. Bligh's Bad Language: Passion, Power, and Theater on the Bounty.* Cambridge: Cambridge University Press, 1992.

Derrida, Jacques. "Racism's Last Word," trans. Peggy Kamuf. In *"Race," Writing, and Difference*, ed. Henry Louis Gates Jr. Chicago: University of Chicago Press, 1986.

Deutsche Kolonial-Ausstellung: Köln 1934. 1. Juli bis 2. Sept. Cologne: Ernst Stauf, 1934.

Du Bois, W. E. B. *The Autobiography of W. E. B. Du Bois: A Soliloquy on Viewing My Life from the Last Decade of Its First Century.* New York: International Publishers, 1968.

————. *The Souls of Black Folk.* Introduction by Nathan Hare and Alain Poussaint. New York: Signet, 1969.

————. "The World War and the Color Line." *The Crisis* 9 (November 1914): 28–30.

Eagleton, Terry. *Nationalism, Colonialism, and Literature; Nationalism, Irony, and Commitment.* Derry, U.K.: Field Day Theater Co., 1988.

Ehlers, Otto E. *Samoa: Die Perle der Südsee à jour gefaßt.* 2d ed. Berlin: Verlag von Hermann Paetel, 1895.

Einstein, Carl. *Werke*. Ed. Marion Schmid with Henriette Beese and Jens Kuasny. Vol. 2 of 5. Berlin: Medusa, 1981.

Elgar, Frank, and Robert Maillard. *Picasso*. Munich: Knaur, 1956.

Embacher, Friedrich. *Lexikon der Reisen und Entdeckungen*. Amsterdam: Meridian, 1961. Originally published in Leipzig in 1882.

Engels, Friedrich. *Herr Eugen Duhring's Revolution in Science (Anti-Duhring)*. Trans. Emile Burns. New York: International Publishers, 1939.

Essner, Cornelia. *Deutsche Afrikareisende im neunzehnten Jahrhundert: Zur Sozialgeschichte des Reisens*. Beiträge zur Kolonial- und Überseegeschichte, ed. Rudolf von Albertini, vol. 32. Stuttgart: Steiner, 1985.

Fabri, Friedrich. *Bedarf Deutschland der Colonien? Eine politische-ökonomische Betrachtung*. Gotha: Friedrich Andreas Perthes, 1879.

———. *Der deutsch-englische Vertrag: Rede, auf der am 1. Juli 1890 zu Köln veranstalteten Volks-Versammlung mit Wißmann-Feier*. Cologne: DuMont-Schauerberg, 1890.

———. *Deutsch-Ostafrica: Eine colonialpolitische Skizze*. Cologne: DuMont-Schauerberg, 1886.

Faïtlovich, Jacques. *Quer durch Abessinien: Meine zweite Reise zu den Falaschas*. Berlin: M. Poppelauer, 1910.

Falkenhausen, Helene von. *Ansiedlerschicksale: Elf Jahre in Deutsch-Südwestafrika 1893–1904*. 2d ed. Berlin: Dietrich Reimer, 1905.

Falkenhorst, C. *Auf Bergeshöhen Deutsch-Afrikas*. Bibliothek denkwürdiger Forschungsreisen, vol. 5. Stuttgart: Union Deutsche Verlagsgesellschaft, 1890.

———. *Durch die Wüsten und Steppen des dunklen Weltteils*. Bibliothek denkwürdiger Forschungsreisen, vol. 6. Stuttgart: Union Deutsche Verlagsgesellschaft, 1890.

Farias, Victor. *Heidegger and Nazism*. Ed. Joseph Margolis and Tom Rockmore, trans. Paul Burrell and Gabriel R. Ricci. Philadelphia: Temple University Press, 1989.

Feuchtwanger, E. J. *Democracy and Empire: Britain 1865–1914*. London: Edward Arnold, 1985.

Fischer, Eugen. *Das Problem der Rassenkreuzung beim Menschen*. Freiburg im Breisgau: Speyer und Kaerner Universitäts-buchhandlung, 1914.

———. *Die Rehobother Bastards und das Bastardierungsproblem beim Menschen: Anthropologische und ethnographische Studien ans Rehobother Bastardvolk in Deutsch-Südwest-Afrika*. Jena: G. Fischer, 1913.

Flad, Joseph Martin. *60 Jahre in der Mission unter den Falaschas in Abessinien*. Gießen: Brunnen-Verlag, 1922.

——. *Zwölf Jahre in Abessinien oder Geschichte des Königs Theodoros II und der Mission unter seiner Regierung*. Schriften des Institutum Judaica in Leipzig, no. 12/13. Leipzig: Dörffling und Franke, 1887.

Forster, Georg. *Werke*. Ed. Deutsche Akademie der Wissenschaft zu Berlin. Berlin: Akademie-Verlag, 1968.

——. *Werke in vier Bänden*. Ed. Gerhard Steiner. Vol. 1. Frankfurt: Insel, 1967.

Frantz, Constantin. *Ahasverus oder die Judenfrage*. Berlin: Wilhelm Hermes, 1844.

Freud, Sigmund. "A Disturbance of Memory on the Acropolis." In *The Standard Edition of the Complete Psychological Works of Sigmund Freud*, 22: 239–48. Trans. James Strachey. London: Hogarth Press and the Institute of Psycho-Analysis, 1964.

——. *The Interpretation of Dreams (first part)*. Vol. 4 of *The Standard Edition of the Complete Psychological Works of Sigmund Freud*, trans. James Strachey. London: Hogarth Press and the Institute of Psycho-Analysis, 1953.

——. *The Interpretation of Dreams (second part)*. Vol. 5 of *The Standard Edition of the Complete Psychological Works of Sigmund Freud*, trans. James Strachey. London: Hogarth Press and the Institute of Psycho-Analysis, 1953.

——. *The Question of Lay Analysis*. Vol. 20 of *The Standard Edition of the Complete Psychological Works of Sigmund Freud*, trans. James Strachey. London: Hogarth Press and the Institute of Psycho-Analysis, 1959.

Freytag, Gustav. *Soll und Haben: Roman in sechs Büchern*. Stuttgart: Parkland, 1977.

Gates, Henry Louis, ed. *"Race," Writing, and Difference*. Chicago: University of Chicago Press, 1986.

Gaudy, Alice Freiin von. *Balladen und Lieder*. Berlin: Verlag von Otto Elsner, 1900.

Geertz, Clifford. *The Interpretation of Cultures*. New York: Basic Books, 1973.

Genschorek. Wolfgang. *Im Alleingang durch die Wüste: Das Forscher-leben des Gerhard Rohlfs*. Leipzig: F.A. Brockhause, 1982.

Gervinus, Georg Gottfried. *Johann Georg Forster*. Vol. 7 of *Sämtliche Schriften*. Leipzig: Brockhaus, 1843.

Gidney, Rev. W. T. *At Home and Abroad: A Description of the English and Continental Missions of the London Society for Promoting Christianity amongst the Jews*. London: Operative Jewish Converts' Institution, 1900.

Gilman, Sander L. *Difference and Pathology: Stereotypes of Sexuality, Race, and Madness*. Ithaca: Cornell University Press, 1985.

Goldhagen, Daniel Jonah. *Hitler's Willing Executioners: Ordinary Germans and the Holocaust*. New York: Alfred A. Knopf, 1996.

Gooding-Williams, Robert. "Philosophy of History and Social Critique in *The Souls of Black Folk*." *Social Science Information* 26 (1987): 99–114.

Grimm, Hans. *Volk ohne Raum*. Munich: Albert Langen, 1926.

Haftmann, Werner. *Emil Nolde*. 7th ed. Cologne: Verlag M. DuMont-Schauerberg, 1978. Originally published in 1958.

Haftmann, Werner, Alfred Hentzen, and William S. Lieber. *German Art of the Twentieth Century*. New York: Museum of Modern Art, 1957.

Harnack, Adolf von. *Entstehung und Entwickelung der Kirchenverfassung und des Kirchenrechts in den ersten zwei Jahrhunderten: Nebst einer Kritik der Abhandlung R. Sohm's: "Wesen und Ursprung des Katholizismus."* Leipzig: J.C. Hinrich'sche, 1910.

Harrison, J. W. *Alexander M. Mackay: Pionier-Missionar von Uganda*. Trans. J. H. Nebinger, introduction by Wilhelm Baur. Leipzig: J.C. Hinrich'sche, 1891.

Hawkesworth, John. *An Account of the Voyages Undertaken by the Order of His Present Majesty for Making Discoveries in the Southern Hemisphere*. London: W. Strahan and T. Cadell, 1773.

Heidegger, Martin. *Being and Time*. Trans. John Macquarrie and Edward Robinson. New York: Harper and Row, 1962.

Hilberg, Raul. *The Destruction of the European Jews*. Chicago: Quadrangle Books, 1961.

Hildesheimer, Rabbi Esriel. *Briefe*. Ed. Mordechai Eliau. Jerusalem: Rubin Mass, 1965.

Holmes, Christine, ed. *Captain Cook's Second Voyage: The Journals of Lieutenants Elliott and Pickersgill*. London: Caliban, 1984.

Hooker, J. R. "The Foreign Office and the 'Abyssinian Captives.'" *Journal of African History* 2, no. 2 (1961): 245–58.

Horkheimer, Max, and Theodor W. Adorno. *Dialectic of Enlightenment*. Trans. John Cumming. New York: Continuum, 1972.

Humboldt, Alexander von. *Kosmos*, ed. Hanno Beck. Quellen und Forschungen zur Geschichte der Geographie und der Reisen, vol. 12. Stuttgart: Brockhaus, 1978.

Husserl, Edmund. *The Crisis of European Sciences and Transcendental Phenomenology: An Introduction to Phenomenological Philosophy*. Trans. David Carr. Evanston: Northwestern University Press, 1970.

Isaacs, Albert Augustus. *Biography of the Rev. Henry Aaron Stern, D.D., for More Than Forty Years a Missionary amongst the Jews Containing an Account of His Labours and Travels in Mesopotamia, Persia, Arabia, Turkey, Abyssinia, and England*. London: James Nisbet, 1886.

JanMohamed, Abdul. *A Manichean Aesthetics: The Politics of Literature in Colonial Africa*. Amherst: University of Massachusetts Press, 1983.

Kafka, Franz. *The Penal Colony: Stories and Short Pieces*. Trans. Willa and Edwin Muir. New York: Schocken Books, 1961.

Kahnweiler, Daniel-Henry. *Der Gegenstand der Ästhetik*. Munich: Heinz Moos, 1971.

———. *Der Weg zum Kubismus*. Stuttgart: Verlag Gerd Hatje, 1958.

Kennedy, Gavin. *The Death of Captain Cook*. London: Duckworth, 1978.

Kessler, David. *The Falashas: The Forgotten Jews of Ethiopia*. New York: Schocken, 1982.

Kissinger, Henry. *Diplomacy*. New York: Simon and Schuster, 1994.

Klotz, Marca. "White Women and the Dark Continent: Gender and Sexuality in German Colonial Discourse from the Sentimental Novel to the Fascist Film." Ph.D. diss., Stanford University, 1994.

Kramer, Fritz. *Verkehrte Welten: Zur imaginären Ethnographie des 19. Jahrhunderts*. 2d ed. Frankfurt: Syndikat, 1981. Originally published in 1977.

Laude, Jean. *La peinture française (1905–1914) et 'l'art nègre': Contribution à l'étude des sources du fauvisme et du cubisme*. Paris: Editions Klincksieck, 1968.

Lewis, David Levering. *W. E. B. Du Bois: Biography of a Race 1868–1919*. New York: Henry Holt, 1993.

Locke, John. *An Essay Concerning Human Understanding*. Ed. Peter H. Nidditch. Oxford: Clarendon Press, 1975.

Lomax, Alfred E., and E. C. Dawson. *Sir Samuel Baker and Henry A. Stern: The Story of Their Lives*. London: Sunday School Union, n.d.

Ludwig, Emil. *Wilhelm der Zweite*. Berlin: Ernst Rowohlt, 1926.

Markham, Clements R. *A History of the Abyssinian Expedition*. London: MacMillan, 1869.

McClintock, Anne. *Imperial Leather: Race, Gender, and Sexuality in the Colonial Conquest*. New York: Routledge, 1994.

Meyer, Michael A. *German Political Pressure and Jewish Religious Response in the Nineteenth Century*. Leo Baeck Memorial Lectures, no. 25. New York: Leo Baeck Institute, 1981.

Mill, John Stuart. *Essays on England, Ireland, and the Empire*. Ed. John M. Robson. Vol. 6 of *Collected Works of John Stuart Mill*. Toronto: University of Toronto Press, 1982.

Mirbach, Ernst Freiherr von. *Die Reise des Kaisers und der Kaiserin nach Palästina: Drei Vorträge*. Berlin: Ernst Siegfried Mittler u. Sohn, 1899.

Neil, Stephen. *Anglicanism*. New York: Oxford University Press, 1958.

Nolde, Emil. *Das Eigene Leben: Die Zeit der Jugend 1867–1902*. 2d ed. Flensburg: Verlagshaus Christian Wolff, 1949.

————. *Jahre der Kämpfe: 1902–1914*. 2d ed. Flensburg: Christian Wolff, 1958.

Noyes, John. "The Capture of Space: An Episode in a Colonial Story by Hans Grimm." *Pretexts* 1, no. 1 (winter 1989): 52–63.

————. *Colonial Space: Spatiality in the Discourse of German South-West Africa, 1884–1915*. Chur, Switzerland: Harwood Academic, 1992.

Obeyesekere, Gananth. *The Apotheosis of Captain Cook: European Mythmaking in the Pacific*. Princeton: Princeton University Press, 1992.

Oguntoye, Katharina, May Opitz, and Dagmar Schultz, eds. *Farbe Bekennen: Afro-deutsche Frauen auf den Spuren ihrer Geschichte*. Berlin: Orlanda Frauenverlag.

Paasche, Hans. *Die Forschungsreise des Afrikaners Lukanga Mukara ins innerste Deutschland*. Schriftenreihe das Andere Deutschland, ed. Helmut Donat, Horst Temmen, and Lothar Wieland. Bremen: Donat und Temmen, 1984; reprint of 7th ed., 1927.

Pan, David. "Kafka as a Populist: Re-reading 'In the Penal Colony.'" *Telos* 101 (fall 1994): 3–40.

Pechstein, Max. *Erinnerungen: Mit 105 Zeichnungen des Künstlers*. Ed L. Reidemiesch. Wiesbaden: Limes, 1960.

Penkert, Sibylle. *Carl Einstein: Existenz und Ästhetik*. Wiesbaden: Franz Steiner, 1970.

Peters, Carl. *Die deutsche Emin-Pascha-Expedition*. Munich: Verlag von R. Oldenbourg, 1891.

————. *Willenswelt und Weltwille: Studien und Ideen zu einer Weltanschauung*. Leipzig: Brockhause, 1883.

Pratt, Mary Louise. *Imperial Eyes: Travel, Writing, and Transculturalism*. London: Routledge, 1992.

Rassam, Hormuzd. *Narrative of the British Mission to Theodore, King of Abyssinia*. London: John Murray, 1869.

Ratzel, F. "Gerhard Rohlfs." In *Biographisches Jahrbuch und Deutsche Nekrologie*. Berlin: G. Reimerm, 1896.

Ritschl, Albrecht. *Die Entstehung der altkatholischen Kirche: Eine kirchen- und dogmengeschichtliche Monographie*. 2d ed. Bonn: Adolph Marcus, 1857.

Ritter, Gerhard A., ed. *Das Deutsche Kaiserreich 1871–1914: Ein historisches Lesebuch*. Göttingen: Vandenhoeck und Ruprecht, 1975.

Rohlfs, Gerhard. *In Abessinien: Im Auftrage Sr. Majestät des Königs von Preussen mit dem Englischen Expeditionskorps in Abessinien. Mit dem Portrait des General Napier und einer Karte von Abessinien*. Bremen: Verlag von J. Kühtmann's Buchhandlung, 1869.

————. *Angra Pequena: Das erste deutsche Kolonie in Afrika*. Bielefeld: Velhagen und Klasing, 1884.

————. *Neue Beiträge zur Entdeckung und Erforschung Africa's.* Kassel: Verlag von Theodor Fischer, 1881.

————. *Quer durch Afrika: Die Erstdurchquerung der Sahara vom Mittelmeer zum Golf von Guinea.* Ed. Herbert Gussenbauer. Stuttgart: Edition Erdmann im K. Thienemanns, 1984.

————. "Reise durch Nord-Afrika vom Mittelländischen Meere bis zum Busen von Guinea: 1865–1867." Part 1, "Von Tripoli Nach Kuka (Fesan, Sahara, Bornu)"; Part 2, "Von Kuka nach Lagos." *Mittheilungen aus Justus Perthes' Geographischer Anstalt über wichtige neue Erforschungen auf dem Gesamtgebiete der Geographie von Dr. A. Petermann* Ergänzungsheft Nr. 25 (1868); Ergänzungsheft Nr. 34 (1872).

Rubenson, Sven. "Ethiopia and the Horn." In *Cambridge History of Africa*, 5:51–98. Ed. John E. Flint. Cambridge: Cambridge University Press, 1976.

————. *King of Kings: Tewodros of Ethiopia.* Hailie Selassie I University Department of History Historical Studies No. 2. Addis Ababa: Hailie Selassie University in association with Oxford University Press, 1966.

Rubin, William, ed. *"Primitivism" in Twentieth-Century Art.* New York: Museum of Modern Art, 1984.

Sacher-Masoch, Leopold von. *Don Juan von Kolomea: Galizische Geschichten.* Ed. Michael Farin. Bonn: Bouvier Verlag Herbert Grundmann, 1985.

Sahlins, Marshall, *How "Natives" Think: About Captain Cook, for Example* Chicago: University of Chicago Press, 1995.

Said, Edward. *Orientalism.* New York: Pantheon, 1978.

Salentiny, Fernand. *Das Lexikon der Seefahrer und Entdecker.* Tübingen: Horst Erdmann, 1974.

Sartre, Jean-Paul. Preface to *The Wretched of the Earth*, by Frantz Fanon. New York: Grove Press, 1968. Originally published in 1961.

Sauerlandt, Max. *Emil Nolde.* Munich: Kurt Wolff, 1921.

Schmidt, Max. *Aus unserem Kriegsleben in Südwestafrika: Erlebenisse und Erfahrungen.* Berlin: Edwin Runge, 1907.

Schorske, Carl E. *Fin-de-Siècle Vienna: Politics and Culture.* New York: Knopf, 1980.

Segalen, Victor. *Essai sur l'exotisme: Un esthétique du divers; et Textes sur Gauguin et l'Océanie.* Paris: Fata Morgana, 1978.

Shepherd, Naomi. *The Zealous Intruders: The Western Rediscovery of Palestine.* San Francisco: Harper and Row, 1987.

Singer, Charles. "The Falashas." *Jewish Quarterly Review* 17 (1905): 142–47.

Sohm, Rudolph. *Wesen und Ursprung des Katholizismus.* Leipzig: 1898.

Sonnenberg, Else. *Wie es am Waterberg Zuging: Ein Beitrag zur Geschichte des Hereroaufstandes.* Berlin: Wilhelm Süsserolt Verlagsbuchhandlung, 1905.

Stanley, Henry M. *Magdala: The Story of the Abyssinian Campaign of 1866–67.* London: Sampson, Low, Marston, 1896.

Stern, Rev. Henry A. *The Captive Missionary: Being an Account of the Country and People of Abyssinia, Embracing a Narrative of King Theodore's Life, and His Treatment of Political and Religious Missions.* London: Cassell, Petter, and Galpin, 1868.

————. *Dawnings of Light in the East; with Biblical, Historical, and Statistical Notices of Persons and Places Visited during a Mission to the Jews in Persia, Coordistan, and Mesopotamia.* London: Charles H. Purday, 1854.

————. *Wanderings among the Falashas in Abyssinia. Together with A Description of the Country and Its Various Inhabitants.* 2d ed. London: Frank Cass, 1968. Originally published in 1862.

Stimmen über Jerusalem: Weihe und Abschiedspredigt gehalten zu London am 7. und 8. November 1841 von Dr. A. M'Caul, Professor der hebräischen und rabbinischen Literatur am King's College, und Dr. M. S. Alexander, Bischof der vereinigten Kirche von England und Irland in Jerusalem. Berlin: Wilhelm Besser, 1842.

Südafrikas Deutsche in englischer Gewalt. Dresden: Heimat und Welt, 1916.

Theweleit, Klaus. *Male Fantasies.* Trans. Stephan Conway in collaboration with Erica Carter and Chris Turner. Minneapolis: University of Minnesota Press, 1987.

Trevenen, J., C. B. Holland, and Henry M. Hozier. *Record of the Expedition to Abyssinia.* London: H. M. Stationery Office, 1870.

Vely, Emma. *Mein schönes und schweres Leben.* Leipzig: Carl Frankenstein, 1929.

Warmbold, Joachim. "Germania in Afrika: Frieda Freiin von Bülow, 'Schöpferin des deutschen Kolonialromans.'" *Jahrbuch des Instituts für deutsche Geschichte* [Tel-Aviv University] 15 (1986): 309–36.

————. *Ein Stücken neudeutsch Erd . . . : Deutsche Kolonial-Literatur; Aspekte ihrer Geschichte, Eigenart, und Wirkung, dargestellt am Beispiel Afrikas.* Frankfurt: Haag und Herchen, 1982.

Warnod, Jeanine. *Bateau-Lavoir: Wiege des Kubismus, 1892–1914.* Trans. Ursula Patzies. Geneva: Weber, 1976.

Wegner, Reinhard. *Der Exotismus-Streit in Deutschland: Zur Auseinandersetzung mit primitiven Formen in der Bildenden Kunst des 20. Jahrhunderts.* Europäische Hochschulschriften, Reihe 28: Kunstgeschichte, vol. 27. Frankfurt: Peter Lang, 1983.

Wernhart, Karl R. *Ethnohistorie und Kulturgeschichte*. Vienna and Cologne: Hermann Böhlaus, 1986.

Wernhart, Karl R., ed. *Ethnohistory in Vienna*. Aachen: Edition Herodot im Rader, 1987.

Wider die Sklaverei! Bericht über die Verhandlungen der Volksversammlung im Gürzenich zu Köln am 27. Oktober 1888. Düsseldorf: Verlag von Felix Bagel, 1888.

Wieland, Christoph Martin. *Kleine Schriften II: 1778–1782*, ed. Wilhelm Kurrelmeyer. In *Gesammelte Schriften*, ed. Deutsche Akademie der Wissenschaften zu Berlin, section 1, vol. 22. Berlin: Akademie, 1954.

Williamson, Joel. "W. E. B. Du Bois as a Hegelian." In *What Was Freedom's Price?*, ed. David G. Sansing. Jackson: University Presses of Mississippi, 1978.

Wulf, Joseph. *Die bildenden Künste im Dritten Reich: Eine Dokumentation*. Gütersloh: Sigbert Mohn, 1963.

Zamir, Shamoon. *Dark Voices: W. E. B. Du Bois and American Thought, 1888–1903*. Chicago: University of Chicago Press, 1995.

Index